T.S. Eliot and the Philosophy of Criticism

T.S. Eliot and the Philosophy of Criticism

Richard Shusterman

New York

Columbia University Press

1988

LIBRARY OF CONGRESS
Library of Congress Cataloging-in-Publication Data

Shusterman, Richard.
  T.S. Eliot and the philosophy of criticism / Richard Shusterman.
    p.   cm.
  Includes bibliographical references and index.
  ISBN 0-213-06742-9
  1. Eliot, T.S. (Thomas Stearns), 1888–1965—Knowledge—
Literature. 2. Literature—Philosophy. 3. Criticism—
History—20th century.   I. Title.
PS3509.L43Z8649 1988
821'.912—dc19   87-32567
                                       CIP

Contents

For
R.N.S.

... And what there is to conquer
By strength and submission, has already been discovered
Once or twice, or several times, by men whom one cannot hope
To emulate – but there is no competition –
There is only the fight to recover what has been lost
And found and lost again and again: and now, under conditions
That seem unpropitious. But perhaps neither gain nor loss.
For us, there is only the trying. The rest is not our business.

'East Coker'

Preface

Though largely appreciative and supportive of many of Eliot's views, this book is not a pious hagiography. Justification and praise are tempered with considerable questioning and criticism. I unashamedly confess, however, that my study of Eliot's philosophy of criticism is guided by what philosophers sometimes call the principle of charity – the idea of making an author's views (or an agent's actions) as coherent and cogent as reasonably possible by one's own lights. But I believe and hope to show that applying this principle to Eliot's critical theory will ultimately prove more charitable and helpful to ourselves than to Eliot. For it will enable us to perceive and profit from those aspects of his thought which are especially relevant and therapeutic for criticism today, but which are typically ignored or misunderstood, since overshadowed by an exaggerated perception of enormous differences between Eliot's outlook and our own postmodernist perspective. Yet Eliot himself, as this study will demonstrate, came to recognize the problems of the modernist critical program he so successfully propounded in his early criticism; and in trying to remedy them, he anticipated some of the directions and dangers of today's postmodernist theories. Eliot, who saw so much himself and is no longer here to profit from the knowledge and viewpoint of the present, surely does not need or deserve our charity in any condescending way. Yet we, I believe, can gain greatly from his guidance.

This book is troublesomely awkward to place in a precise genre. It does not pretend to be an essay in pure, scholarly literary history or intellectual biography, though I hope it is adequately informed by and reflective of such scholarship. Nor can it claim to be a purely philosophical inquiry into certain issues of literary and critical theory pursued single-mindedly for their own sake no matter how far from Eliot they take us. I have rather aimed at making my philosophical points while trying to suggest a cogent (though far from complete and systematic) narrative of Eliot's development as critic and theorist, an evolution which, I argue, reflects illuminatingly a major course of development in twentieth-century philosophy.

I have therefore striven to structure and pursue my own philosophical views and arguments in a way that does not impede or distract excessively from the central story line but instead enhances it. This has often been extremely difficult, necessitating some mediating balance between the

ix

urge for narrative clarity and simplicity and the often conflicting desire for depth of philosophical analysis and argumentation. I am aware that some readers may not be satisfied with some of the balancing bargains I have struck, desiring either more detailed and systematic exposition of Eliot or more philosophy. It is painful to think that my effort to achieve a fruitful union and hybrid of literary study and philosophy might be taken by some as a mongrelized misfit – a muddle of superficial scholarship and shallow philosophizing. Such disappointed readers will at least find here an anticipatory apology and warning. I hope, however, that recognition of the book's compound character and aims will enable its readers better to appreciate whatever merits it has.

The book's dual literary-philosophical nature is reflected in the different professional journals where some of its material first appeared. I thank the editors and publishers of *ELH*, *Philosophy and Literature*, *Orbis Litterarum*, *The Journal of the History of Ideas*, *The British Journal of Aesthetics*, *Philosophy and Phenomenological Research*, and *The Monist* (the journal where Eliot himself published his only two full-length articles of professional philosophy) for permission to re-use and rework this material. Thanks are also due to a number of Eliot scholars and philosophers whose critical comments on various parts of my manuscript have been very helpful. Among the former I wish particularly to note Shyamal Bagchee, Lyndall Gordon, Victor Li, A.V.C. Schmidt, and Ronald Schuchard; among the latter T.J. Diffey, Chuck Dyke, Richard Eldridge, John Fisher, A.C. Grayling, P.M.S. Hacker, Joseph Margolis, Graham McFee, Richard Rorty, J.O. Urmson, and Gerald Vision. I am also grateful to Mrs. Valerie Eliot for her encouragement and permission to consult Eliot's unpublished writings in the Houghton Library at Harvard University and in Kings College Library, Cambridge; and I should like to thank Dr Michael Halls who greatly facilitated my work at Kings.

Much of this book was written while on a year's sabbatical leave from Ben-Gurion University of the Negev. I spent that year of 1984-85 at St. John's College, Oxford, where I had been a student. It is with pleasure and gratitude that I recall the fine facilities and good company I once again enjoyed there. When my sabbatical year and funds ran out, I was most fortunate to be awarded a visiting research fellowship at Temple University's Department of Philosophy. This afforded me the time and resources to complete the book, which has been carefully typed and repeatedly retyped by Nadia Kravchenko. She has my thanks, as do Bob and Heidi Shusterman, who were wonderfully helpful in getting me settled in Philadelphia. My stay at Temple has rewarded me with much more than the completion of this book. I have had the privilege of working in one of the world's finest centers of aesthetics; and I am grateful to its faculty and graduate students for the ambience of intellectual stimulation and welcoming warmth which made work a pleasure.

This book is fortunate to appear in time to greet the centenary year of

Eliot's birth. But for the early trust and enduring support of my English publisher, this would not have been possible. I also wish to thank Jennifer Crewe of Columbia University Press for her interest and efforts in arranging the book's simultaneous publication in Eliot's native land.

Finally, on the most personal level, I wish to thank those who have had to follow this project (and me) through three continents: my children – Damon, Aelia, and Eden – and especially their mother, Rivka. She gave me so much in so many ways. Not in any hope of compensation, but in gratitude and witness, I dedicate this book to her.

Philadelphia   R.M.S.
May 1987

Abbreviations

In this book I refer to many of Eliot's major works by abbreviations. The abbreviations and editions I use are as follows:

SW   *The Sacred Wood* (London: Methuen, 1968), first published in 1920.

FLA   *For Lancelot Andrewes* (London: Faber, 1970), first published in 1928.

SE   *Selected Essays* (London: Faber, 1976), first published in 1932.

TUP   *The Use of Poetry and the Use of Criticism* (London: Faber, 1964), first published in 1933.

ASG   *After Strange Gods* (New York: Harcourt, Brace and Company, 1934).

EAM   *Essays Ancient and Modern* (London: Faber, 1936).

ICS   *The Idea of a Christian Society* (London: Faber, 1982), first published in 1939.

NDC   *Notes Toward the Definition of Culture* (London: Faber, 1962), first published in 1948.

OPP   *On Poetry and Poets* (London: Faber, 1957).

KE   *Knowledge and Experience in the Philosophy of F.H. Bradley* (London: Faber, 1964).

TC   *To Criticize the Critic, and other writings* (London: Faber, 1978) first published in 1965.

CPP   *The Complete Poems and Plays of T.S. Eliot* (London: Faber, 1969).

SP   *Selected Prose of T.S. Eliot*, edited by Frank Kermode (London: Faber, 1975).

Occasional abbreviations of other writings of Eliot as well as those of other authors will be explained in the footnotes.

Chapter 1

Introduction

> We shall not cease from exploration
> And the end of all our exploring
> Will be to arrive where we started
> And know the place for the first time.
>
> 'Little Gidding'

I

This book is a study of Eliot's critical theory and of its relevance for contemporary philosophy of criticism. In reaching canonical status, Eliot's critical thought (as his poetry) has already been the focus of so much scrutiny and discussion that my book is already prefaced by a host of works on this topic, some of them quite substantial and informative. This might make not only my preface but my entire project seem gratuitous. That the project is worthwhile I hope will emerge by the end of the book, but perhaps some preliminary justifications and explanations of intent are needed to encourage readers that my study of Eliot's philosophy of criticism is not just one more redundant refrain of an already tiresomely dated song.

Whatever one thinks of the merit of Eliot's critical thought, its enormous influence on twentieth-century critical theory and practice cannot be denied. We surely may say of Eliot what he himself said of Yeats: 'he was one of those few whose history is the history of their own time, who are part of the consciousness of an age which cannot be understood without them' (*OPP*, 262). That his theoretical ideas and critical judgments are now so often and sharply attacked by today's theorists in their polemics against the long-entrenched Anglo-American 'schools' of criticism which were largely inspired (though never unequivocally supported) by him, is powerful testimony to his lasting significance. It is also a telling indication that despite the breathless industry and ambition of the past twenty years of critical theory (since Eliot's death in 1965), we still have not altogether escaped the age of Eliot. And if his long and wide-ranging influence has secured his status as a permanent orientation or point of reference for criticism and theory, his incontestable stature as a poet will only further

1

consolidate and magnify his central place in the literary-critical tradition.

Once we thus place Eliot firmly in the tradition, we may borrow and expand his famous doctrine of tradition to justify our renewed study and reinterpretation of his thought. In maintaining that the meaning of an artist's work derives largely from the tradition to which he belongs (and to which he may contribute), Eliot asserts that 'no artist of any art has his complete meaning alone' but that 'his significance, his appreciation is the appreciation of his relation to the dead poets and artists ...; you must set him, for comparison and contrast among the dead' (*SE*, 15). Eliot here is only telling half the truth. As long as the tradition is alive, you must also set your object of study among the living, for similar relations of comparison and contrast. One reason for reexamining Eliot's much examined critical theory is to provide a greatly needed study of its relation to twentieth-century philosophers who are either living or recently deceased and whose philosophies are still very much alive. Such a study should shed light on the different terms of relation and increase our understanding not only of Eliot but of contemporary critical theory and philosophy. By this line of argument one can confidently claim that with a developing theoretical tradition there will always be room for a reinterpretation of Eliot in terms of contemporary perspectives.

Another distinctive feature of my treatment of Eliot is the nature of my philosophical perspective. For better or for worse, I come to Eliot as a philosopher trained in the Anglo-American analytic tradition, not as an English scholar with an interest in theory. While a spate of studies have been devoted to Eliot's relation to Bradley and idealist thought and to his literary predecessors and cohorts in modernist theory, Eliot's connection with analytic philosophy has been almost totally neglected, and sadly misunderstood when not ignored.[1] Much of the reason for this is the general unfamiliarity of Eliot scholars with analytic philosophy (despite Eliot's own manifest knowledge of it) and their inadequate grasp of its variety of doctrines, branches, and issues. For example, Eliot's obvious distaste for Russell's atheistic *Weltanschauung* and liberalist ethics has prevented previous scholars from appreciating his early admiration and adaptation of Russell's doctrines and strategies in logic, epistemology, and the philosophy of language. One aim of my book is to provide long overdue recognition of Eliot's link and affinity with the analytic philosophical tradition, primarily with respect to Russell but also to Wittgenstein, Moore, and

---

[1] For some examples of such studies focusing on Bradley, see A.Bolgan, 'The Philosophy of F.H. Bradley and the Mind and Art of T.S. Eliot: An Introduction', in S.P. Rosenbaum (ed.), *English Literature and British Philosophy* (Chicago: University of Chicago Press, 1971); L. Freed, *The Critic as Philosopher* (LaSalle: Purdue University Press, 1979); M.Allan, *T.S. Eliot's Impersonal Theory of Poetry* (Lewisburg: Bucknell University Press, 1974). The list could go on to unmanageable length, and other examples will only be cited when they apply directly to our discussion. For a recent and quite comprehensive account of Eliot's debt to his literary modernist predecessors – primarily Ford, Pound, Lewis, and Hulme – see M.H. Levenson, *A Genealogy of Modernism* (Cambridge: Cambridge University Press, 1984).

contemporary Anglo-American philosophers.

However, my examination of Eliot's critical theory will not be confined to the Anglo-American perspective. It will endeavor to show how Eliot's later theory anticipates and converges with certain currents in contemporary continental philosophy, most strikingly with the hermeneutic philosophy of Gadamer on the topics of interpretation and tradition. This seemingly unnatural coupling of analytic philosophy with hermeneutics through the medium of Eliot is not an attempt at eclectic comprehensiveness. It reflects a significant movement in recent analytic philosophy toward historicist, holistic and non-realist points of view which converge with those urged by contemporary hermeneuticians in the continental tradition. Eliot's own theoretical development, as I hope to show, neatly reflects this development of twentieth-century Anglo-American philosophy: a movement from early scientific realism and objectivism (inspired by the revolt against the Hegelian idealist tradition represented by Bradley) to a growing awareness of the historicist, non-foundational, pragmatic character of human understanding. Here again, Eliot's intellectual history is an illuminating model of that of our recent past and thus a valuable tool for understanding the present and forming the future.

Though seeking to avoid excessive narrowness, my philosophical perspective on Eliot is not without significant limitations. But, of course, as Eliot himself points out, any perspective or point of view must necessarily be limited in scope and leave concealed that on which it does not focus. Perhaps the most obvious limitation of my study is its lack of attention to the Christian aspect of Eliot's critical thought. Two points are offered to extenuate this omission. First, as a 'free-thinking', secular Jew (the sort Eliot once viciously condemned as a corruptive danger that western society could not tolerate),[2] I consider my capacity for understanding Eliot as a Christian to be limited. Secondly, and more importantly, though Christianity is certainly a significant aspect of Eliot the man and thinker, its importance for his philosophy of criticism has been overemphasized. Though he recognized that literary criticism must ultimately lead into and be supplemented by moral, social, and religious criticism, and though he applied his religious beliefs to his practical criticism, Eliot did not use his Christian faith as a device or foundation to provide incorrigible certainty or absolute objectivity for his or any possible critical system. Unlike Berkeley and Descartes, Eliot did not invoke God to secure the possibility of permanently stable and absolutely objective knowledge of matters of this world. On the contrary, he ultimately maintained a non-foundational, non-absolutist, pragmatic view of human knowledge.

From my secular point of view, Eliot's Christianity seems very much a

---

[2] See *After Strange Gods* (1934), 20: 'reasons of race and religion combine to make any large number of free-thinking Jews undesirable'. Despite its important theory of tradition Eliot never allowed this work to be reprinted. One can hopefully assume that this decision reflects his repentance for its anti-semitism.

red-herring for understanding the value of his critical theory. Since so many of his New Critical followers and interpreters endorse a distinctly Christian critical outlook and emphasize Eliot's Christianity, it has been assumed that Eliot's theory of criticism can only be understood in Christian terms. Uncritically accepting the New Critical Christian interpretation of Eliot as exclusively correct, and violently rejecting both New Criticism and Christianity, contemporary theorists glibly dismiss Eliot's theory as obviously unhelpful and inadequate for secular literary theory. I hope to show that a secular understanding of Eliot's critical thought is possible and fruitful.

Contemporary philosophers have revealed a similar but enormously more significant mistake of seventeenth-century thought, when the wealth of Aristotle's philosophy was hastily discredited and repudiated because it was understood as interpreted by and closely associated with medieval Christian philosophy and scholasticism. In philosophy's recent dissatisfaction with the Cartesian tradition, there has been a renewed appreciation and application of Aristotelian ideas, particularly in philosophy of mind and ethics. Eliot seems to anticipate and manifest this move both by repudiating Cartesianism[3] and, as I shall show in detail, by his frequent praise and implementation of Aristotelian doctrines and strategies. Here too, then, Eliot's thought seems both topical and representative of the age.

Apart from these general aims, I hope to correct a number of distorted views of Eliot's theory which have gained wide dissemination, but which tend to devalue the breadth, depth, complexity, and development of his thought. In this introduction I shall confine myself to discussing briefly five of these distortions, whose correction, along with others, will emerge more fully in later chapters.

II

(1) Eliot has often been censured as a representative of the narrow-minded insularity of Anglo-American criticism, that of the New Criticism and 'the English school'. Such criticism is condemned as stubbornly refusing possible enrichment from continental sources and models of literary theory; as essentially cutting literature off from other concerns (like politics, sociology, philosophy); and as confining literary appreciation and criticism entirely to the detailed interpretation of particular works and to a purely aesthetic response to their qualities of form and structure. Thus Christopher Norris contrastively praises American deconstructionist

---

[3] Eliot's most severe condemnation of Descartes is in his unpublished Clark Lectures (1926), where he blames Descartes for (mis)leading philosophy away from Aristotelian, scholastic realism toward sceptical, self-centered psychologism. The famed argumentation of the Cartesian *Meditations* is denounced by Eliot as an extraordinarily crude and stupid piece of reasoning which gave rise to the whole pseudo-science of epistemology which has haunted the nightmares of the last three hundred years (Lecture II, p. 41).

opponents of New Criticism for their 'openness to continental European sources – Heidegger, Derrida, Walter Benjamin – not so much for their specific ideas as for the fact that they fly in the face of everything "British" and post-Eliotic'. The point is that their very foreignness and intellectual concerns are a welcome challenge to the insularly English, aesthetically formalist 'orthodox Eliotic standpoint'.[4] Similarly, Terry Eagleton (simplistically impugning Eliot with the deficiencies of some of his New Critical epigoni) claims that Eliot treated literature only from a narrowly aestheticist perspective, one where literature is 'sealed from history, ... where "sensibility" may play in its purest, least socially tainted form'. Not only does Eagleton falsely belittle Eliot's criticism as restricted to poetry and drama, but he further condemns it as 'strikingly uninterested in ... "thought" ' and 'in what literary works actually *say*', being instead 'almost entirely confined to qualities of language, styles of feeling, the relations of image and experience.'[5] In short, Eliot is glibly and gleefully dismissed by today's fashionable theorists as representative of Anglo-American parochialism and rigidly narrow aesthetic formalism.

This picture of Eliot is as grossly distorted as it is obviously inimically tendentious. For Eliot himself vociferously decried the insularity of English letters and sought to introduce European ideas and models into his critical thought, and through it into English criticism in general. Rémy de Gourmont, Charles Maurras, Julien Benda, Jacques Maritain, Ramon Fernandez are but a few examples of continental thinkers whose thought Eliot tried to inject into the world of English letters. Many pages of Eliot's journal *The Criterion* were devoted to the work of contemporary European thinkers, Eliot often translating them himself. Suspicious of smug confidence in the special English genius (*SE*, 27-28), Eliot was always more interested in the mind of Europe, believing in and hoping to promote 'an international fraternity of men of letters within Europe' (*NDC*, 118).

If Eliot was the opposite of parochial in his assimilation and dissemination of continental thought, he was also far from any aestheticist insularity which limited criticism to the interpretation and appreciation of particular works in terms of their formal qualities. In the first place, Eliot always preferred to treat an author as a whole and generally avoided interpretative studies of individual works. Secondly, from the mid-1920s, Eliot recognized the futility and the dangers of isolating literature and its criticism from other human interests, since literature itself necessarily involves such non-literary interests. Though in his early essays he successfully sought to make room for a relatively autonomous field of literary criticism (i.e. one not wholly subordinate to other disciplines), he

---

[4] See C. Norris, *Deconstruction: Theory and Practice* (London: Methuen, 1982), 97, 118.

[5] T. Eagleton, *Literary Theory: An Introduction* (Oxford: Blackwell, 1983), 50-51. The range of Eliot's literary criticism also includes novels, short stories, literary critical essays, and works of philosophy, theology, and social and political theory. One need only consult the list of periodical entries in D. Gallup, *T.S. Eliot: A Bibliography* (London: Faber, 1969).

none the less warned that 'isolating the concept of literature [will] destroy the life of literature', since 'even the purest literature is alimented from non-literary sources, and has non-literary consequences. Pure literature is a chimera of sensation.'[6] From this, of course, it follows that a purely 'literary appreciation' is an equally chimerical 'abstraction' or 'figment' (*SE*, 271; *TUP*, 98, 109).

Eliot therefore insists that one's appreciation of poetry 'cannot be isolated from one's other interests and passions', nor should it be. We must not ignore 'the doctrine, theory, belief, or "view of life" presented in a poem' to concentrate exclusively on formal embellishments, for such an isolating focus deprives us of the enrichment poetry can give and leaves us not with pure poetry but only with 'the debris of poetry' (*TUP*, 36, 96-98). And questions of thought and belief figure centrally in Eliot's criticism of Shelley, Hardy, and Lawrence (*TUP*, 88-98; *ASG*, 59-66). This is not to deny that Eliot was always very much concerned with qualities of language and styles of feeling, as in his particular self-conceived role of poet-critic he thought he should be. But Eliot pluralistically recognized the legitimacy of a variety of critical functions and concerns, among them the philosophical and ideological. Moreover, Eagleton's mistaken view that Eliot's concentration on language and feeling betrays his disdainful indifference to thought ('the contempt for the intellect of any right-wing irrationalist')[7] is itself undermined by betraying a dubious assumption of sharp contrast or division between language, feeling, and thought. The idea that language is an ornamental supplement or distracting corruption of thought, not essential and formative of thought itself, has recently been the target of much philosophical criticism in both continental and Anglo-American philosophy. We shall consider these recent views in relation to Eliot's ideas and arguments for the intimate interdependence of language, thought, and feeling, which will be discussed in Chapter Seven.

The case for Eliot's critical concern with 'thought' and 'extra-literary' matters hardly needs to rely on his claims for language. For he openly asserts that literary criticism must not avoid ideology, that 'literary criticism should be completed by criticism from a definite ethical and theological standpoint' (*SP*, 97). Moreover, far from claiming that art and criticism are 'sealed from history' and social forces, Eliot in fact insists that they are largely constituted and changed through history, primarily 'due to elements which enter from the outside', most especially 'social changes' (*TUP*, 21, 75, 127, 150).[8] Indeed, his recognition of art and criticism's inextricable embeddedness and dependence on the culture and ideology of a society, led him (as it earlier led Arnold and Ruskin) to devote increasingly more attention to the independent study of culture and

[6] See T.S. Eliot, 'The Idea of a Literary Review', *Criterion* 4 (1926), 3-4.

[7] Eagleton, 40-41.

[8] It is worth noting that Eliot discusses with approbation Trotsky's views on the deep dependence of art on social forces (*TUP*, 135-136).

education, which issued in lengthy monographs: *The Idea of a Christian Society, Notes Toward the Definition of Culture*, and *The Aims of Education*.

(2) Closely related to this twofold misreading of Eliot as narrowly Anglo-American and still more narrowly formalist is the misconception that he is non-rational, anti-intellectual, and unphilosophical. Eagleton and Norris[9] again unite to propagate this error, though with slightly more reason and support. For numerous Eliot commentators are led to roughly this sort of view in response to the embarrassing number of apparently conflicting statements that can be culled from Eliot's mammoth critical corpus.[10] Many of these inconsistencies may be readily explained in terms of a rational development of Eliot's thought, earlier views being modified or rejected as he matured and saw the changing needs of criticism. Many others may be explained away by showing that the appearance of contradiction derives from considering statements out of their original context and/or taking the vague and problematic terms in which they are often made as unambiguous and fixed in meaning. Eliot himself frequently warns us of the elusive, wobbly nature of words and the inescapable contextual factor in their meaning, whether in poetry or in prose.

But we may well exhaust these explanatory stratagems without thereby rendering Eliot's critical writings into a wholly consistent and harmoniously structured theoretical system. This problem of consistency is made much more tolerable to Eliot apologists by Eliot's own apparent disclaimers of philosophical prowess. 'I am not a systematic thinker', Eliot confessed privately in a letter of 1934;[11] and in his most extensive treatment of literary and critical theory he repeatedly pleaded his incapacity for 'abstruse reasoning' and all too 'limited qualifications' for the high-level thought of philosophical aesthetics (*TUP*, 77, 143, 149-150).

In the light of such remarks and in the face of awkward tensions and apparent aporias in the Eliot corpus, some find it congenial to regard Eliot's theoretical writing not as rational, intellectual theorizing at all, but simply as emotive expression in prose of his current feelings, attitudes, and desires regarding literature and criticism. It is thus viewed like his poetry, a

---

[9] Apart from the works cited in notes 5 and 6, see C. Norris, *William Empson and the Philosophy of Literary Criticism* (London: Athlone, 1978), 128-129, 174; and more recently, C. Norris, *The Contest of Faculties: philosophy and theory after deconstruction* (London: Methuen, 1985), 12-16, where Eliot's alleged formalist intolerance of theoretical, rational reflection (literature and its criticism being 'in a sealed-off aesthetic domain ... leaving no room for theory on the one hand or historical reflection on the other', p. 14) is explicitly linked with his ideological conservatism.

[10] For a detailed survey of such commentators (critics and apologists) see F-P. Lu, *T.S. Eliot: The Dialectical Structure of His Theory of Poetry* (Chicago: University of Chicago Press, 1966), 3-21. Wollheim also notes in Eliot 'a certain fear of the intellect' and a tendency for 'inconsistencies' in critical judgements. See R. Wollheim, 'Eliot and F.H. Bradley: An Account' in G. Martin (ed.), *Eliot in Perspective: A Symposium* (London: Macmillan, 1970), 190.

[11] See Eliot's letter to Paul Elmer Moore of 20 June 1934, quoted in J.D. Margolis, *T.S. Eliot's Intellectual Development, 1922-1939* (Chicago: University of Chicago Press, 1972), xv.

working out of essentially personal concerns with more affective than rational or cognitive aims and import.[12]

It would be foolish to claim that Eliot's theorizing is not significantly influenced by his personality and his particular situation and needs. But does such influence and orientation preclude rationality? Would it be rational for the literary theorist entirely to ignore his personal convictions and situation? Further pursuing this line of questioning we might ask: Granted that Eliot's critical writings contain some contradictions and present no rigorous and systematic edifice of theory, no elaborate and long-distance flights of abstruse reasoning, must we infer that Eliot is an anti-rational, unphilosophical theorist, and that a book on Eliot's philosophy of criticism is a book without a subject? Such inferences surely are as wrong as they are harsh. What perhaps implicitly lends them a seductive air of plausibility is our Cartesian scientistic prejudice of narrowly equating the rational, the intellectual, and the philosophical with the methodically argued and the rigorously systematic.

But Eliot himself clearly rejected Cartesianism's identification of reason with method and its divorce of the intellect from feeling. Far from irrationalism, Eliot's campaign for classicism was a call for 'a higher and clearer conception of Reason' which involved a unified sensibility of thought and feeling, with the education 'and serene control of the emotions by Reason'.[13] Far from feeling contempt for the intellect, Eliot, in his polemic against Middleton Murry's romantic Bergsonian intuitionism, declares himself 'on the side of the intelligence'. More importantly, he repudiates Murry's apparent dichotomy between intellect and intuition as 'following Bergson in a tradition which derives from Descartes'. The point Eliot insists upon is that to affirm the intellect is not to exclude the value of intuition. For in the first place some forms of intuition (e.g., concerning mathematical axioms) are highly intellectual, and secondly, any intuition, in order to prove its value, 'must always be tested ... in a whole of experience in which intellect plays a large part'.[14] Those who are quick to accuse Eliot of narrow-minded irrationalism should consider whether it is not their own conception of rationality which is excessively narrow.

[12] See B. Lee, *Theory and Personality: The Significance of T.S. Eliot's Criticism* (London: Athlone, 1979), 18-28. Lee indeed recommends that we read Eliot's critical essays 'as *expression*, not as theory; as one might read literature, continuous with poetry – with Eliot's own poetry'. Eliot's theorizing 'isn't theory at all' (19, 23). E. Lobb, *T. S. Eliot and the Romantic Critical Tradition* (London: Routledge and Kegan Paul, 1981) more moderately maintains that Eliot's critical theory is unphilosophical 'rhetoric', 'an art of persuasion rather than a science of "proof" ' or 'reasoned argument' (94, 7, 158). Lobb's thesis sadly begs the question that philosophy is or should be a science and never an art of persuasion involving argumentation that is neither inductive nor deductive but which might be characterized as rhetorical. Besides the many contemporary philosophers who would challenge this constricted conception of philosophy and reasoning, Eliot himself asserted that 'philosophy is not science' (*TUP*, 60).

[13] 'The Idea of a Literary Review', 5.

[14] T.S. Eliot, 'Mr. Middleton Murry's Synthesis', *Criterion* 6 (1927), 340-347; quotations from 342-343.

To be guilty of occasional contradiction and to take account of personal feelings and needs in theorizing about literature and its criticism is not to be anti-rational. Nor are philosophy and theory confined to the erection of well-wrought systems or the formulation of necessary, unexceptionable principles and methods. As Richard Rorty has recently argued (and as Eliot much earlier may have learned from Hulme) there is a perfectly respectable form of philosophy which is intentionally unsystematic but instead pragmatic or edifying.[15] Recognizing the historicity of human knowledge, it does not pretend to provide a comprehensive unshakeable system of unchanging truths, but instead offers pragmatic strategies for ordering and coping with a field of inquiry, and for obtaining desirable modifications of it which have particular validity for a certain time or context. Eliot's critical theory, as I shall show, was essentially of this pragmatic variety, neither advocating nor employing any fixed and uniformly applicable method or formulable principle, but rather reacting to changing circumstances and needs and motivated chiefly by aims of improving practice rather than theoretically reflecting the existent 'truth' about it. (This pragmatic theoretical stance is coupled with an historicist meta-theory or philosophy which affirms that poetry and criticism will not admit of unchanging systems or methods or essentialist principles, but rather change over and by means of history.)

In the scientistic ideology which has cramped Western philosophy since Descartes, theoretical rationality is apt to be narrowly construed as necessarily involving systematic methods or foundationalist principles. But a number of contemporary philosophers, in both analytic and continental traditions, have, in their general rebellion against Cartesianism, revived and emphasized an Aristotelian notion of practical wisdom, an intellectual virtue of deliberative intelligence which cannot be reduced to law or method, but which is none the less essential to human understanding.[16] Eliot, too, despite some early yearnings for more rigorous and standardized scientific methods in criticism, generally insisted that good judgment in criticism and in theory cannot depend on mere adherence to method. Here, says Eliot 'there is no method except to be very intelligent'; and it is not surprising that this advocacy of practical wisdom comes from a passage where Aristotle (whom Eliot describes as the perfect critic) is praised for providing an exemplary theoretic model 'not of laws or even of method' but 'of intelligence' (*SW*, 11). I shall discuss the pragmatism of Eliot's theory and its Aristotelian sources in Chapter Eight.

[15] See R. Rorty, *Philosophy and the Mirror of Nature* (Princeton: Princeton University Press, 1979). For Hulme's clear anticipation of these Rortian views on philosophy, see pp. 37-38 below, and more fully, my 'Remembering Hulme: A Neglected Philosopher-Critic-Poet', *Journal of the History of Ideas*, 46 (1985), 559-576.

[16] For two renowned representatives, see H. Putnam, *Meaning and the Moral Sciences* (London: Routledge and Kegan Paul, 1979), 5, 66-67; and H-G. Gadamer, *Truth and Method* (New York: Crossroad, 1982), 278-288; *Reason in the Age of Science* (Cambridge, Mass.: MIT Press, 1983), 69-138.

Contemporary theorists' belittling caricature of Eliot as a narrow and anti-intellectual aesthete, propounding an anti-rational criticism to serve an irrational reactionary religious and political ideology is a very neat, though embarrassingly transparent, strategy for dismissing the importance and complexity of Eliot's critical thought. Since so many of us secular liberals instinctively tend to regard religion and reactionary politics as irrational, we are tempted to a fallaciously facile dismissal of Eliot's critical theory, as if it must be entirely corrupted by the putative irrationality of his religion and politics. But the dubious rationality of this inference is what instead should be questioned, as should the motive of the strategy. One obvious motive is to magnify the novelty and hence importance of contemporary critics' excursion into theory and cultural criticism by systematically ignoring or denying the achievements of an influential progenitor which still painfully dwarf their own.

(3) Though it hardly seems to tally with his putative unreflective irrationalism, another popular misconception depicts Eliot's critical theory as rigidly objectivist, seeking to minimize if not altogether extinguish the subjective factor and the role of the reader, who is essentially reduced to impersonal detachment and neutral passivity. Thus, the literary theorist David Bleich censures Eliot for his scientific objectivism which misled generations of critics to dismiss the relevance and authority of subjectivity and to disguise personal response and value judgment 'in the form and syntax of fact'. By now we should not be surprised to meet once again the favorite strategy of linking whatever seems repellent in Eliot's critical thought to what is assumed *a priori* most objectionable – his religious outlook. Thus Bleich, postulating an essential 'association of religious interests and the objective paradigm', emphasizes that in Eliot's critical program 'two aspects of the objective character are combined – the religious assumption that ministers have special access to the absolute truth and the scientistic assumption that an object of art is independent of human perception.'[17] If critical objectivism is not odious enough, its association with religion should certainly make it so.

Unfortunately, the misapprehension of Eliot as an uncompromising critical objectivist is also often shared by Eliot's sectaries and sympathizers. Thus Sean Lucy confidently claims: 'The whole of Eliot's theory of criticism is based on a firm belief in objective standards of excellence in art ... As in his theory of poetry, ... he insists on the exclusion of the personal element from criticism, and on the search for the thing itself rather than a personal vision of it.'[18]

However, apart from an early (though enormously influential) advocacy of objectivism, Eliot explicitly and repeatedly rejected the idea of criticism as an objective science (e.g. *TUP*, 60; *OPP*, 117). And, as we shall see in

[17] D. Bleich, *Subjective Criticism* (Baltimore: Johns Hopkins University Press, 1978), 33-34.
[18] S. Lucy, *T.S. Eliot and the Idea of Tradition* (London: Cohen and West, 1960), 44.

Chapter Three, at least one version of his early objectivism in no way involved the implausible view that a work of art be understood as 'independent of human perception'. As his thought developed, Eliot clearly and definitively distanced himself from any impersonal objectivism which would deny a place for the personal factor of response and the active role of the reader in appreciation and criticism. For he indeed insists throughout his mature writing (at least from as early as 1930)[19] that the meaning of a literary work is a function of its meaning to its readers and to some degree differs from reader to reader; and he unequivocally draws the conclusion that 'a valid interpretation [of a literary work] ... must be at the same time an interpretation of my own feelings when I read it' (*OPP*, 113-114). Similarly, rather than recommending the exercise of an impersonal and pure aesthetic taste, Eliot inculcates that there simply is no such thing, nor should there be. One's literary judgment 'cannot be isolated from one's other interests and passions'; and if you attempt to exclude or bracket out your personal beliefs and attitudes regarding what the poem expresses, you risk 'cheating yourself out of a great deal that poetry has to give to your development' to pursue 'some illusory *pure* enjoyment' or appreciation (*TUP*, 36, 98). The exemplary critic is no longer a depersonalized master of impersonal rules and techniques, 'the critic must be the whole man', bringing to bear his personal 'convictions ... and experience of life' (*OPP*, 116). The role of the reader and critic is thus not one of inertly neutral reflection of a 'thing in itself' but an engaged and complex response whose character will be delineated in Chapter Six.

Since the conventional view of Eliot's critical theory as strict scientistic objectivism is so very wrong, must we then regard his theory as sceptically subjectivist or radically relativist, as some sympathetic critics seem tempted to do? This, I think, would be an overly hasty, extreme, and simplistic reaction, which naively neglects non-scientistic models of objective validity and uncritically assumes that the objective/subjective distinction marks a clear and rigid dichotomy, where all judgments involving a subjective factor are precluded from having any objective validity or truth. Eliot's treatment of the question of objectivity is too complex to be simply branded as objectivist, subjectivist, or relativist, and it will be the topic of Chapter Three.

(4) A major reason for failing to grasp the complexity of Eliot's account of objectivity (and also for regarding him as an irrationally inconsistent thinker) is the failure to pay sufficient attention to the development of his thought. As Eliot matured, his theoretical views developed significantly though not always sharply. On some issues (e.g. the legitimacy of interpretation, the desirability of impersonal 'scientific' criticism, the virtual exclusion of non-poets from the ranks of valuable critics of poetry)

[19] See Eliot's 'Introduction' to G. W. Knight, *The Wheel of Fire* (London: Methuen, 1930), xiii-xx, especially xvi, xviii. In this essay Eliot first recanted his previous scepticism of the legitimacy of interpretation in criticism.

the change is salient and self-conscious; while on others (e.g. the nature of tradition) it is much less remarkable though still quite significant. Of course, many who closely followed Eliot's critical career have noted (and sometimes mourned) important changes in his theory and outlook.[20] However, the dominant recent trend is to minimize or deny altogether the development of his thought. His biographer, Ackroyd, speaks for many in asserting that 'Eliot did not develop as a "thinker": he merely elaborated on the implications of his previous convictions' held as early as 1916 when he began his critical career, if not still earlier.[21] (His striking conversion to Anglicanism in 1927 is apparently one of these non-developments!) Though the borders between mere elaboration and development may be fuzzy, I find this non-developmental view misleading and unproductive and shall try to demonstrate significant developments in Eliot's thought on a number of topics.

The attraction of the non-developmental view derives chiefly from a very powerful, positive motivation to maintain the essential unity of Eliot's thought. Unity, for Eliot, was an extremely important value, perhaps the supreme value. His craving for it was deep and pervasive, not only in art and criticism but in non-aesthetic thought and society. His high praise, not only of Shakespeare, Dante, and Goethe but also of Bradley, is largely in terms of the fundamental unity of their work. Advocates of the non-developmental view may also point out that Eliot seems to take pains to emphasize the essential unity of his own thought. He often does this by citing in confirmation his earlier assertions and by playing down apparently sharp changes of view by asserting their underlying continuity or coherence (*SE*, 23; *OPP*, 104, 115, 151-161; *TCC*, 23-24).

Undeniable as it is, Eliot's commitment to the ideal of unity needs to be understood in terms of two further considerations. First, Eliot was also exceedingly committed to the ideal of development, which equally informs his high praise of Yeats, Shakespeare, Joyce, Pound, and James; and which leads him to describe development as 'one of the greatest capacities of genius'.[22] Secondly and more importantly, it would seem, at least in Eliot's eyes, that there is no reason to regard development as incompatible with unity. He defines Shakespeare's unity purely in terms of development (*SE*, 193, 203), and likewise the unity of Bradley's thought 'is not the unity of mere fixity ... attained by a man who never changes his mind' (*SE*, 453). Moreover, the interconnection of unity and development is extremely important for Eliot's theory of culture and

---

[20] See, for example, F.W. Bateson, 'Criticism's Lost Leader', in D. Newton-De Molina (ed.), *The Literary Criticism of T.S. Eliot* (London: Athlone, 1977), 1-19.

[21] See P. Ackroyd, *T.S. Eliot* (London: Hamish Hamilton, 1984), 75.

[22] From Eliot's remarks on Joyce in B. Gheerbrant, *James Joyce; sa vie, son oeuvre, son rayonnement* (Paris: Le Hune, 1949), n. pag. Quoted on p. x of the 'Preface' to Margolis which also documents Eliot's praise of development in other writers.

tradition, which will be discussed in Chapter Seven along with the question of the possibility of a developing structure of unity.

Whatever our view on the general connection of unity and development, it is clear that neglect or denial of development can be used to simplify and unify Eliot's theoretical views, reducing difficult complexities to a facile monolithic stance or label. Most typically this is done by ignoring later developments to embalm Eliot's theory in the early objectivism expressed in *The Sacred Wood* (1920), 'The Function of Criticism' (1923) and other essays of his pre-conversion period. This reduction, though false and brutally impoverishing, sometimes seems charitably motivated by the fear that the Eliot corpus might otherwise be dismissed as an unprofitably murky muddle.

(5) A more sophisticated strategy of unification for reducing the apparent development and diversity of Eliot's theoretical views to a common unitary core would be to claim that they all are essentially generated and informed by a central philosophical source. Since the belated publication of Eliot's doctoral thesis, *Knowledge and Experience in the Philosophy of F.H. Bradley*, in 1964, this has been an increasingly popular strategy, where the entirety of Eliot's critical theory is explained as the product and elaboration of Eliot's doctoral absorption in and interpretative adaptation of Bradley's philosophy. Thus Ann Bolgan (who rescued the thesis from the oblivion to which Eliot had consigned it) confidently declares of Eliot that Bradley's mind 'lies ... behind every major theoretical concept appearing in his literary criticism'.[23] Lewis Freed similarly maintains that 'the philosophy in his critical prose, late and early, is the version of Bradley sketched in *Knowledge and Experience*'.[24]

The view that Eliot was essentially and undeviatingly a Bradleyan disciple throughout his career is a fifth misconception which needs to be exposed. Moreover, even the more limited view that Bradleyan philosophy is the major philosophical influence at work in his early criticism is also mistaken.

It is easy to understand the attraction to interpret Eliot's critical theory in terms of general philosophy, and particularly that of Bradley. We must remember that most of Eliot's formal academic education and professional training was not in literary scholarship but in philosophy. While studying for his doctorate in philosophy at Harvard (1911-1914), he was employed as a teaching assistant in the philosophy department and was for a time the President of the University's Philosophical Society.[25] His courses there covered a wide range of topics from symbolic logic to Indian metaphysics (in

[23] Bolgan, 252.

[24] Freed, xii.

[25] For these and other details of Eliot's Harvard and Oxford education, see B. Bergonzi, *T.S. Eliot* (New York: Macmillan, 1972), 24-37; R. Sencourt, *T.S. Eliot: A Memoir* (London: Garnstone Press, 1971), 38-49; L. Gordon, *Eliot's Early Years* (Oxford: Oxford University Press, 1977), 21-22, 49-58; P. Gray, *T.S. Eliot's Intellectual and Poetic Development, 1909-1922* (Sussex: Harvester, 1982), 90-174; and Ackroyd, 40-75.

which for some period he took an intense interest). Earlier (1910-1911) he had spent a year in France studying Bergson, but ultimately settled on the philosophy of F.H. Bradley as the topic of his doctoral research, under the supervision of the renowned Harvard idealist Josiah Royce, whose work Eliot also closely studied.[26]

Having completed his course requirements and with the aid of a travel scholarship, he further pursued his study of philosophy; first briefly in Marburg, Germany (July 1914) and then for three terms at Merton College, Oxford (1914-1915), where he studied Aristotle at Bradley's college with Bradley's closest disciple, H. Joachim. Eliot's doctoral thesis on Bradley, originally titled 'Experience and the Objects of Knowledge in the Philosophy of F.H. Bradley', was completed and sent to Harvard by April 1916, most of it probably having been written during Eliot's stay at Oxford.[27] The thesis was enthusiastically received by the Harvard faculty, Royce describing it as the work of an expert; and only Eliot's failure to return for the oral defence of his thesis (chiefly because of his young wife's reluctance that he go) prevented him from being awarded a doctorate in philosophy. In the years immediately following the completion of his thesis, his literary criticism and theory began to grow and blossom in a variety of short essays and reviews, some of the best of which were gathered into Eliot's first critical collection, *The Sacred Wood* (1920), which established him as an important critic before he had achieved equal fame as a poet. Between 1916 and 1918 Eliot had also published two articles in the respected philosophical journal *The Monist*, as well as numerous reviews of philosophical books in the *International Journal of Ethics* and the *New Statesman*.[28]

Given the extent of Eliot's philosophical training, it is most reasonable to believe that his critical views were influenced by his philosophical interests and can be better understood in the light of more general philosophical perspectives. Our present study similarly assumes that a philosophical approach to Eliot is pertinent and illuminating. But given Eliot's intensive study of Bradley, the fact that his critical theory immediately follows that study, and finally his high praise and avowal of indebtedness to Bradley, it

[26] See Gray, 90-174, who (while giving pride of place to Bradley) makes the most substantial case for Royce's influence on Eliot, in terms of Roycean emphases on community and history, which Gray links to Eliot's idea of tradition. Though Royce was an idealist like Bradley, his philosophy had acquired a strong pragmatist orientation by the time Eliot studied under him. Acknowledging his debt to Peirce, Royce called his philosophy 'absolute pragmatism'. See J.E. Smith, 'Josiah Royce', in P. Edwards (ed.), *Encyclopedia of Philosophy* (New York: Macmillan, 1967), vol. 7, 225-229. Royce's pragmatism may well have nourished the pragmatic tendency of Eliot's thinking and the pervasive pragmatism of his doctoral thesis which Gray fails to address. On the pragmatism of Eliot's thesis, see W. Michaels, 'Philosophy in Kinkanja: Eliot's Pragmatism', *Glyph* 8 (Baltimore: John Hopkins University Press, 1981), 170-202.

[27] See Ackroyd, 69.

[28] It was Russell who secured for Eliot the two commissioned *Monist* articles and the reviewing. See Eliot's 'Preface' *to Knowledge and Experience*, 11, and Ackroyd, 68-69. It would hardly be surprising therefore to expect a growing philosophical influence of Russell on the budding critic and theoretician. This influence will be delineated in Chapter Two.

is also very tempting to explain his theory as fundamentally an elaboration of his Bradleyan philosophy and essentially informed by it. It is this claim I want to contest, though I hardly wish to claim that Bradley had no notable influence on Eliot. Certainly, as Eliot himself remarks, there seems to be some trace of Bradley in his prose style, and who can fathom the mysteries of poetic creativity to gainsay Eliot's claim that Bradley's 'personality as manifested in his works' influenced Eliot's poetry (*KE*, 10-11, *TCC*, 20)? Nor is it convincing to deny categorically that any affinities can be found or connections made between Bradley, Eliot's Bradleyan thesis, and Eliot's critical theory. Several long studies claim to demonstrate substantial connections, and since all three allegedly connected terms have proven open to widely variant interpretations, the project of totally refuting the claim seems a daunting and futile exercise. I hope to achieve a certain dislodging of the dominant Bradleyan interpretation of Eliot's critical theory (particularly his earlier theory) by interpreting it instead in terms of other and, I think, more rewarding philosophical perspectives – those of twentieth-century philosophy rather than Bradley's essentially nineteenth-century thought.

However, let me offer here some brief remarks to suggest why Eliot's early critical theory seems both remote from Bradley and significantly different (and hence a salient development) from the Bradleyan philosophy of his thesis. As Wollheim convincingly demonstrates, Bradley's whole philosophy was essentially motivated by a radical repudiation of empiricist thought.[29] This involved both a denial of the existence of a plurality of facts and a rejection of the method of analysis. Facts were condemned as mere abstractions, while analysis was decried as a mutilating alteration of reality, which is essentially and necessarily *one*.[30] Such an attitude surely seems alien to Eliot's early criticism with its insistent and often shrill advocacy of precisely these two notions – facts and analysis – and with its distinct leanings toward an empiricist outlook, where 'all knowledge ... is in perception' and a favored strategy of critical intelligence is 'the analysis of sensation to the point of principle and definition' (*SW*, 10, 11). Throughout *The Sacred Wood* and other writings of that period, Eliot relentlessly inculcates that 'the critical attitude is to attempt to analyze', that analysis is one of the chief 'tools' and aims of the critic, just as facts are

[29] See R. Wollheim, *F.H. Bradley* (Harmondsworth, UK: Penguin, 1969), 43-127. When presented with the task of relating Eliot to Bradley, Wollheim wisely concentrates on Eliot's thesis and Harvard philosophy papers and only sketchily suggests a few 'very general tendencies of thought' that Eliot's criticism seems to share with Bradley. Wollheim revealingly cautions that any attempt to undertand Eliot's criticism through his Bradleyan philosophy is apt to yield 'bewilderment'. See 'Eliot and F.H. Bradley: An Account', 170-193. It is unfortunate that such an accomplished analytic philosopher as Wollheim never attempted to consider Eliot in relation to analytic philosophy.

[30] Consider, for example: 'Reality is one. It must be single, because plurality, taken as real, contradicts itself.' 'It is a very common and most ruinous supersition to suppose that analysis is no alteration.' F.H. Bradley, *Appearance and Reality* (Oxford: Clarendon, 1930), 28; and *Principles of Logic* (Oxford: Clarendon, 1922), 95.

both his necessary data and among the valuable results of his endeavor. The critic thus needs a 'sense of fact', and his presentation of relevant facts, especially 'facts which are capable of generalization, ... is a service of value' (*SW*, 60, 5, 37, 14, 96, 124).

There are, then, serious obstacles to viewing the distinctly empirical and analytic emphases of Eliot's early theory as deeply consistent with, let alone inspired by, Bradley's own philosophy. Nor do such difficulties dissolve if we confine ourselves to Eliot's interpretation and application of Bradley in his thesis, which though generally sympathetic is not entirely uncritical of Bradley's philosophy and thus needs to be distinguished from it. For here as well there are sharp differences from his early criticism on such important issues as fact, interpretation, and objectivity. The thesis shares Bradley's rejection of fact: 'The true critic ... refrains from statements which pretend to be literally true; he finds fact nowhere.' Repudiation of fact means that all truth is 'only an interpretation', for indeed 'any assertion about the world [and its objects] ... will inevitably be an interpretation'. Consequently, there is necessary value in the 'sort of interpretation ... that the historian, the literary critic, and the metaphysician are engaged with' (*KE*, 164-165).

It is obviously a very different Eliot who repeatedly claims in the early critical essays that 'the work of art cannot be interpreted; there is nothing to interpret'; and that the critic's 'chief task' of so-called interpretation 'is the presentation of relevant historical facts which the reader is not assumed to know' (*SW*, 96). For now Eliot 'is fairly certain that "interpretation" ... is only legitimate when it is not interpretation at all, but merely putting the reader in possession of facts'. The critic should not only be 'dealing with his facts' but should endeavor to have the nebulous feelings and meanings of poetry 'clarified and reduced to a state of fact' (*SE*, 31-32). He should never 'take leave' of his factual 'data' for interpretative passage into 'the frontiers of metaphysics or mysticism' (*SW*, 13, 59).

With this striking reversal of the valencies of fact and interpretation, there is a similar reversal of the valencies of the private, the subjective, and the internal versus the public, objective, and external. While Eliot's thesis awkwardly combines the rejection of any firm and substantial 'distinction between inner and outer', subjective and objective (*KE*, 20-21, 31, 138-139) together with a firm assertion that 'all significant truths are private truths', which 'as they become public ... cease to become truth' (*KE*, 165), his early postdoctoral criticism contrastingly insists on firmly distinguishing objectivity, shared public truth, and 'Outside Authority' from the private subjectivity of 'the Inner Voice', elevating the former and violently repudiating the latter (*SE*, 26-33).

If there seems to be such significant difference between Eliot's doctoral philosophy and the philosophy which informs his early criticism, what then makes the difference? The answer, to be delineated in the next chapter, is Russell and his philosophy of logical, analytic empiricism, particularly as it was most powerfully expounded between the years 1914-1924, chiefly under the more specific label and doctrine of 'logical atomism'. If the difference between Eliot's Bradleyan philosophy and his early criticism seems so obvious, why has it been so easy to ignore? Apart from the motives of unity and simplification previously mentioned, there is also the fact that Eliot's conversion to hard-line empiricist objectivism was short lived, and he later reverted to a hermeneutical philosophical perspective which shared the irrealism of his thesis and recognized that the objectivities of our human world are largely constituted by interpretative thought. Eliot's philosophical development, from his early discarding of Bradleyan Absolute Idealism for an analytic empiricist realism, which in turn was abandoned for a non-realist hermeneutical perspective emphasizing the historicity and holistic nature of human understanding, is a simulacrum of the history of much of twentieth-century philosophy. In England this history begins, as we shall, by forsaking Bradley for the project of analytic philosophy.

Chapter 2

Eliot and Analytic Philosophy

The greatest debts are not always the most evident.

'What Dante Means to Me'

I

Analytic philosophy was essentially born of Moore and Russell's rebellion against Bradley. Though originally disciples of Bradleyan idealism (and students of the Cambridge absolute idealist McTaggart), Moore and Russell soon came, at the turn of the century, to attack not only the idealism but the monism of Bradley's philosophy. They advanced in its stead a realist philosophy which insisted on the independent reality of different objects and facts (and, at least for a time, of concepts, propositions, and values) as well as maintaining the possibility of real or non-internal relations between them.[1] Though it was Moore who initiated the analytic anti-idealist revolt, by the time Eliot encountered analytic philosophy around 1914, Russell had become the more productive and leading thinker and had begun to formulate an extremely powerful, comprehensive, and systematic philosophy which he came to call logical atomism.[2] Over the

[1] Moore in fact first began his realist, pluralist revolt by asserting that concepts and the (true) propositions in which they are related are real and indeed all that is ultimately real. See G.E. Moore, 'The Nature of Judgement', *Mind* 8 (1899), 176-193. Russell's *The Principles of Mathematics* (London: Allen and Unwin, 1903) displays a similar if not even more opulent platonistic realism. Both philosophers later took a far more empiricist and reductive line. For a concise and helpful account of Moore and Russell's revolt against Bradley, see J. Passmore, *A Hundred Years of Philosophy* (Harmondsworth, UK: Penguin, 1980), 201-217.

[2] Logical atomism may roughly be said to date from 1914 with the publication of Russell's *Our Knowledge of the External World* (London: Allen and Unwin), though many of its ideas (including some which influenced Eliot) were already adumbrated in his earlier works. The term was introduced in Russell's course of lectures 'The Philosophy of Logical Atomism', given in the first months of 1918 in London and subsequently published in *The Monist* (1918-19). Russell's philosophical position was further strengthened by the publication in December 1917 of *Mysticism and Logic* (London: Allen and Unwin), a very influential collection of previously published essays similarly expressing the logico-analytic empiricist approach of his logical atomism, and so popular that by 1925 it had received more than five reprintings.

next two decades, Russell's logical atomism was impressively developed both by himself and by Wittgenstein, and then further clarified, applied, and critically refined by others (e.g. Ramsey and Wisdom).[3] It thus became the leading philosophical theory in England throughout the period of Eliot's earlier analytic and objectivist criticism, which can be said to begin in 1916 with the completion of his doctoral thesis and which seems to have run its course by 1927, the year of his conversion. By 1928 Eliot himself confessed that his critical interests began to shift from close analysis of poetry as an autonomous object to a consideration 'of the relation of poetry to the soul and spiritual life' (*SW*, viii); and the motivating spirit and tone of his criticism had begun to turn from revolutionary, avante-garde zeal to reactionary conservatism and then ultimately to benign sage-like moderation.[4]

In order to argue that Eliot's early criticism – which has so far proved his most seminal and potent – was influenced by Russell's analytic philosophy, I shall first show that Eliot, the young critic, was very much aware of and impressed by this philosophy. Then I shall demonstrate that several major themes of Eliot's early criticism reflect central doctrines of logical atomism and are more or less straightforward applications of these doctrines in the field of literary criticism. Finally, I shall show that the only apparent alternative (and generally accepted) source for these early Eliotic critical doctrines – T.E. Hulme – was himself powerfully and avowedly influenced by Russell and Moore's analytic philosophy.

II

Eliot was immediately impressed by Russell when the English philosopher came to Harvard as a visiting professor in 1914, while Eliot was a graduate student working on Bradley's philosophy. However, at this stage Eliot was only attracted to Russell's personality and not to his philosophy. Though he attended Russell's course on symbolic logic, he did not then warm to or distinguish himself in this subject, and doubted

---

Logical atomism more or less dominated English philosophy until about 1936 with the publication of A.J. Ayer's *Language, Truth and Logic* (London: Gollancz). Much of my account of logical atomism is based on J.O. Urmson's classic history of analytic philosophy, *Philosophical Analysis: Its Development Between the Two World Wars* (Oxford: Oxford University Press, 1967).

[3] See L. Wittgenstein, *Tractatus Logico-Philosophicus* (London: Kegan Paul, 1922); F.P. Ramsey, *The Foundations of Mathematics* (London: Kegan Paul, 1931); and J. Wisdom, 'Logical Constructions', *Mind*, 1931-33, in five parts.

[4] Eliot once suggested that his critical career could be divided into three periods: approximately, 1915-1918, 1918-1930, 1930-1961 (*TC*, 17-18; and Kermode in *SP*, 11-12). However, it is clear that his conversion marks a turning in his criticism, a change avowed in his preface to the 1928 edition of *The Sacred Wood*. This is not to suggest that the conversion actually caused the change or that the change was total, sudden, and violent rather than partial and gradual.

whether it had 'anything to do with reality'.[5] Eliot's philosophical inclinations were then distinctly idealistic, reflecting the idealistic bias of his undergraduate training and reflected in his attraction to the philosophy of Bradley. Even when, as a graduate student, he saw his department adopt the New Realist position with its stress on mathematics and the exact sciences, Eliot (lacking adequate background in either) could not accept the change and turned first to Indian philosophy and then to Bradley.[6]

Eliot's attitude toward Russell's philosophy quickly changed after he came to England to study Bradley. Already in his first vacation from Oxford (Christmas, 1914) he was deeply absorbed in the study of Russell's *Principia Mathematica*.[7] There can be little doubt that in the next few years Eliot was exposed to and interested in subsequent developments of Russell's philosophy, at least as much as one is naturally interested in the work of a close friend in a field which was recently one's own primary interest. For in 1915, shortly after his marriage and the consequent break with his family in America, Eliot and Russell's friendship was renewed with tremendous intensity when Eliot and his bride moved into Russell's London flat. During their extended stay and indeed for the next ten years, Russell played an influential role in the couple's unhappy personal life, trying to relieve their marital problems (though probably actually exacerbating them) and ease their financial difficulties. At this point Eliot regarded Russell almost as a father, and Russell wrote of Eliot: 'I have come to love him, as if he were my son.'[8]

Most scholars and biographers of Eliot regard Russell's influence as entirely personal, and maintain that Eliot was always indifferent if not hostile to Russell's philosophy. This view can find some support from a parenthetical remark in Russell's autobiography denying that he and Eliot influenced each other.[9] And Eliot clearly disapproved of Russell's secularist liberal ideology and political thought. However, closer study will reveal that Russell's analytic philosophy was a significant influence on Eliot's early critical thought, though an influence Eliot never adequately acknowledged. Its aims, methods and spirit not only served Eliot as a paradigm of rigorous critical thought, but represented ideas and values which Eliot sought to emulate in his early criticism.

The first point to note is that Eliot's critical writings in this period contain several remarks which show Eliot's awareness and admiration of Russell's philosophical achievement. *The Sacred Wood*'s important essays (written between 1917-1920) provide at least three clearly sympathetic

[5] Quoted in L. Gordon, *Eliot's Early Years*, 49. The biographical information in this and the following paragraph come from Gordon, 49-59, 74-84; B. Bergonzi, *T.S. Eliot*, 32-36; and R. Sencourt, *T.S. Eliot: A Memoir*, 40-49. These three works are cited in full in ch. 1, n. 25.

[6] See Gordon, 21. See also Eliot's own confession of weakness in these subjects (*TC*, 45).

[7] See Sencourt, 49.

[8] B. Russell, 'Letter to Ottoline Morrell' (Nov. 10, 1915), repr. in *The Autobiography of Bertrand Russell*, vol. 2 (Boston: Little, Brown, 1969), 64.

[9] *The Autobiography of Bertrand Russell*, vol. 2, 9.

references to Russell's philosophy. In 'The Perfect Critic' Eliot refers to Russell's philosophy of mathematics to argue that the abstract may nevertheless be clear and exact, as in the abstract yet precisely defined objects of mathematics (*SW*, 9). In 'The Possibility of Poetic Drama' Eliot praises Russell's renowned essay of philosophical analysis 'On Denoting' as 'a work of art'; 'clear and beautifully formed thought' (*SW*, 66). In yet another essay of this small collection Eliot alludes to the existence and importance of the new philosophy of logical atomism propounded by Russell and his Cambridge colleagues; for among the list of 'contemporary' scientific advances of 'very great value', Eliot mentions 'a new philosophy arose at Cambridge' (*SW*, 75). Moreover, outside *The Sacred Wood*, Eliot praises Russell for helping (together with other modern logicians) to make English into an excellent language, 'a language in which it is possible to think clearly and exactly on any subject. The *Principia Mathematica* are perhaps a greater contribution to our language than they are to mathematics.'[10] In his 1918 review of Russell's *Mysticism and Logic*, which demonstrates detailed knowledge of the different works and development of Russell's philosophy, Eliot praises Russell's thought as 'a victory ... of science' which liberated English philosophy from German influence. He presents Russell's philosophy (and even his style) as superior to Bradley's; it is not a sceptical 'perfection of destruction' but the constructive, promising work 'of a man of science ... who has invented a new method and ... will probably carry this method further'.[11]

Scholars who maintain the commonly accepted view that Eliot was resistant to Russell's philosophy might try to discount such evidence as mere lip service to the work of a personal friend and benefactor, or to the widely held view that Russell's work was a major philosophical achievement. The best way to show that Eliot's admiration for Russell's philosophy was indeed sincere and that Eliot's criticism was influenced by it is to demonstrate that Eliot himself shared and articulated in his own critical writings many of the central ideas of Russell's philosophy. This will be done by presenting four central themes of Russell's logical atomism and demonstrating how these same themes are central to Eliot's criticism.

III

I shall not attempt here to give an adequate sketch of logical atomism, for many of its important doctrines are of narrowly philosophical interest and could have no real relevance for literary criticism. J.O. Urmson, whose

[10] T.S. Eliot, 'Commentary', *The Criterion*, 6 (1927), 291.
[11] See T.S. Eliot, 'Style and Thought', *The Nation*, March 23, 1918, 768-770. Eliot's knowledge and admiration of Eliot's analytic philosophy is further displayed in the following places: '[A Review of] *A Defence of Idealism*', *New Statesman* (22 Sept. 1917), 596; 'A Commentary', *Criterion*, 2 (1924), 233; and 'Mr. Middleton Murry's Synthesis', *Criterion*, 6 (1927), 341. Alongside the praise of Russell's technical philosophy Eliot directs sharp criticism

Philosophical Analysis provides a clear and detailed study of logical atomism, suggests that this philosophy has two major aspects which are closely related: the methodology and ideology of logical and linguistic analysis, and the atomistic metaphysics which is, on the one hand, the product of analysis and, on the other hand, its justification and rationale.[12] We shall not be much occupied here with the metaphysical doctrines of logical atomism (e.g. that the world is ultimately composed of atomic facts which are in turn composed of particulars and their attributes or relations); for remote as these doctrines are from literature, they seem to have little, if any, expression in Eliot's criticism. However, the major methodological tenets of logical atomism, which by their general methodological nature could be applicable to most disciplines, are frequently and fervently echoed and applied by Eliot in his early critical writings.

(1) The most fundamental and important of the methodological doctrines of logical atomism is the view that (philosophical) knowledge is to be obtained primarily from analysis. The notion and role of analysis is so central here that logical atomism together with the philosophies it later engendered (e.g. logical positivism and ordinary-language philosophy) are commonly referred to as 'analytic philosophy'. Russell clearly affirmed the centrality of analysis to his philosophy. In 'Logical Atomism'[13] he writes:

> The business of philosophy, as I conceive it, is essentially that of logical analysis, followed by logical synthesis. ... Although, moreover, comprehensive construction is part of the business of philosophy, I do not believe it is the most important part. The most important part, to my mind, consists in criticizing and clarifying notions which are apt to be regarded as fundamental and accepted uncritically. As instances I might mention: mind, matter, consciousness, knowledge, experience, causality, will, time. I believe all these notions to be inexact and approximate, essentially infected with vagueness, incapable of forming part of any exact science. (*RLA*, 162)

Russell indeed is so aware of the fundamental importance of analysis that he earlier admits that 'to justify the sort of philosophy I wish to advocate would consist in justifying the process of analysis' (*RLA*, 32). Atomistic metaphysics (whose truth is to be revealed through analysis) is an essential part of that justification, while additional justification comes from the solution of logical confusions and conceptual unclarities, where

---

at his liberal, humanist *Weltanschauung*. See, for example, the *Criterion* 'Commentary' just mentioned and 'Why Mr. Russell is not a Christian', *Criterion*, 6 (1927), 177-179.

[12] Urmson, 45, 47.

[13] B. Russell, 'Logical Atomism' (1924), more or less a condensation of the earlier lectures, repr. in D. Pears (ed.), *Russell's Logical Atomism* (London: Fontana, 1972). Pears' book also contains Russell's, 'The Philosophy of Logical Atomism' (1918). All page references to both these essays will be to Pears' edition, hereinafter referred to as *RLA*. For those interested in the exact source of each citation, the earlier essay extends from pp. 31-142, the latter from pp. 143-165.

the aim is to 'pass from the vague to the precise by the method of analysis and reflection' (*RLA*, 33).

If we look carefully at Eliot's early criticism, we find the same stress on analysis as perhaps the most basic and important activity of literary criticism. In 'The Function of Criticism' Eliot asserts that 'comparison and analysis ... are the chief tools of the critic' (*SE*, 32); and this assertion is basically a development of the view expressed in 'The Perfect Critic' that the proper aim and direction of criticism is 'analysis and construction', 'you either begin to analyse and construct, to "ériger en lois", or you begin to create something else' (*SW*, 5). The similarity between these assertions and Russell's remarks above is certainly striking. Moreover, throughout *The Sacred Wood* we find evidence of Eliot's view that analysis is of the essence of criticism. He chides Swinburne for not employing enough 'dissection and analysis' (*SW*, 21); Whibley is censured because he 'is not an analyst' (*SW*, 36); and we are told that 'the only cure for Romanticism is to analyse it' (*SW*, 31) and that 'the critical attitude is an attempt to analyse' (*SW*, 66). More important, however, than Eliot's praise of analysis is his actual use of it, which we shall now consider.

As Urmson points out, Russell employed two different types of analysis.[14] One was reductive analysis which aimed at getting to the metaphysically basic by reducing certain alleged entities to non-existence, e.g. by showing them to be merely logical constructions or logical fictions (as in the analysis of material objects into sense-data, or the analysis of 'the average man' into a quotient of real men). Secondly, there was same-level analysis which aimed simply at elucidating expressions, propositions, or concepts into a clearer, more exact, and less misleading form (as, for example, in Russell's theory of descriptions). It is significant that Eliot uses both these forms of analysis.

In 'Reflections on *Vers Libre*' Eliot cleverly employs reductive analysis to argue that the notion of *vers libre* is merely an empty 'battle-cry' and that there really is no such thing as free verse. He first analyzes the notion of *vers libre* into three possible definitions, then he shows that none of them designates any distinct type of verse associated with the term '*vers libre*', and therefore concludes that *vers libre*, as a verse-form, does not really exist.

> *Vers libre* does not exist, and it is time that this preposterous fiction followed the *élan vital* and the eighty thousand Russians into oblivion.... If *vers libre* is a genuine verse-form it will have a positive definition. And I can define it only in negatives: (1) absence of pattern, (2) absence of rhyme, (3) absence of metre. ... [Moreover, analysis shows] that it is not defined by absence of pattern or absence of rhyme, for other verse is without these; that it is not defined by non-existence of metre, since even the *worst* verse can be scanned; and we

[14] Urmson, 27-41.

conclude that the division between Conservative Verse and *vers libre* does not exist, for there is only good verse, bad verse, and chaos. (*TCC*, 183, 184, 186)

Eliot's essay 'Rhetoric and Poetic Drama' provides an excellent example of the second, clarificatory sort of analysis, which according to Russell 'consists mainly in passing from those obvious, vague, ambiguous things that we feel quite sure of, to something precise, clear, definite, which by reflection and analysis we find is involved in the vague thing that we start from, and is, so to speak, the real truth of which that vague thing is sort of a shadow' (*RLA*, 33). In this essay Eliot attempts to rescue the term 'rhetoric' (which we believe to stand for some real aesthetic quality) from its confused and degenerate usage where 'the word is merely a vague term of abuse for any style that is bad' (*SW*, 78). As Russell assigned to philosophy the primary task of 'criticizing and clarifying' the fundamental and uncritically accepted notions of mind, matter, knowledge, etc., so Eliot argues that criticism must clarify the notion of rhetoric. For clearly, 'the word cannot be used as synonymous with bad writing. ... It is one of those words which it is the business of criticism to dissect and reassemble' (*SW*, 79). Eliot then endeavors to show, through analysis of certain works, that 'a precise meaning can be found for it' and that this meaning applies to both good and bad writing.

(2) Closely connected with logical atomism's doctrine of analysis as the major tool of philosophical inquiry stands the doctrine that a major obstacle to philosophical progress is the misleading nature of language and the philosopher's misunderstanding of it. Philosophical errors, it is maintained, often arise from unjustified inferences from the form or nature of ordinary language to the form or nature of reality. Russell explains how the subject-predicate form of the Indo-European languages engendered the substance-attribute metaphysics which mistakenly maintains that all facts are of this form and thus inevitably leads to monism, 'since the fact that there were several substances ... would not have the requisite form' (*RLA*, 152). He also notes the tendency 'to suppose that one word must stand for one object', which with abstract words implies the existence of corresponding single universals; 'but certainly there are many abstract words which do not stand for single universals – e.g. triangularity and rationality' (*RLA*, 152, 151). Thus, Russell maintains that 'language misleads us both by its vocabulary and by its syntax' (*RLA*, 151) and that 'practically all traditional metaphysics is filled with mistakes due to bad grammar, ... failure ... in what we may call philosophical grammar' (*RLA*, 128-9).

Eliot not only shared the belief that much metaphysical confusion is generated by language, but he further maintained that critical confusion is similarly generated. His attack on *vers libre* is a case in point. The literati, he argued, were misled by the 'battle-cry of *vers libre*' to assume that there really is a genuine verse form designated by this name, whereas according to Eliot there is none, and *vers libre* is but a fiction.

Eliot believed that language is most dangerous and misleading when it is general, vague, and abstract, and he therefore condemns 'the abstract style in criticism' as a 'verbal disease' which breeds confusion and empty critical babbling (*SW*, 2, 8, 9). Similarly, Hegel and his followers (always a prime target for the jibes of analytic philosophers) are chided by Eliot for having 'taken for granted that words have definite meanings, overlooking the tendency of words to become indefinite emotions' (*SW*, 9). The 'verbalism' of these professional philosophers has had a contaminating effect on literature and criticism; 'their corruption has extended very far' so that 'words have changed their meanings. What they have lost is definite, and what they have gained is indefinite' (*SW*, 9).

One remedy for this verbalism and its consequent confusions is logical analysis and elucidation; and Eliot indeed calls for such an analytic enterprise. 'Now, there is an urgent need for experiment in criticism of a new kind, which will consist largely in a logical and dialectical study of the terms used ... so that we may know at every moment what we mean.'[15] But there is also a prophylactic against linguistic error and confusion – to use clear and precise language in the first place. This brings us to the third theme of logical atomism that we shall consider – the nature of language and the linguistic ideal of precision.

(3) Philosophers have generally recognized that an essential function of language, if not *the* essential function, is to represent reality and thus enable us to describe the world. A central tenet of logical atomism is that language represents reality by 'mirroring' or 'picturing' facts. Russell asserts that in a logically correct language 'there will always be a certain fundamental identity of structure between a fact and a symbol for it; ... there is an objective complexity in the world, and that is mirrored by the complexity of propositions' (*RLA*, 52).

As the best sort of mirror would be one that provides a reflection of great clarity and precision, so it might seem to follow that the best language would be precise and unambiguous. Moreover, since Russell holds that philosophy aims at transforming the vague into the precise, he wants philosophical language to be as clear and precise as possible. Thus, though recognizing the indispensability of ordinary language for everyday life, Russell complains of its 'logical imperfections' for philosophy, since its 'words are all ambiguous' (*RLA*, 52) and 'more or less infected with vagueness, by which I mean that it is not always clear whether they apply to a given object or not' (*RLA*, 159).

Russell tries to characterize what a logically perfect language would be like. He asserts, for example, that 'in a logically perfect language, there will be one word and no more for every simple object, and everything that is not simple will be expressed by a combination of words, by a combination

---

[15] T.S. Eliot, 'Experiment in Criticism', *The Bookman* 70 (1929), 232.

derived, of course, from the words for the simple things that enter in, one word for each simple component' (*RLA*, 52). Implicit in this idea of language is the theory that meaning is ultimately equated with reference. The meanings of complex expressions depend on those of the simple words that compose them, and Russell equates the meaning of a simple word with the object it names (*RLA*, 48). In Russell's ideal of language the link between word and object is exceedingly close and direct.

Eliot seems to echo many of the motifs of Russell's theory of language. I shall not try to argue that his enigmatic notion of the objective correlative ('a set of objects, a situation, a chain of events' which can adequately represent or be the formula of a particular emotion, because of its 'exact equivalence' to it, *SW*, 100) is based on the atomistic model of mirroring and identity of structure, though there is strong resemblance between the two notions. What is undeniably clear, however, is Eliot's early acceptance of the atomist's ideal of precision.

Throughout *The Sacred Wood* (e.g. pp. 9, 43, 67) Eliot emphasizes the importance and superiority of the precise, clear, particular, and definite, while deploring the vague, general, and indefinite; not only in literary criticism but in literature itself. He not only sees 'the necessity for greater precision in the phrases we apply' in criticism (*SW*, 78), but he sees Shakespeare's superiority over Massinger as that of 'precise vigour' and 'the particular image' over 'the general forensic statement' (*SW*, 126). Elsewhere in this period, Eliot argues for the superiority of Herbert over Vaughan, and Marvell over Morris in terms of the superiority of clarity and precision over mistiness and vagueness.[16] Similarly, the prose of Lancelot Andrewes is praised for its clarity and 'precision in the use of words', and so is Russell's prose (*SE*, 344; *SW*, 66). One could go so far as to suggest that Eliot's early emphasis on visual imagery is connected with atomism's desire for precision (visual imagery, by nature, being most concrete and precise), and particularly connected with atomism's picture theory of language, where language, as it were, graphically represents the world.

Moreover, Eliot seems to embrace Russell's referential theory of meaning, stressing the direct and indissoluble link between word and object in proper and healthy language. Consider his criticism of Swinburne's verse:

> The morbidity is not of human feeling but of language. Language in a healthy state presents the object, is so close to the object that the two are identified. They are identified in the verse of Swinburne solely because the object has ceased to exist, because the meaning is merely the hallucination of meaning ... (*SW*, 149)

[16] See T.S. Eliot, 'The Silurist', *The Dial*, 83 (1927), 262; and 'Andrew Marvell' (1921), (*SE*, 299-300).

The same view of language is suggested in Eliot's praise of Donne and others, in whose language 'sensation became word and word was sensation' (*SW*, 129). The association of this view with Russell's theory of language is particularly tempting when we recall that for Russell the paradigmatic objects of precise words were sense-data.

(4) The subject of sense-data brings us to the final theme we shall consider in Russell's logical atomism – its rigorous empiricism. One can distinguish at least three salient elements of this empiricism which are echoed in Eliot's early criticism: first, that sense perception is the prime source and basis for knowledge and language; secondly, the superiority of science over traditional philosophy in getting at the truth; and thirdly, the emphasis on the strictly factual over the speculative and the interpretative.

(a) For Russell, all meaning, and hence all language and all knowledge of truths depend ultimately upon knowledge by acquaintance, i.e. direct sensory perception. The meanings of complex expressions, according to Russell, are a function of the meanings of simple expressions. And the meanings of a crucial class of simple expressions – proper names – are the particular sense-data which they refer to or name. Therefore, the meaning of these expressions (and hence also of all the complex expressions based on them) can be learned only by direct sensory acquaintance. All linguistic knowledge and 'all analysis ... always depends, in the last analysis, upon direct acquaintance with the objects which are the meanings of certain simple symbols' (*RLA*, 48). Moreover, aside from their linguistic and epistemological primacy, we must not forget that sense-data were for Russell 'part of the ultimate constituents of the world' (*RLA*, 134).

Eliot clearly seems to share this view of the primacy of sense-perception. In *The Sacred Wood* he declares: 'Not only all knowledge, but all feeling, is in perception' (*SW*, 10). And still earlier he asserted that 'all thought and all language is based ultimately upon a few simple physical movements'.[17] Moreover, we must recall Eliot's praise of certain Elizabethan and Jacobean writers for having 'the intellect ... immediately at the tips of the senses', and his contrasting criticism of Massinger for 'the decay of the senses' which caused failure in the poetic task 'of perceiving, registering, and digesting impressions'. 'Had Massinger a nervous system as refined as that of Middleton, Tourneur, Webster, or Ford, his style would be a triumph' (*SW*, 129, 131).

(b) Russell, we remember, discounted most of traditional metaphysics as arising from confusions about symbolism and the philosophical grammar of ordinary language. In contrast to philosophy, which is essentially questionable, science is conceived as much more reliable and veridical:

science is what you more or less know and philosophy is what you do not know ... [but] choose to have opinions about ... Therefore every advance in

[17] T.S. Eliot, 'Studies in Contemporary Criticism', *Egoist*, 5 (1918), 114.

knowledge robs philosophy of some problems which formerly it had, ... the moment they become soluble, they become to a large class of philosophical minds uninteresting, because to many of the people who like philosophy, the charm of it consists in the speculative freedom, in the fact that you can play with hypotheses. (*RLA*,141)

Russell therefore concludes that since 'science has a much greater likelihood of being true ... than any philosophy', we would 'be wise to build our philosophy upon science' (*RLA*, 160).

Eliot's early critical writings express very much the same attitude, distrust of most philosophy and admiring faith in science. In 'The Perfect Critic' he uses 'philosophic' as a pejorative term for the abstract and vague verbalism of speculative philosophy. It is used 'to cover the unscientific ingredients of philosophy; to cover, in fact, the greater part of the philosophic output of the last hundred years' (*SW*, 8). In contrast to this derogatory sense of 'philosophic', Eliot praises 'the scientific' and the scientific philosopher as exemplified by Aristotle. Aristotle is presented as the perfect critic because he has 'the scientific mind – a mind which ... might better be called the intelligent mind. For there is no other intelligence than this' (*SW*, 13). And since he virtually identifies all intelligence (including critical intelligence) with science, the young Eliot feels compelled to point out that his favorite modern critic, Rémy de Gourmont, was 'an excessively able amateur in physiology' (*SW*, 13-14).[18]

(c) Closely connected with this view of science's superiority to speculative philosophy is the empiricist emphasis on hard facts over interpretation and speculation. Though Russell realized that some prefer to remain in the philosophic realm where uncertainty allows much 'speculative freedom' and 'play of fancy', he held that one must strive to transform the uncertain into scientific knowledge, to fact rather than speculation, even if 'it makes it dry, precise, methodical, and in that way robs it' of its speculative charm (*RLA*, 141). One should aim at getting to the facts (which according to logical atomism are what constitutes reality); and these empirical facts must be given full weight and not be discounted or distorted by philosophical interpretations of them which accord them only a 'minor degree of truth' or mere truth of appearance. For, as Russell argues, errors are more likely

---

[18] The early Eliot was so impressed with the scientific mind that he sometimes described not only criticism but even poetry in terms of science. 'A poet, like a scientist, is contributing toward the organic development of culture ... It is exactly as wasteful for a poet to do what has been done already as for a biologist to rediscover Mendel's discoveries. The French poets in question have made 'discoveries' in verse ... To remain with Wordsworth is equivalent to ignoring the whole of science subsequent to Erasmus Darwin.' [T.S. Eliot, 'Contemporanea', *Egoist*, 5 (1918), 84.]

Eliot however became increasingly disenchanted with positivist science and severely critical of its pretensions to complete cognitive dominance and superiority over philosophy and 'wisdom'. This development (largely due to recognizing the historical and societal dependence, contingencies, and limitations of science) is discussed in Chapter Eight.

in 'abstract argument' and 'interpretation' than in the empirical facts of
science (*RLA*, 160-161).

Like logical atomism, Eliot's early critical theory is much preoccupied
with facts and their importance; and it is equally distrustful of interpretation and fanciful speculation. Eliot insists that 'a critic must have a
very highly developed sense of fact', since the goal is to reduce the vague
and 'narcotic fancies' of unsystematic criticism to the 'sphere of fact, of
knowledge, of control' (*SE*, 31).

> To the member of the Browning Study Circle, the discussion of poets about
> poetry may seem arid, technical, and limited. It is merely that the
> practitioners have clarified and reduced to a state of fact all the feelings that
> the members can only enjoy in the most nebulous form; the dry technique
> implies, for those who have mastered it, all that the member thrills to; only
> that has been made into something precise, tractable, under control. That, at
> all events, is one reason for the value of the practitioner's criticism – he is
> dealing with his facts … (*SE*, 31-32)

The echoes of Russell are certainly pronounced here. For Eliot, facts are
the essential data of criticism (as the facts of science are, for Russell, the
data on which to build philosophy). Eliot therefore asserts that 'any book,
any essay, any note … which produces a fact even of the lowest order about
a work of art is a better piece of work than nine-tenths of the most
pretentious critical journalism, in journals or in books' (*SE*, 33). Besides
advocating the importance of collecting facts (even apparently useless ones
like 'Shakespeare's laundry bills'), Eliot expresses keen distrust of
interpretation with its tendency to fanciful speculation. 'But it is fairly
certain that "interpretation" … is only legitimate when it is not interpretation at all, but merely putting the reader in possession of facts which he
would otherwise have missed', e.g. 'a selection of the simpler kind of facts
about a work – its conditions, its setting, its genesis' (*SE*, 32). Eliot admits
(like Russell) that facts may be dull and boring; 'but *fact* cannot corrupt
taste,' while interpretations, which tend to create more than elucidate, are
'the real corrupters' which 'supply opinion or fancy' rather than truth (*SE*,
33).

IV

I have demonstrated that Russell's empiricist analytic philosophy was
familiar to and admired by Eliot during the period in which he was
producing his early, revolutionary, and probably most influential criticism,
and that several major themes of Russell's philosophy find frequent
expression and powerful application in Eliot's early critical writings. For
instance, Eliot's emphasis on analysis, logic, clarity, precision, sensation,
the scientific, and the factual can readily be explained as influenced by
aspects of Russell's philosophy. I submit that this indeed is how these
critical emphases should be explained and that Russell's influence on

Eliot's critical theory was substantial though never properly acknowledged.

Many of the aspects of Eliot's early criticism which I have traced to Russell are often attributed instead to the influence of T.E. Hulme, who advocated precision and restraint and 'dry, hard, classical verse'.[19] Some, like F.O. Matthiessen, have denied this Hulmian influence by arguing that though Eliot knew of Hulme (but never met him) through Ezra Pound and had read Hulme's poetry, 'he had not read any of Hulme's essays before they were published [in 1924] by which time Eliot's own theory of poetry had already matured'.[20] But more recent scholarship has convincingly shown that Eliot must have been previously acquainted with a few of Hulme's prose writings, i.e. translations of and notes on Bergson and Sorel.[21] None the less, it is clear that these writings do not present Hulme's definitive, classicist critical views which Eliot later praised.[22] And it seems far more likely that the Eliotic critical doctrines I discussed were due to the influence of Russell, whose work and person were certainly familiar to Eliot, and whose philosophical doctrines have been shown to be strikingly akin to the critical tenets of the young poet-critic. In any case, though the question of Hulme's influence on Eliot's early critical theory may remain an interesting puzzle for scholars, it ultimately poses no significant threat to my thesis that this theory bears a great debt to Russell. For I maintain that Hulme's own mature, classicist views were largely influenced by the analytic philosophy of Russell and Moore.

The major obstacle to seeing Hulme's debt to analytic philosophy is his long-entrenched misinterpretation as utterly Bergsonian. He indeed began as a zealous disciple of Bergson, and his formidably famous (mis)interpreters, Krieger and Kermode, need to see him that way for the plausibility of their attempt to depict both New Criticism and modernism as essentially mere elaborations of romantic poetics.[23] Hulme, as a recognized source of both these movements and yet as a vehemently explicit opponent of romanticism, poses a problem. The solution is to view Hulme, *malgré lui*, as essentially a romantic thinker by completely

---

[19] T.E. Hulme, 'Romanticism and Classicism' in T.E. Hulme, *Speculations* (1924, London: Routledge and Kegan Paul, 1960). All further references to this work will be to this edition, hereinafter abbreviated as *Spec*. I shall also refer to Hulme's posthumously published *Further Speculations* (Minneapolis: University of Minnesota Press, 1955), employing the abbreviation *FS*.

[20] F.O. Matthiessen, *The Achievement of T.S. Eliot* (New York: Oxford University Press, 1959), 71.

[21] See R. Schuchard, 'Eliot and Hulme in 1916: Toward a Revaluation of Eliot's Critical and Spiritual Development', *PMLA*, 88 (1973), 1083-1094.

[22] On the changes and development of Hulme's thought, see M. Levenson, *A Genealogy of Modernism*, 37-47, 80-102. See also, R. Shusterman, 'Remembering Hulme: A Neglected Philosopher-Critic-Poet', *Journal of the History of Ideas*, 46 (1985), 559-576.

[23] M. Krieger, *The New Apologists for Poetry* (Minneapolis: University of Minnesota Press, 1956), 31-45; and Frank Kermode, *Romantic Image* (London: Routledge and Kegan Paul, 1961), 119-137.

identifying him with the romantic philosophy of Bergson, which he had forsaken by the time of his influential modernist-classicist essays.

Thus Krieger, who ultimately aims to present Hulme as a Coleridgean, ignores Hulme's self-proclaimed anti-romanticism and explicit reversal of Coleridge's privileging of imagination over fancy, and instead focuses on Hulme's early exposition of Bergson where, according to Krieger, the poet's activity is described in terms 'nearly as transcendental as Coleridge's': the poet presents not the world of our senses but 'the real world beyond, which he somehow intuits'. Krieger concludes from his interpretation of Hulme's interpretation of Bergson that Hulme himself advocated a theory of imagination 'not far removed from the imagination invoked by Coleridge'.[24]

One is therefore obliged to assert what any straightforward reading of Hulme's work should make evident, that Hulme was not a confused Coleridgean romantic who thought that poetry took us beyond the senses to a metaphysical intuition of the essence of reality. Hulme, even when expounding Bergson, always insisted that the aim of poetry is to capture and convey particular physical things and visual images, not metaphysical essences. Thus, even in his essay on 'Bergson's Theory of Art', Hulme maintains that the poet's aim is not to render the Bergsonian metaphysical flux but 'to express the individual thing which he has seen' (*Spec.*, 160), and that good poetry is poetry which captures and conveys the 'presence of a vividly felt physical and visual scene' (*Spec.*, 164). Elsewhere, we read that the poet's job is 'recording impressions by visual images', 'seeing "solid" things'; the greatest poets being those who 'saw solid, definite things and described them' (*FS*, 73, 78, 80). Finally, in his more definitive and influential 'Romanticism and Classicism', Hulme's opposition to the romantic conception of the poet's role as transcendental seer could hardly be clearer. The goal of poetry is not visionary metaphysical truth; rather 'the aim is accurate, precise, and definite description. ... It always endeavours to arrest you, and to make you continuously see a physical thing, ... an actually realised visual object ... It doesn't matter if it were a lady's shoe or the starry heavens' (*Spec.*, 132, 134, 137). And in contrast to the romantic poetics of Wordsworth and Coleridge, the light in which Hulme's poet should see these objects 'is always the light of ordinary day, never the light that never was on land and sea' (*Spec.*, 127).

Krieger's additional attempts to identify Hulme's theory with Coleridge are equally weak and ineffective. The fact that Hulme notes (parenthetically, in the course of a diatribe on how romantic thought deteriorates clear meanings) that Coleridge's term 'vital' originally had a clear and definite sense, denoting the phenomenon of organic unity, and was only subverted into a vague and mysterious notion by later romantics; and the fact that Hulme goes on to assert that the notion of organic unity is important to Bergson's philosophy and to aesthetics in general, are taken

---

[24] Krieger, 34.

by Krieger as strong evidence of Hulme's Coleridgean romanticism as opposed to his claimed allegiance to 'the old classical view'.[25] Krieger seems strangely unaware that the notion of organic unity is not the invention of Coleridge, Bergson, or romanticism, but was originally an important classical concept, clearly formulated in Aristotle's *Poetics* and frequently employed and interpreted in pre-romantic thought.[26]

Frank Kermode's misinterpretation of Hulme is similar in spirit and substance to Krieger's, but different in particulars because he has a slightly different axe to grind. In *Romantic Image* he too wishes to show that certain romantic tenets about poetry, most importantly that 'the image ... is the primary pigment of poetry', 'are none the less fundamental to much twentieth-century thinking about poetry', even 'for critics and poets who are militantly anti-Romantic'.[27] But Kermode is not fixated on Coleridge and rather views Hulme's theory in a broader romantic context, characterizing the theory as 'a modernized, but essentially traditional, aesthetic of Symbolism'.[28] Like Krieger, Kermode dismisses Hulme's fervent anti-romantic proclamations and maintains that his theory is simply a 'version of the Magic Image, or Romantic anti-positivism'.[29]

Again, Bergson is the philosopher's stone which converts Hulme's anti-romantic pronouncements into mainstream romanticism. Hulme, we are told, 'was a devoted admirer of Bergson' from whom he imbibed 'his strong affiliation to that organicist, anti-positivist stream of ideas that stems from the Romantic movement'.[30] Hulme's poetic theory is thus said to assert that 'poems are concerned with intuited truth' of a metaphysical nature, the poet succeeding to 'pierce the veil' of ordinary sensual perception and to grasp through special intuition 'a higher but finite order of truth'.[31]

Though Kermode is more scrupulous than Krieger and much closer to Hulme, the same sort of objections hold against his reading. He takes Hulme's early enthusiasm for Bergson as the continuously dominant factor in Hulme's poetic theory; he takes Hulme's exposition of Bergson's views on art for Hulme's own considered views, and even further gives them primacy and dominance over Hulme's more mature and independent theoretical statements (e.g. 'Romanticism and Classicism' and 'Humanism and the Religious Attitude'). Moreover, we must again insist that throughout Hulme's writings, even in his exposition of Bergson, poetry is essentially

---

[25] *Ibid.*, 39-40.
[26] See Aristotle's *Poetics*, chapters 7, 8. For discussion of pre-romantic treatment of organic unity, see W.K. Wimsatt and C. Brooks, *Literary Criticism: A Short History* (Chicago: University Press, 1978), vol. 1, 28-34, 123. See also J. Benziger, 'Organic Unity: Leibniz to Coleridge', *PMLA*, 66 (1951), 24-48.
[27] Kermode, vii.
[28] *Ibid.*, 121.
[29] *Ibid.*
[30] *Ibid.*, 121-122.
[31] *Ibid.*, 128, 130.

concerned not with intuited *truths* but with concretely perceived *things* and visual impressions; it does not aim at transcendental 'higher' truth but at the surprisingly difficult task of accurately rendering the solid things and concrete images of non-transcendental experience.

Finally, we must again point out that Hulme's apparent organicism is no proof of his romanticism, nor is the acceptance of the importance of intuition and non-discursive knowledge any proof of romantic anti-positivism, if the term 'positivism' is meant to include philosophical thinking that can be characterized as scientific and systematic. On the contrary, the notions of organic unity and intuition play leading roles in the moral and aesthetic philosophy of G.E. Moore;[32] and the idea of a non-discursive, direct knowledge (especially of sensual images or sense-data), 'knowledge by acquaintance', forms the very foundation of Bertrand Russell's theory of meaning and epistemology.[33] These two systematic or scientific philosophers are surely not to be linked, simply by their embracing such notions, to the anti-positivist romantic stream which issued Bergson. Yet Russell and Moore may be profitably linked to Hulme, as positive influences in the development of his later philosophical thinking. Their influence will now be made explicit.

Having been interested in philosophy as an undergraduate at Cambridge in 1902-1904 (and then again in 1912), Hulme had long been aware of the reputation and importance of the philosophy of Moore and Russell (who were both at Cambridge).[34] However, not until the later years of his life did Hulme actively address their thought and incorporate it into his own philosophy. It seems idle to speculate about the reason for this delay of interest, for Hulme gives a lengthy account of it in his admiring discussion of Moore and Russell as leaders of 'Neo-Realism' (*Spec.*, 39-45).

Having lived at Cambridge at various times during the last ten years, I have naturally always known that the only philosophical movement of any importance in England is that which is derived from the writings of Mr. G.E. Moore. I now find these writings extremely lucid and persuasive, yet for years

[32] See G.E. Moore, *Principia Ethica* (Cambridge: University Press, 1903, repr. 1978), viii-x, 6-12, 18-22, 27-36. For an account of Moore on organic unity, see my paper 'Osborne and Moore on Organic Unity', *British Journal of Aesthetics*, 23 (1983), 352-359.

[33] See B. Russell, 'Knowledge by Acquaintance and Knowledge by Description', *Proceedings of the Aristotelian Society*, 11 (1911), repr. in *Mysticism and Logic* (London: Penguin, 1953), 197-218; and also *The Problems of Philosophy* (London: Home University Library, 1912; republished London: Oxford University Press, 1971). References to Russell's *The Problems of Philosophy* will be to the 1971 edition.

[34] For these and other biographical facts concerning Hulme's early schooling, undergraduate vicissitudes, and philosophical interests and pursuits, see A.R. Jones, *The Life and Opinions of T.E. Hulme* (London: Gollancz, 1960), 17-24, 54-67, 76-90. It is worth noting that in 1910 Hulme became a member of the Aristotelian Society, which was then chaired by Moore and largely dominated by the philosophical thought of Moore and Russell. Jones notes that in the company of such powerful scientific philosophers 'Hulme was strangely silent' and 'uncharacteristically passive' (p. 76), probably because he came to the Society's meetings more to listen and learn than to contribute.

was entirely unable to understand in what lay their value. It was not so much
that I did not agree with what was said, as that I was entirely unable to see
how any meaning could be attached to some of its main contentions. (*Spec.*,
39)

Hulme then relates how his reading of Husserl and Husserl's followers
led him to understand and appreciate the 'intellectualist' and 'realist'
philosophy of Moore and Russell; and he goes on to explain his circuitous
course to a philosophical enlightenment which from the start was at his
doorstep as representative of 'the typical difficulties of the dilettante' who,
since 'he only reads what he finds interesting', is unlikely to come into close
contact with a philosophy unless it involves topics or methods close to his
own views or interests (*Spec.*, 39-40). Hulme thus relates:

> When, with entirely empirical and nominalist prejudices, I read Moore and
> Russell, there was no foothold for me; they dealt with logic and ethics, and
> holding, as I did, entirely relativist views about both, I naturally found
> nothing familiar from which I might have started to understand the rest. The
> Germans I mentioned were useful in this way; they made the intellectualist,
> non-empirical method comprehensible to me, by enlarging its scope –
> applying it not only to logic and ethics, but to things which at the time did
> interest me. This provided me with the required foothold. (*Spec.*, 41-42)[35]

If Hulme came to understand and appreciate Moore and Russell, what
sustenance did he draw from their philosophy? I have already suggested
that whatever commitment Hulme had to the importance of intuition and
the principle of organic wholes would have been greatly reinforced by
Moore's *Principia Ethica*. For here all ethics is based on the intuition of the
indefinable property of goodness, whose presence in anything is organically
not reducible to its presence in the parts of that thing, and where a major
part of the ideal life is the appreciation of aesthetic organic wholes.[36]
Russell, too, though sharply critical of Bergson's exaggerated claims for
intuition and instinct, accords intuition a fairly wide and important
cognitive role in his own philosophy.[37]

Hulme probably derived greater profit from Moore and Russell's realism,
which he found so congenial and which, in its variety of aspects, bolsters his
theory of poetry and broadens his conception of philosophy. One aspect of
that realism was the reality of sense-data or sensibilia. In rejecting
idealism and its view that the objects of perception are only in our mind,
Moore and Russell maintained that the sensual images or sense-data we

[35] Hulme's remarks here refer specifically to Moore and Russell's non-empirical approach to
logic and ethics (i.e. respectively non-psychologism and non-naturalism), and do not cast
doubt on the saliently empiricist aspects of their epistemology and ontology.

[36] *Principia Ethica*, 188-202.

[37] 'On Intuitive Knowledge' in *The Problems of Philosophy*, 64-68. It is worth noting that
Eliot makes use of Russell's notion of intuition and favorably contrasts it to Bergson's. See 'Mr.
Middleton Murry's Synthesis', 33-35.

see are real entities that actually exist outside the mind.[38] Russell went so far as maintaining that sense-data are physical and real even when they are the stuff of hallucinations, illusions, and dreams; and he regarded them as 'ultimate sources of both meaning and truth'.[39] Though 'sense-data' was used as a general term to cover all the senses, both Moore and Russell concentrated mainly on visual sense-data.

All this dovetails very nicely with Hulme's imagist poetic, where the poet's goal in capturing and conveying reality is not a transcendental truth but a definite visual image, 'to get a physical image', 'a vividly felt actual sensation', 'a vividly felt physical and visual scene' (*Spec.*, 135, 151, 164). Hulme also treats meaning as ultimately dependent on (visual) sense-data, complaining that in ordinary language 'we replace meaning (i.e. *vision*) with words', which tend to lose the images they originally were to represent (*FS*, 77). His allegorical heroine, Aphra, 'sees each word with an image sticking on to it', and we are urged to 'regard each word as a picture, then a succession of pictures' (*FS*, 78, 83). Though the style is surely different from Russell's, the idea is surely close to Russell's picture theory of language, where 'in a logically perfect language the words in a proposition would correspond one by one with the components of the corresponding fact'.

Indeed, the theme of the ambiguity, vagueness, and often obfuscatory nature of ordinary language, and the need to struggle to free thought from linguistic snares and make language more precise and reflective of reality, is a major theme that Hulme shares with Moore and Russell. Moore's dissatisfaction with the typical ambiguity of language and his meticulous attempts to render philosophical questions and assertions more precise by unpacking these ambiguities became a legend which inspired not only philosophers but also his wide-ranging Bloomsbury devotees. And we have already noted Russell's critique of language.

Similarly, Hulme decries the vagueness and clumsiness of ordinary language (a 'large clumsy instrument', *FS*, 83) and inveighs against the 'dignified vagueness' of romanticism (*Spec.*, 137). For Hulme:

> The great aim is accurate, precise, and definite description. The first thing is to recognise how extraordinarily difficult this is. It is no mere matter of carefulness; you have to use language, and language by its very nature ... expresses never the exact thing but a compromise – that which is common to you, me and everybody. But each man sees a little differently, and to get out

---

[38] See G.E. Moore, 'The Refutation of Idealism' (1903) and 'The Status of Sense Data' (1913-14), both reprinted in Moore's *Philosophical Studies* (London: Kegan Paul, Trench, Trubner, 1922); and B. Russell, 'The Relation of Sense-Data to Physics' (1914) reprinted in *Mysticism and Logic*.

[39] See D. Pears, *Bertrand Russell and the British Tradition* (London: Collins, 1968), 32. For a good discussion of Moore's and Russell's views on the reality of sense-data and on other aspects of their philosophical realism, see A.J. Ayer, *Russell and Moore: The Analytic Heritage* (London: Macmillan, 1971).

clearly and directly what he does see, he must have a terrific struggle with language ... Plain speech is essentially inaccurate. (*Spec*. 132, 137)

Having noted that Hulme shared Moore and Russell's critique of language and ideal of precision, let us return to their realism that Hulme so appreciated. This was not confined to maintaining the reality of sense-data and physical things, but affirmed the reality of concepts, propositions, and objective values. The objective reality of concepts, propositions, and values was very important to Hulme in his criticism of what he called 'the philosophy of humanism', which is the major target of Hulme's philosophical and aesthetic polemics and underlies his attack on romanticism, which Hulme regards as but an expression of the humanist spirit.

Essential to Hulme's attack on humanism is his denial that all truth and value is in essentially human terms and is man-dependent. Now though Moore and Russell might be characterized as humanist in their ideology or *Weltanschauung*, Hulme helped himself (as did Eliot for a time) to their rich realism, which afforded a realm of being, truth, and value beyond the relativism of human experience and desires. Hulme found in these 'intellectualist and realist' philosophers (*Spec*., 40) a realism which not only balked at reducing the physical world to mental experience but which, employing a non-empirical reasoning to achieve *a priori* conceptual knowledge, also refused to reduce concepts to psychological ideas, propositions to mental acts or linguistic expressions, or ethical values to human desires and attitudes. After making some relevant quotations from the writings of Moore and Russell, Hulme draws the following conclusions:

> A proposition ... is not something relative to the *human*. 'A proposition ... does not itself contain words ... it contains the entities indicated by words.' ... Logic, then does *not* deal with the laws of human thought but with these quite *objective* sentences. In this way the anthropomorphism which underlies certain views of logic is got rid of. Similarly, ethics can be exhibited as an objective science, and is also purified from anthropomorphism.
>
> All these subjects are thus placed on an entirely objective basis, and do not in the least depend on the human mind. The entities which form the subject-matter of these sciences are neither physical nor mental – they 'subsist'. They are dealt with by an investigation that is *not* empirical. Statements can be made about them whose truth does not depend on experience. When the empirical prejudice has been got rid of, it becomes possible to think of certain 'higher' concepts, those of the good, of love, etc. as at the same time, *simple*, and not necessarily to be analysed into more *elementary* (generally sensual) elements. (*Spec*., 44-45)

Hulme felt that his belief in a realm of truth and value beyond the mentalism of idealist philosophy and the subjectivism of humanist ethics found strong support in the early radical realism of Moore and Russell, and in Moore's doctrines of the non-natural, simple (i.e. unanalyzable), yet objective nature of the good, which Russell also (following Moore) initially advocated,[40] though later rejected (perhaps too late for Hulme to notice) for ethical subjectivism. Hulme in fact explicitly acknowledges his debt to Moore in 'the establishment of the objective character of ethical values ... The school of Moore and Husserl break the humanist tradition ... in as far ... as they free ethical values from the anthropomorphism involved in their dependence on human desires and feeling' (*Spec.*, 62, 83)

Mention of Husserl brings us to still another central idea that the mature Hulme came to share (though in a slightly different perspective) with Moore, Russell, and, of course, Husserl. This is the belief that philosophy may be pursued as an objective, 'impersonal and exact science', 'a difficult investigation into the relations between certain very abstract categories', through a 'method ... as purely scientific and impersonal as that of mathematics' (*Spec.*, 14-15). Asserting that 'pure philosophy ought to be, and may be, entirely objective and scientific', Hulme praises Husserl's account of philosophy as '*strenge Wissenschaft*' as the best account of scientific philosophy. But he also suggests defining such philosophy 'as the *science of what is possible* as contrasted with the *science of what is*' (*Spec.*, 18). Compare this with Russell's definition of philosophy (not cited by Hulme but in an article from which Hulme elsewhere cites): 'philosophy is the science of the possible.'[41]

Hulme joins Russell and Husserl in demanding 'a clear separation' between 'purely scientific philosophy' and the personal, expressive *Weltanschauung*, which 'has often injuriously affected the scientific part of the subject' (*Spec.*, 29). However, while Husserl and Russell demanded this separation merely to protect scientific philosophy from contamination by unscientific, creative *Weltanschauung*, Hulme desired it also because he felt that this unscientific philosophy deserved to be considered and pursued in its own right. He believed that despite the value of scientific philosophy, it has no claim to exclusivity, nor does it satisfy all of man's philosophical needs and give him the satisfaction he seeks in philosophy. Here Hulme saw an essential and ultimately superior role for the unscientific, hermeneutic philosophy of *Weltanschauung*, whose study he accordingly dubbed the 'Critique of Satisfaction' (*Spec.*, 20).

Weltanschauung for Hulme is the 'expression of an attitude towards the world' or 'the interpretation of life' (*Spec.*, 14, 25), whose purpose is to help man cope with the world by giving him a satisfying outlook on it, a satisfying 'final picture' of man's nature and destiny (*Spec.*, 15-16). Hulme thus infers that a *Weltanschauung* is not necessarily connected with a systematic philosophy, since 'the effort to find some "interpretation of life"

---

[40] Russell advocated the objectivity of value in his essay 'The Elements of Ethics' in *Philosophical Essays* (London: Allen and Unwin, 1910) where he confesses his debt to Moore in this matter. Moore's theory is, of course, found in his *Principia Ethica*.

[41] B. Russell, 'Scientific Method in Philosophy' in *Mysticism and Logic*, 108. We must be careful to note that Hulme (like Eliot) admired only Russell's scientific philosophy but rejected his ideology or *Weltanschauung* as too humanist and Romantic.

... may find expression not only in philosophy ... but in literature', which also deals with such questions of man's state whose answers constitute 'Wisdom' (*Spec.*, 24). Nor can the *Weltanschauung* or hermeneutic interpretation of life claim any immutable, foundational truth or validity, since with historical change new circumstances may well require new interpretations.

> The truth is that there are no ultimate principles, upon which the whole of knowledge can be built once and for ever as upon a rock. But there are an infinity of analogues, which help us along, and give us a feeling of power over the chaos when we perceive them. The field is infinite and herein lies the chance for originality. Here there are some new things under the sun.(*Spec.*, 233-234)

Hulme rebukes systematic philosophers for trying to smuggle their *Weltanschauung* into their scientific philosophy 'to make it seem not so much a particular *attitude* as a *necessary* fact', and he emphasizes the 'unsystematic' hermeneutic philosopher's sense and use of history to show that such attitudes are neither necessary nor inevitable by showing how in fact they were contingently generated in history and were neither necessary nor convincing for other epochs (*Spec.*, 31-38).

Hulme's account of this unsystematic, historicist, hermeneutic philosophy and its relations and ultimate superiority to foundationalist scientific philosophy clearly adumbrates Richard Rorty's recent and influential privileging contrast of hermeneutical 'edifying philosophy' over 'systematic philosophy'.[42] More relevant to our present concern, Hulme's advocacy of hermeneutical historicism proved extremely important for Eliot. But it was not Eliot's early objectivist criticism that it nourished. On the contrary, the publication of Hulme's *Speculations* in 1924 seems to have encouraged Eliot's drift away from analytic, scientific objectivism and towards an increasingly historicist and hermeneutical outlook. His subsequent appeals to Hulme's theorizing emphasize this historicism.[43]

V

Pursuit of Eliot's historicism should be postponed till we better understand his early critical objectivism and the problems which engendered its abandonment. That will be undertaken in the next chapter. However, having spent most of the present chapter arguing for Eliot's early critical debt to Russell, we cannot be allowed to conclude without addressing an irrepressible question.

[42] See R. Rorty, *Philosophy and the Mirror of Nature*. A detailed comparison of Hulme's and Rorty's metaphilosophical views is found in my 'Remembering Hulme: A Neglected Philosopher-Critic-Poet'.

[43] See, for example, 'Second Thoughts about Humanism' (1929) in *SE*; *TUP*, 149; and the Clark Lectures, 41.

If Russell's philosophy was indeed a significant influence on Eliot's early criticism, why did Eliot never acknowledge this debt? Apart from the fact that Eliot (Old Possum) could be very secretive and likely to conceal such matters,[44] there are certain personal, psychological reasons which could powerfully explain this silence. Eliot at this early period was still striving and struggling for independence. He had already been financially dependent upon Russell, and also emotionally dependent upon him through Russell's very close and rather questionable involvement in Eliot's unhappy marriage. Perhaps it was too much for Eliot then to admit that some of his major critical ideas also owed something to Russell. Eliot's personal relations with Russell, particularly concerning the philosopher's attention to Eliot's young bride, provide a rich mine of psychological complexities which I cannot pause to investigate here.[45]

There is also good reason for Eliot's failure to acknowledge Russell's influence even after he achieved independence and comparable fame of his own. By that time, which was after Eliot's religious (and philosophical) conversion, Russell's philosophy with its scientific, anti-theological outlook had become repugnant to Eliot; and he thus did not wish to associate it with his early criticism, which he never repudiated though he did abandon. Surely there is no need to argue that the content and spirit of Russell's thought are hardly compatible with Eliot's devout Anglicanism or with his later hermeneutic outlook. Indeed already in 1927, the year of his conversion, we find criticism of Russell's 'scientific' philosophy for being 'crude and raw and provincial (though infinitely more technical and scientific)', for showing 'lack of wisdom' and for 'denying what we know to be true' (*SE*, 449, 454).[46]

Having attained a higher religious and philosophical perspective, Eliot lost his interest in and respect for atomistic analytic philosophy. One should note that parallel to this loss, he lost (by his own confession) his zeal for the analytic and technical study of poetry *qua* poetry, and devoted his criticism instead to 'the relation of poetry to the spiritual and social life' (*SW*, viii). It is fitting that this change in philosophical outlook should terminate the phase of seminal critical activity which I have argued was significantly influenced, perhaps even inspired, by Russell's philosophy. If my thesis is correct, then the debt of modern literature to analytic philosophy is very much greater than has hitherto been acknowledged.

Moreover, I think it reasonable to conjecture that his early esteem for Russell's philosophy helped Eliot choose a career as poet-critic rather than

[44] One might find other unacknowledged influences on Eliot's theory. See, for example, my papers, 'Eliot and Ruskin', *Journal of Comparative Literature and Aesthetics* (1984), 35-49, and 'Wilde and Eliot', *T.S. Eliot Annual*, 1 (London: Macmillan, 1988).

[45] For detailed and rather sexually explicit accounts of this triangle, see R. Bell, 'Bertrand Russell and the Eliots', *American Scholar*, 52 (1983), 309-325; and Ackroyd, 63-71.

[46] In the same essay of 1927 ('Francis Herbert Bradley') there is even a kind word for Bergson and Hegel – the targets of harsh criticism in *The Sacred Wood*. This too seems to indicate a change from the philosophical outlook of Eliot's early criticism.

professional philosopher. When at the crossroads of career choice, Eliot realized that analytic philosophy was and promised to remain the dominant philosophy of the period; when he further realized that he could not adequately compete with Russell or even excel in such philosophy, since with no mathematical or scientific training, he appeared to lack some of its most important tools; finally, when he must have felt some competition with Russell, even over the affection and control of his wife, Eliot must have been powerfully motivated to avoid a hopeless competition in philosophy by pursuing a literary career instead. If this thesis is correct, then modern literature's debt to analytic philosophy is enormously greater still.

Chapter 3

The Mutations of Objectivity

... I am not eager to rehearse
My thought and theory which you have forgotten.
These things have served their purpose: let them be.

'Little Gidding'

I

Eliot's poetic and critical theory is deservedly renowned for its intense concern with objectivity. Two of his most famous theories – the theory of 'the objective correlative' and 'the Impersonal theory of poetry' – whatever their merit, have become landmarks of literary theory, inspiring great polemical and exegetical discussion. These influential theories refer specifically to objectivity in the art of the poet rather than that of the critic. But here, as elsewhere, Eliot's critical theory closely resembles his poetic theory, since as Eliot himself so often insisted, his criticism was essentially a by-product of his poetic enterprise. It is not surprising, then, that Eliot's theory of criticism reveals a similar concern with objectivity and impersonal analysis, which is largely responsible for his being claimed as a father of the New Criticism and identified as an uncompromising champion of critical objectivism.[1]

However, to portray Eliot as a naive and unequivocal objectivist would be falsely simplistic and unfair to the complexity of Eliot's thought. For just as Eliot's poetry, despite all its claims and devices of impersonality and

[1] For discussion of the objectivism of Eliot's critical theory, see, for example, S. Spender, *Eliot* (London: Fontana, 1975); B. Bergonzi, *T.S. Eliot* (London: Macmillian, 1972); and R. Sharrock, 'Eliot's Tone', in D. Newton-DeMolina (ed.), *The Literary Criticism of T.S. Eliot* (London: Athlone, 1977). Spender describes Eliot's theory as advocating 'criticism as scientific analysis' and 'fact-finding' (pp. 73, 79, 80). Bergonzi asserts that despite Eliot's personal aims as a poet, his criticism is that 'of the disengaged critic' and his critical theory advocates that 'criticism ... must conclude in something objective' (pp. 58-60). Sharrock maintains that though Eliot's actual criticism was sometimes subjectively colored and personal in tone, his theory of criticism was strongly objectivist, with its 'plea for impersonal objective methods' (p. 167), 'disinterested critical intelligence' (p. 170), and 'new objective canons of literary taste' (p. 181). All these critics, of course, link Eliot with the New Criticism.

41

objectivity, contains a highly personal dimension, closely related to Eliot's own personal problems; so Eliot's poetic and critical theory, for all its concern with objectivity, contains and recognizes a significant dimension of subjectivity.

One of the tasks of this chapter is to establish the significance of the subjective in Eliot's critical theory by historically tracing its role and oppositional relationship to objectivism in Eliot's early and later theorizing. Such a survey will show a very clear general trend of development which strengthens our general thesis that his thought underwent significant changes and needs to be understood in terms of its developmental and temporal context. In the first part of the chapter I shall briefly outline the trend of his development on this issue, from his early fierce objectivism to his growing acceptance of and emphasis on the subjective and personal.

Moreover, apart from demonstrating the complexity and development of Eliot's thought, our scrutiny of the dynamics and problematics which motivated his changing views on the objectivity/subjectivity issue will shed light on basic issues regarding the aim and function of literary criticism, and the relation of theory to practice, which are of great importance for literary theory and aesthetics. Finally, as I hope to show in the latter part of this chapter, Eliot's struggle with the question of objectivity can be used to elucidate (as it itself is reciprocally elucidated by) the most fundamental and general philosophical questions concerning the very nature of objectivity and the range and measure of its possibility and desirability.

II

In attempting to chart the relations between the objective and subjective in Eliot's critical theory, I shall assume that these correlative binary notions are initially sufficiently intelligible to make my discussion meaningful. This may be assuming too much, for the uses of these terms are very varied and confused, and their proper meaning essentially contested. Indeed the very validity and value of the objective/subjective distinction as a clear and rigid dichotomy of binary opposites has recently been convincingly challenged from such diverse perspectives as deconstruction, hermeneutics, Frankfurt-school critical theory, and analytic philosophy. Eliot himself, as we shall see, became aware of the serious difficulties which plague this privileging opposition. We must defer our deeper probe into the problematic nature of objectivity and subjectivity until we have our initial sketch of Eliot's changing treatment of this issue. But even to understand this sketch we might be asked for some rough preliminary characterization.

Very crudely and tentatively then, we may say that the *objective* is what is perceived as independent of the individual human mind and its particular contingencies of perception, belief, and desire; what is grasped as free from personal feeling and individual or group prejudice. The *subjective* may be defined as the opposite of (and by contrast to) the objective; the terms indicating, as it were, the two poles of a scale of varying degrees of dependence on the personal and particular. But since, as we shall later see, these absolute poles are unrealizable abstractions (given the inherent linguistic-conceptual nature of all human thought), the objective/subjective distinction is, in actual practice, drawn relatively. One's supervisor's view of one's thesis is more objective than one's own, but it is less objective than the view of one's dissertation committee, and still less than that of the general philosophical community. The quest for objectivity thus seems to demand that one transcends some limitation of what is specific to one's own person or group; the idea being that the more external or detached from oneself one's point of view of an object is, the more closely will it coincide with the way the object really is in itself.[2]

There is a closely related but perhaps distinguishable notion of 'objective' that has been employed in aesthetic and literary theory and which seems pertinent to Eliot's critical theory, i.e. concentrating on or relating wholly or principally to the object (the work of art itself) rather than the subjects chiefly involved with it (its author and reader). Eliot's early advocacy of this sort of objectivism, his recognition of the text's measure of independence from the author's psychological state and the reader's personal impressions, surely presents him as a source of the New Critical doctrines of the verbal icon and the intentional and affective fallacies.

III

If we trace, then, the values of objectivity and subjectivity in Eliot's critical theory along the axis of time, we get a very clear general trend. Eliot's early theory is, in essential drift and professed intent, zealously objectivist, advocating that objectivity is essential for valid criticism, which he would like to conceive on the model of natural science: impersonal, objective, and constituted of facts rather than opinion. In the mid-1920s his explicit advocacy of objectivism seems to wane, perhaps partly as a result of his avowed change of critical interest from poetry *qua* poetry to 'the relation of poetry to the spiritual and social life' (*SW*, viii); and by the 1930s we find a growing acceptance of the subjective and the personal in criticism, and even increasing doubts as to the possibility and desirability of a criticism that is altogether objective. Before suggesting the reasons for this

[2] This account of the objective/subjective distinction is roughly similar to that offered by Nagel who sees the terms as constituting 'a polarity' over a 'spectrum'. The quest for greater objectivity is pursued 'by detaching more and more from our own point of view', involving 'not only a departure from one's individual viewpoint' but also 'a transcendence of one's type', even 'so far as possible, departure from a specifically human or even mammalian viewpoint.' See T. Nagel, 'Subjective and Objective', in *Mortal Questions* (Cambridge: Cambridge University Press, 1979), 196-213. Quotations here are from 206, 208-209.

development, let us briefly document it.

Already in 1916, his first year as a professional critic, Eliot notes the importance of objectivity and impersonality, chastizing a fellow critic for lacking the essential critical 'gift of detachment'; and in 1918, in comparing criticism to science, he speaks of the critic's 'laboratory work' and his need for greater emphasis on objective facts and analyses generated by the application of standard 'methods' as 'a recognized set of tools'. By 1919, with the development of his famous impersonal theory of poetry, Eliot could argue more confidently and powerfully for a similar impersonality and objectivity in criticism, maintaining that 'critics are impersonal people ... and avoid intimacies with authors.'[3] In his famous article of 1920, 'The Perfect Critic', he sharply and systematically criticizes the personal, subjective approach of the impressionistic critics, Symons and Pater, and he complains that Coleridge's criticism is biased by his personal and emotional metaphysical interest (*SW*, 2-8, 12-13). In contrast to the evils of subjective criticism, Eliot maintains that good criticism is objective and impersonal, 'the disinterested exercise of intelligence' which looks 'solely and steadfastly at the object' (*SW*, 12, 11). Since personal emotion is obviously one of the major obstacles to objectivity, Eliot maintains that 'a literary critic should have no emotions except those immediately provoked by a work of art – and these are ... perhaps not to be called emotions at all' (*SW*, 12-13). Eliot concludes the essay by echoing Arnold's ideal of critical objectivity, 'to see the object as it really is', an ideal which requires 'a pure contemplation from which all the accidents of personal emotion are removed' (*SW*, 14-15). Thus, as Eliot writes in another essay of this period, the proper critical attitude to literature is 'to detach it from ourselves, to reach a state of pure contemplation', the aim being 'to establish a criticism which should be independent of temperament' (*SW*, 40).

The ideal of impersonal objectivity is further pursued and developed in another early seminal essay, 'The Function of Criticism' (1923). Here the critic is urged to suppress personal opinion and ignore 'the inner voice', and instead to confine himself to facts and common principles that are 'outside the individual' (*SE*, 25-29). 'The critic', says Eliot, 'should endeavour to discipline his personal prejudices and cranks ... and compose his differences with as many of his fellows as possible, in the common pursuit of true judgment' (SE, 25). The critic's goal is thus to reach an objective judgment, 'something outside of ourselves which may provisionally be called truth', and therefore his chief tools are the facts of scholarship and the objective procedures of comparison and analysis (*SE*, 33-34).

Eliot's early critical stance is thus clearly and avidly objectivist; and perhaps since it is his early criticism which has been the most influential, we are apt to picture Eliot as an uncompromising opponent of the personal

---

[3] See T.S. Eliot, 'Thomas Hardy', *Manchester Guardian*, 803 (23 June, 1916), 3; 'Studies in Contemporary Criticism', *Egoist*, 5 (Oct., Dec., 1918), 113-114, 131-132; 'Marivaux,' *Art and Letters*, 2 (1919), 80.

and subjective. This, however, is a very inaccurate picture. For Eliot's later and more mature critical theory not only accepts the personal and subjective but even insists upon them as essential.

In Eliot's most extensive and definitive essay on criticism, *The Use of Poetry and the Use of Criticism*, written in 1932, we find him condemning the demand for purely objective and detached appreciation on at least two counts. First, such appreciation simply can be no more than an impossible ideal, 'so long as the appreciation of art is an affair of limited and transient human beings existing in space and time' (*TUP*, 109). For 'one's taste in poetry cannot be isolated from one's other interests and passions ..., and must be limited as one's self is limited' (*TUP*, 36). But secondly and more importantly, such an ideal has become for Eliot intrinsically gainless and unworthy; because such impersonal objectivity or pure appreciation would greatly deplete our experience of poetry and the value we derive from it, since these require that we engage the poem with our self and entire personality. Thus Eliot warns that if in reading poetry you make 'a deliberate effort to put out of mind all ... convictions and passionate beliefs about life, ... you are in danger of seeking from poetry some illusory *pure* enjoyment, of separating poetry from everything else in the world, and cheating yourself out of a great deal that poetry has to give to your development' (*TUP*, 97-98).

Eliot similarly argues that just as it is profitless to suppress or 'bracket out' our own personal convictions, it is equally senseless to try to ignore or edit out the convictions expressed by the poet and to confine ourselves to the places in his verse where we find only 'poetry itself'. For, says Eliot, 'what you get in the end by this process is ... but a mere unrelated heap of charming stanzas, the debris of poetry rather than the poetry itself' (*TUP*, 97-98). A poem is written by an individual in a particular context in order to express something, thus 'if you adopt no attitude towards what the poet has to say, you will tend to evacuate it of all significance' (*TUP*, 64). Eliot, by this time, had come to realize that poetry and its appreciation are not entirely timeless and unchangeable essences, but are integrally related to and largely influenced by society and the changing needs of the individuals who constitute it (*TUP*, 21-25).

Such, then, was Eliot's acceptance of the subjective in the definitive critical work of his middle years, written at the prime and mature age of forty-four. Almost twenty-five years later, in one of Eliot's last important critical essays, 'The Frontiers of Criticism' (1956), his commitment to the subjective or personal is still as strong, if not stronger. Eliot makes two central subjectivist claims in this essay. The first is that the meaning of poetry is equivalent neither to authorial intention nor to some objective impersonal textual meaning, but is always to *some* degree a personal matter, potentially differing from reader to reader; and therefore, as a corollary of this, that one's interpretation must include and relate to one's own feelings. Since 'the meaning of the poem as a whole ... is what the poem means to different sensitive readers, ... a valid interpretation must be at the same time an interpretation of my own feelings when I read it' (*OPP*, 113-114). In contrast to this advocacy of personal, affective criticism, there is the warning that pure impersonal analysis and presentation of facts about a poem (formerly the pillars of Eliot's critical theory) tend to harm the enjoyment of the poem, leaving it as a lifeless 'machine taken to pieces' (*OPP*, 114).

The second subjectivist claim of the essay is a reiteration of the demand for the critic to involve his entire personality and his individual outlook on life when he is criticizing poetry. For, as Eliot remarks, 'the literary critic is not merely a technical expert, who has learned the rules to be observed by the writers he criticizes: the critic must be the whole man, a man with convictions and principles, and of knowledge and experience of life' (*OPP*, 116).

Eliot thus ends up embracing a meta-critical outlook with a distinctly subjectivist dimension,[4] an outlook which is sharply opposed to his initial objectivist stance which condemned the personal emotion and subjective response of impressionistic criticism, and championed the dry technical analysis of the poet-critic and the impersonal comparative analysis and fact-gathering of the scholar.

IV

The striking development in Eliot's theorizing from the ardent demand for impersonal objectivity to an acceptance of the necessary and invaluable role of the subjective and personal is not only significant for Eliot scholarship but may have more general relevance for critical theory. It is certainly an encouraging fact for defenders of the subjective factor in criticism, since Eliot is so often regarded and invoked as one of the authoritative prophets of objectivity.[5] Moreover, if we examine the deeper dynamics of Eliot's conversion to acceptance of critical subjectivity, we may reach more interesting and compelling arguments against a rigid and exclusive meta-critical objectivism.

Eliot's critical conversion involves some paradoxes and incongruities. First, though Eliot clearly seems to abandon his early commitment to critical impersonality and objectivity, he does not retrospectively repudiate his early criticism as essentially wrong and misguided. Secondly, though his early objectivist theory is likely to strike us as unconvincing, naive, and inferior to his later views, it is hard to deny the almost unanimous verdict that Eliot's early criticism is far more powerful than

---

[4] Eliot's final acceptance of the subjective factor can also be seen in his very late essay 'To Criticize the Critic' (1961), *TC*, 11-26.

[5] See, for example, David Bleich, *Subjective Criticism* (Baltimore: Johns Hopkins University Press, 1978), 34.

that of his later years.[6] How are these apparent inconsistencies to be explained?

I think they may be explained most simply and adequately by the basic and crucial distinction between practical criticism and meta-criticism or critical theory. Though the young Eliot zealously professed a radically objective and impersonal theory of criticism, he did not practice what he preached. Quite the contrary. Eliot's early criticism was in fact deeply colored and essentially controlled by his own personal needs and ambitions as an aspiring young poet. One could readily show that Eliot's praise of the metaphysical poets, Elizabethan poets, and Dante, and his censure of Milton, Shelley, and the Georgians essentially derived from the fact that the former were congenial to and a helpful influence on the sort of poetry he was writing and wanted to write, while the latter were unhelpful or a hindrance to his verse and represented other, competing poetic qualities.

However, though this dependence of Eliot's early critical judgments on his own personal needs as a poet could be easily demonstrated, it is unnecessary to do so, since we have Eliot's own subsequent confession to that effect. In his retrospective essay, 'To Criticize the Critic' (1961), he avows: 'in my earlier criticism, both in my general affirmations about poetry and in writing about authors who had influenced me, I was implicitly defending the sort of poetry that I and my friends wrote' (*TC*, 16). Eliot in fact had already expressed much the same view almost twenty years earlier in 'The Music of Poetry' (1942), maintaining that the poet-critic, in his critical writings, 'is always trying to defend the kind of poetry he is writing, or to formulate the kind that he wants to write. Especially when he is young, and actively engaged in battling for the kind of poetry which he practices, he sees the poetry of the past in relation to his own: and his gratitude to those dead poets from whom he has learned, as well as his indifference to those whose aims have been alien to his own, may be exaggerated' (*OPP*, 26). Eliot elsewhere goes on to assert that such a personal critical bias 'is not only inevitable, it is right' (*OPP*, 159); and the decisive influence of his own personal needs as a 'battling' poet-critic is perhaps most striking in his evaluation of Milton, which changes dramatically from condemnation to approval once Eliot's poetic battle was won.[7]

Thus, though Eliot's early critical theory professed objectivity and impersonality, his actual critical practice has a strongly subjective character, essentially dependent on his personal needs as a poet. One could interpret this resistance of his practice to conform to his objectivist theory as a testimony to the pervasive power and ineradicable presence of the subjective in criticism. Alternatively, and more penetratingly, one could

[6] See, for example, F.W. Bateson, 'Criticism's Lost Leader', in *The Literary Criticism of T.S. Eliot*, 9, 17.

[7] For a fuller discussion of Eliot's changing evaluation of Milton and its meta-critical significance, see R. Shusterman, 'Evaluative Reasoning in Criticism', *Ratio*, 23 (1981), 145-146. See also Chapter Eight below, 202-203.

interpret his early objectivist critical theory as an ingenious method to disguise the essentially subjective and self-seeking character of his early criticism. For it is interesting to note that as Eliot's status as a poet became more firmly established and he had less need to battle for his poetry, his critical theory became more accepting of the subjective, while his actual critical judgments became generally more disinterested or objective. It seems, then, that once Eliot had achieved the early poetic and critical aims he was striving for, it was no longer necessary to disguise his self-promoting critical judgments as the objectively true product of an impersonal and objectivist critical methodology. Eliot's success similarly allowed him to make his later critical judgments more disinterested or detached from his poetic aims, since these had either been realized or had become less urgent.

However, no matter how we interpret it, there is, in Eliot's early criticism, a gaping inconsistency between theory and practice. And I believe there is an even more embarrassing and philosophically damaging inconsistency, a deep contradiction in the theory itself, with respect to its ideal of objectivity and the primacy of the poet-critic.

We have already shown how Eliot's early critical theory maintains that criticism should be detached, impersonal, and objective, 'the disinterested exercise of intelligence', and thus that the critic should suppress personal bias in the 'pursuit of true judgment' and the 'aim to see the object as it really is'. Yet when Eliot turns to theorize about who in fact makes the best critic, we find that it is not, as one would expect, an informed but detached observer of that ideal order of poetic tradition which Eliot describes in 'Tradition and Individual Talent'. It is rather, surprisingly, the practicing poet, who is likely to be far more interested in the struggle to win acceptance for his own poetry than in the common pursuit of true judgment.

In the very same two essays in which Eliot most powerfully urges the critical ideals of objectivity and disinterestedness ('The Perfect Critic' and 'The Function of Criticism'), he also tells us that the best criticism is that of the practicing poet: 'the artist is ... oftenest to be depended upon as a critic; his criticism will be criticism, and not the satisfaction of a suppressed creative wish – which, in most other persons, is apt to interfere fatally' (*SW*, 7). Eliot similarly maintains that since 'a critic must have a very developed sense of fact', there is 'peculiar importance' and value in the poetic practitioner's criticism; for 'he is dealing with his facts, and he can help us do the same' (*SE*, 31, 32). 'The practitioners have clarified and reduced to a state of fact all the feeling that ... [other critics and lovers of poetry] can only enjoy in the most nebulous form'; the poet-critic with his mastery of fact and poetic technique can make the magic of poetry 'into something precise, tractable, under control' (*ibid*.).[8]

---

[8] In other early writings Eliot expressed not only the view that 'the best criticism of poetry is the criticism of poets' but the more extreme claim 'that the only valuable criticism is that of the

In these essays which advocate factual objectivity and impersonal, disinterested analysis, and which claim superiority for the practicing poet's criticism because of his mastery of fact and technique, Eliot seems to ignore the fact that the practicing poet, for all his objective knowledge of fact and technique, is not likely to use this knowledge objectively and disinterestedly in the pure pursuit of true judgment. For the poet-critic's major aim in criticism is not really pure contemplation and impersonal judgment, but the furthering of his own poetic achievement (if also that of his poetic allies).

This patently personal motivation of poet-critic, though conveniently ignored in the two famous objectivist essays, is strikingly present elsewhere in Eliot's early writings on critical theory. In an essay of 1920 he states that 'every form of genuine criticism is directed toward creation ...; the poetic critic is criticizing poetry in order to create poetry.'[9] And in one of the less familiar sections of *The Sacred Wood*, he similarly claims that the critic needs 'a creative interest. ... The important critic is the person who is absorbed in the present problems of art, and who wishes to bring the forces of the past to bear upon the solution of these problems' (*SW*, 37-38).

Thus, Eliot's ideal of the practicing poet-critic, who intrinsically is personally involved and not disinterested or detached, simply does not and cannot tally with his other ideal of critical objectivity and impersonal detachment. One of these ideals would have to be sacrificed to maintain a consistent critical theory; and we have seen that Eliot chose to abandon objectivism and to accept the place and value of subjectivity in criticism. This move has the advantage of not only rendering his critical theory more internally consistent, but also making it more consistent with his actual practice, which, of course, reveals much of the subjective bias and interest of the poet-critic who is criticizing in order to create and defend his creation.

Eliot, then, provides testimony, both in theory and in practice, that the poet-critic is and *should be* pursuing in his criticism goals other than objective judgment or truth, goals like the advancement or acceptance of a new style of poetry. English criticism and poetry would have been poorly served indeed, if Eliot (and Dryden, Wordsworth, and Coleridge before him) had exorcized their literary aims and interests from their criticism and confined themselves to impersonal fact and neutral contemplation. This testimony, I think, points to a more general meta-critical lesson which I have argued for extensively elsewhere:[10] viz., that some valid and fruitful

workman'. See, respectively, T.S. Eliot, 'The Criticism of Poetry', *Times Literary Supplement*, 953 (1920), 256; and 'The Local Flavour', *Athenaeum*, 4676 (1919), 1333.

[9] T.S. Eliot, 'A Brief Treatise on the Criticism of Poetry', *Chapbook*, 2 (1920), 3. In this essay Eliot emphasizes that the best kind of critic must be something of a poet since criticism requires knowledge of technique. 'And you cannot understand the technique of poetry unless you are to some extent capable of performing this operation.' And of Remy de Gourmont, he says, 'unless he had been a poet he could not have been a critic' (*ibid.*).

[10] See R. Shusterman, 'The Logic of Interpretation', *Philosophical Quarterly*, 28 (1978), 310-324; 'The Logic of Evaluation', *Philosophical Quarterly*, 30 (1980), 327-341; 'Evaluative

types of literary criticism are not and do not aim to be objectively true (nor indeed subjectively true). For there are valid critical aims, both in interpretation and evaluation, other than the pursuit of objective (or subjective) truth; and this variety of critical aims engenders a variety of valid but often incommensurable critical frameworks which cannot be reduced to a single logical base, let alone a common methodology.

We should recall, however, that Eliot's mature acceptance of critical subjectivity was not confined to the practicing poet's criticism. He rather came to insist that subjectivity is not only a condition and privilege of the poet-critic, but that it is, to some degree, the lot of all critics, who as human beings with limitations, needs, and contingencies cannot attain the state of a purely impersonal and detached objective contemplation of poetry, but who, perhaps precisely for that reason, can better understand and respond to poetry, or indeed appreciate it at all.

                                    V

The danger of pointing out Eliot's acceptance of the subjective factor in criticism is that it temptingly suggests that this must make him a subjectivist who rejects the idea of any objective validity or standards outside the individual critic's consciousness. Though Eliot may have ceased his polemics for objectivist theory, he never professed or applied the subjectivist or radical relativist idea that whatever an individual thinks is right and that one man's judgment of poetry is as good or correct as any other. On the contrary, he surely continued to claim the compelling validity and rightness of some views, and the contrasting wrongness of others (no matter how sincerely they may have been held, and even when it was he himself who had sincerely held them).

This suggests the more general point that any thorough-going subjectivism or radical relativism seems self-refuting. For if any view or judgment is as good as another, there is no compelling reason at all to adopt the subjectivist's as the correct one. Is Eliot then an objectivist or a subjectivist? Can one reject a personality-denying objectivism without thereby committing oneself to subjectivism? The inhibiting feeling that one logically cannot, despite the gut-feeling that one can and should, reflects some of the philosophical cramps and dangers of simplistic binary thinking on the objectivity/subjectivity issue.

It therefore seems worthwhile to probe more deeply into the ideal of objectivity and Eliot's early (and ultimately abandoned) attempt to formulate and advocate it as the critical goal. For not only was this attempt extremely influential, but the issue of objectivity is still a very live issue in critical theory today. Do literary texts have objective meaning and value?

Reasoning in Criticism' and *The Object of Literary Criticism* (Amsterdam: Rodopi, 1984), 148-224.

What would be the nature of objective interpretation or evaluation of literature, if indeed there can be such objectivity? Concern regarding the nature and possibility of objectivity is *not*, it should be emphasized, a mere parochial worry of the literary critic and aesthetician, but is rather one of the most topical and pressing concerns of general philosophy today. Several leading philosophers have recently felt obliged to struggle with the problematic notion of objectivity in order to salvage a reasonably clear conception of it that is both workable and worthy.

This philosophical task is obviously very difficult, since so many philosophers have so long and so freely tossed about the terms 'objective' and 'subjective' in advocating a wide variety of so-called objectivist and subjectivist theories on a wide variety of subjects, thus providing an apparently bewildering variety of models and meanings of objectivity. Even in the single, limited domain of contemporary meta-ethics, as Richard Hare complains, though almost all philosophers advocate either objectivism or subjectivism, 'hardly any of them give any clear idea of how they are using the terms "objective" and "subjective" '; and Hare goes on to deplore the fact that these ambiguous terms have provided more confusion than illumination in moral philosophy.[11]

It would be unfair, however, to present dissatisfaction with the notions of objectivity and subjectivity as an entirely recent phenomenon. For as early as 1856, John Ruskin challenged the value of these terms most vehemently:

> German dullness, and English affectation, have of late much multiplied among us the use of two of the most objectionable words that were ever coined by the troublesomeness of metaphysicians – namely, 'Objective' and 'Subjective'. No words can be more exquisitely, and in all points, useless; and I merely speak of them that I may, at once and forever, get them out of my way and out of my reader's. But to get that done, they must be explained.[12]

Ruskin's extremely simple and obviously inadequate explanation of the subjective/objective distinction as that between felt sensation (subjective) and dispositional 'power of producing that sensation' (objective) surely will not lay these terms to rest. And however vague and problematic the terms may be, they seem too deeply entrenched to be facilely dismissed from theoretical discourse; though we may strive to avoid them in practice, and even, by clarificatory analysis, somewhat loosen their grip of mystification in theory.

In any event, Eliot's early theorizing struggles, like contemporary philosophy, with the problem of providing an adequate account of objectivity, and we may pursue our study of Eliot by examining the major

---

[11] R.M. Hare, *Moral Thinking* (Oxford: Oxford University Press, 1981), 207.
[12] J. Ruskin, 'Of the Pathetic Fallacy', repr. in *English Critical Essays (Nineteenth Century)*, ed. E.D. Jones (London: Oxford University Press, 1946), 378.

views of objectivity in current philosophical discussion. Perhaps the two most central and fundamental of these are: (1) objectivity as accurate correspondence to an independent object or more generally to reality; and (2) objectivity as agreement or consensus among a community of competent discussants or practitioners. These two conceptions are clearly logically independent (achieved agreement not precluding the possibility of particular inaccuracy of correspondence, nor accuracy itself entailing agreement); and since the first notion seems to demand an ultimately exclusive and univocal standard of objectivity, there would appear to be an ineliminable possibility of tension between the two notions, making it ultimately impossible to embrace both together.[13] Eliot's early struggle to maintain objectivism is plagued by the uneasy relations between these notions of objectivity. In this struggle, to preview my narrative, Eliot conflatingly entertains them both and vacillates between them in an attempt to reach an account of objectivity which would meet his needs as a poet and critic, and which would stand up to the sort of sceptical scrutiny that he, as a trained philosopher, would instinctively direct at it. His failure to distinguish sufficiently between these two fundamentally different conceptions of objectivity may have made him insufficiently aware that the impossibility of one does not entail the hopelessness of the other and thus led to his abandoning the project of theorizing how and how far criticism could and should be objective. To understand Eliot's problem of objectivity, and our own, we should examine the correspondence and consensual views more closely.

VI

The correspondence theory of objectivity is essentially linked to and built upon the idea of an independent external object to which perception or judgment is directed (and from which the term 'objective' seems to have etymologically derived). The 'objective' properties of such an object are those properties that the object independently has irrespective of whether or how we perceive it. This first conception of objectivity thus presupposes the existence of an autonomous external object which our (subjective) sensations or impressions must faithfully correspond to or accurately mirror in order for our perception to be objective. The system or order of such external objects constitutes external reality, and we can thus see how this concept of objectivity is ineluctably tied to ontological realism and perhaps also to ontological essentialism, where the essence of an object is

---

[13] Rorty, in a recent article, goes so far as to suggest their mutual incompatibility and exclusiveness; since strong commitment to a consensual community ('solidarity') frustrates the correspondence ideal of perfectly detached and neutral accuracy of reflection, while the ideal of detachment tends to isolate one from and disrupt the consensual community. See R. Rorty, 'Solidarity or Objectivity', *Nanzan Review of American Studies*, 6 (1984), 1-20; reprinted but somewhat altered in J. Rajchman and Cornell West (eds.) *Post-Analytic Philosophy* (New York: Columbia University Press, 1985), 3-19.

precisely those properties which really 'objectively' belong to and constitute the object as opposed to others we merely attribute to the object as a result of the vagaries of our perception or conceptual scheme.

The more accurately we mirror or represent this external reality, the more objective our perceptions or judgments are, and the closer we come to absolutely objective knowledge, i.e. to knowledge of things as they really are. We may never be able to achieve such absolute objectivity, since we may never be able to rid ourselves utterly of distorting features in our perception or conceptual scheme. But we should strive to approximate it as closely as possible, and should measure our theories against this ideal – or perhaps, more precisely, against a standard derived from it, since we hardly seem to have it to measure against but rather seem to be striving to achieve it. (In this way we can interpret Popper's move from the ideal standard of truth to the actual standard of verisimilitude.)[14]

The centrality of this notion of objectivity in traditional philosophical and scientific thought is attested to by even its severe critics. Richard Rorty, who aims to undermine completely this notion of objectivity as correspondence, sadly complains how it and its mirror metaphor underlie and misguide the entire epistemological enterprise of modern philosophy, and he mordantly characterizes the role it gives the philosopher as perennially cleaning, polishing, or adjusting the mirror so as to provide the clearest and most faithful reflection of the independently real.[15] Joseph Margolis, also critical of this notion of objectivity and particularly of its foundationalist and essentialist connections, similarly recognizes that it has governed and motivated modern philosophical and scientific thought; and he even seems willing to grant that at least in some cognitive areas it may in part have real validity: 'objectivity in the physical sciences presupposes an existent order independent of ... the shifting interests of human investigators.'[16]

But not to lose sight of Eliot and the literary domain, we must remember that this correspondence or realist notion of objectivity had been borrowed from philosophy and science and erected into a literary critical ideal by Eliot's avowed progenitor, Matthew Arnold, who formulated it in the famous injunction 'to see the object as in itself it really is'.[17] Much of Eliot's

---

[14] See K.R. Popper, *Objective Knowledge* (Oxford: Oxford University Press, 1979), 57-60.

[15] R. Rorty, *Philosophy and the Mirror of Nature* (Princeton: Princeton University Press, 1979). Rorty's most concentrated discussion of objectivity is on pages 333-342.

[16] J. Margolis, 'Relativism, History, and Objectivity in the Human Studies', *Journal for the Theory of Social Behavior*, 14 (1984), 1-23. I here cite from p. 4.

[17] M. Arnold, 'The Function of Criticism at the Present Time', in L. Trilling (ed.), *The Portable Matthew Arnold* (New York: Viking, 1949), 234. Of course, Eliot's sympathies with Arnold were never complete, and he sharply criticized several of Arnold's views (especially later in *TUP*, 103-119). However not only is Arnold's general influence recognized in Eliot's early objectivist period (e.g. in the 1921 'Introduction' to *SW*), but Eliot's specific advocacy of objectivism explicitly invokes 'the words of Arnold' (*SW*, 15).

early advocacy of objectivism was expressed in the spirit of this realist, correspondence notion of objectivity; and before examining Eliot's use of it, we should consider its criticism and the claims of alternative notions of objectivity, and foremost among these alternatives, the notion of objectivity as agreement or consensus.

As we have already intimated, the idea of a purely objective order or reality, wholly independent of and unmodified in human perception and against which we can measure the objectivity of our judgments, seems a rather unworkable idea. For, in the first place, how can we employ this objective reality as a standard unless we know it; and how can we ever know we know it? Against what would such alleged foundationalist knowledge be measured? Moreover, not only does the idea of correspondence to the independent and uninterpreted order of the real fail as a practical touchstone for objectivity of judgment, it also seems unworkable even as a normative ideal that is beyond our achievement but still directing our inquiry. For even such an ideal would seem to require some reasonably definitive sense in order to function adequately; yet what real sense can we give it, debarred as we seem to be in principle from knowledge of what this objectivity amounts to? What real sense can we give to the idea of 'seeing the object as in itself it really is, uninterpreted by any conventions of perception and conceptual scheme', besides the obviously unsatisfactory sense of seeing the object as it is not seen and cannot be seen by human perception?

For reasons somewhat similar to these, Rorty denies the validity of the realist-correspondence notion of objectivity, and instead insists that 'our only usable notion of "objectivity" is "agreement" rather than mirroring'.[18] In other words, 'objective' is to be construed simply as 'characterizing the view which would be agreed upon as a result of argument undeflected by irrelevant considerations', objectivity being 'a property of theories which, having been thoroughly discussed, are chosen by a consensus of rational discussants'.[19] Margolis, at least in the domain of 'human studies' (including, of course, literary studies), similarly denies the validity of the realist notion of objectivity as correspondence, and expounds a notion of objectivity as agreement, which is richer than Rorty's and which will prove quite helpful in understanding Eliot's objectivism. 'Objectivity in the human studies must be fundamentally *consensual* ... There *is* nothing independently "there" to discover, but making or doing things in the consensually accepted way signifies that one's understanding *is* objective, that is, "belongs" within the life of a given society.'[20]

Realist opponents of the consensual notion of objectivity may avail

---

[18] *Philosophy and the Mirror of Nature*, 333, 337.

[19] *Ibid.*, 333-34, 338. See also 361.

[20] Margolis, 7, 9. It is important to emphasize that Margolis and Rorty's model of consensuality is far from mere idealist intersubjective agreement of judgment. It is essentially pragmatist, involving agreement in practices entrenched in a real social world.

themselves of the Moorean argument that after rational consensus has been achieved concerning a judgment, we can always meaningfully ask whether this rationally and consensually endorsed judgment is objectively true or merely a product of common, reasonable error, and that this question seems to be an open one. They may further maintain that since within so many cognitive areas we find conflicting judgments or theories, each commanding a community of consenting rational discussants, we seem compelled either to assume that conflicting judgments can be objectively true or that none of the conflicting judgments can be objective simply because none commands total consensus in the field. Either alternative seems decidedly unattractive. The realist therefore insists that the only way out of this dilemma, the only possibility for conclusively determining which of the rival consensual judgments is objectively true, and the only hope of maintaining a notion of objective truth unassailable and uncorruptible by fashion, is by appeal to an external, independent reality as final arbiter, at least in principle, if impossible in practice.

In rejoinder, the consensualist might again challenge the view that any real sense or use can be made of such a posited objective reality, and he might simply deny what Rorty calls 'the dogma that only where there is correspondence to reality is there the possibility of rational agreement', since 'we are able to eliminate the possibility of perpetual, undecidable rational disagreement only in those areas whose unquestioned links to external reality provide a common ground for the disputants'.[21]

The *prima facie* plausibility of this alleged dogma is partly that we seem to require something outside the agreement itself to be agreed about, which seems to push us again towards some external reality. Moreover, the consensualist might seem pressured outside his circle of agreement by the need not only to posit what agreement is about, but also to determine what constitutes the measure of agreement itself. To such charges the consensualist may wish to reply that the objects of agreement and also the measure of what constitutes agreement are simply other agreements, and that we simply move in ever wider circles of agreement, there being nothing beyond agreement that is necessary for rational agreement to be anchored upon. This sort of defense is available to Rorty, who rather seems to defend the possibility that firm rational agreement and objectivity can exist on a purely consensual basis, mainly by suggesting that the burden of proof rests on those who deny such a possibility. Margolis is perhaps more helpful in suggesting a model to show how such rational and stable agreement may be secured, maintained, and extended without positing transcendentally external realities, laws, or standards to anchor them.

The objectivity of the human studies, then, is ... fundamentally grounded in the idea of the *natural* acquisition of a language and a culture – which is not an appeal to essentialism or any cognitive privilege but rather to the

[21] *Philosophy and the Mirror of Nature*, 337.

irresistible assumption that the members of a human society, groomed from
infancy to acquire the skills and habits that constitute the very life of that
society, cannot be supposed to be generally uncomprehending or inept about
its regularities.[22]

Margolis's 'participant model' of consensual objectivity draws heavily on
Wittgenstein for three major points. First, it is not a mere matter of
consensus on propositions, but involves a certain agreement in action,
practice, and ways of living. Secondly, 'the members of a society cannot
generally be wrong in their characterization of the central practices of their
own worlds', though 'they can go wrong in determinate instances'. Thirdly,
'understanding these practices by way of social membership entails, as
Wittgenstein explicitly says, knowing "how to go on", how to extend a
practice beyond the contingent instances one is already familiar with'.[23]
The upshot of this third point, as elaborated by Margolis, is extremely
important for Eliot's treatment of objectivity (and for his social and cultural
theory as well).

> A living practice, then, has its improvisational power, whether in composing
> fugues or displaying good manners or producing effective insults; and what
> may count as an objective understanding of such a practice includes a sense of
> continuous, diachronic, even multiply divergent lines of development for
> which, correspondingly, shifting idealized rules could (perhaps) be
> provided.[24]

The notion of a 'living practice' that Margolis describes as constituting
the core of objectivity in human studies, though explicitly derived from
Wittgenstein's idea of 'form of life', very clearly echoes Eliot's central notion
of a 'living tradition' and 'the historical sense' which grasps it and guides its
present and future development. In his theory of tradition we find Eliot
embracing the participant-consensual notion of objectivity with an
enthusiasm equal if not superior to that with which he embraced the
objectivism of correspondence. Eliot's problem, I maintain, was failing to
distinguish sufficiently between these two forms of objectivity but rather
conflating them. Therefore, when he came to feel the inadequacies of the
correspondence model and lost faith in it, he tended to abandon his explicit
advocacy of objectivity altogether, even though he still went on to maintain
the basic tenets (those of the theory of tradition) which would support his
continued affirmation of objectivity in the consensual sense. But before
scrutinizing the uneasy conjunction of these two notions of objectivity in
Eliot's early theorizing, we should briefly note some other (apparently less
central) senses of objectivity which may be distinguished in current

[22] Margolis, 18.

[23] *Ibid.*, 8. See also 10-11.

[24] *Ibid.*, 9. For further elaboration of Margolis's theory, see J. Margolis, *Pragmatism Without
Foundations* (Oxford: Blackwell, 1986).

philosophical writing, one of which is very relevant to Eliot's poetic and critical theory.

These other senses of objectivity are conveniently catalogued in Hare's analysis of this concept, which interestingly does not include the two rival notions of objectivity we have so far discussed.[25] According to Hare, the term 'objective' may be variously used to characterize: (1) a statement descriptive of any fact; (2) a statement descriptive of a publicly observable fact (e.g. 'She has blue eyes' but *not* 'I love her', which, however, may be objectively true in sense (1)); (3) any (i.e. not necessarily descriptive) utterance about an observable object (e.g. 'Shut the door'); (4) judgment that is unbiassed (e.g. judging that my beloved daughter sings well when she is regularly off key would in this sense *not* be objective); (5) judgment which can be determined by 'physical measurement' or other mechanically applied standard (e.g. judging a competition in speed skating versus one in figure skating); (6) in a narrowly legal sense, that a particular provoked reaction would have been provoked in any reasonable man (objective) and was not merely in point of fact provoked in the man in question (subjective); and finally, (7) 'a judgment made from an impersonal standpoint'.

This last sense of objectivity as impersonality, which Hare admits is closely allied to the sense of 'unbiassed' and claims as 'the most crucial sense of "objective" for ethics',[26] is certainly a crucial notion for Eliot's aesthetics of objectivity. We can hardly ignore the fact that Eliot's objectivist poetic was advanced under the title 'the Impersonal theory of poetry' and that his objectivist theory of criticism was also frequently formulated in terms of impersonality. Must we then posit a third basic notion of objectivity to examine in our study of this concept in Eliot?

I think not, for this notion of impersonality seems reducible to the two basic notions of objectivity already discussed: correspondence and consensuality. Indeed, its embracing both these notions may explain why impersonality was itself such an attractive and serviceable notion for Eliot and yet such a problematic one, which he had frequently to redefine or reinterpret in order to go on maintaining it after having jettisoned his early radical objectivism.[27]

Impersonality may indicate, first of all, not being governed or distorted by narrowly individual, private, or personal prejudice or outlook, but rather conforming (deliberately or not) to the accepted more-than-personal norms, criteria, or methods of viewing or judging things of the given sort in the given culture. Here, clearly, 'impersonal' essentially means 'more than narrowly personal', and impersonality essentially amounts to consensual

---

[25] Hare, 206-212. It might be an interesting project to try to map Hare's classification onto the binary scheme that we have presented, but this will not be attempted here, except with respect to the one of Hare's senses of objectivity which is clearly relevant to Eliot's objectivism.

[26] *Ibid.*, 211.

[27] See, for example, Eliot's reinterpretation of impersonality in his late essay on Yeats to show that it can be consistent with 'the greater expression of personality' (*OPP*, 299).

objectivity, i.e. what would be accepted as valid and pertinent by competent discussants or participants in the given community, tradition or practice. This sense of impersonality is at the heart of Eliot's advocacy of poetic impersonality and objectivity through adherence to tradition. It also clearly underlies his famous plea for impersonal objectivity in the critic, who is implored 'to discipline his personal prejudices and cranks ... and compose his differences with as many of his fellows as possible, in the common pursuit of true judgment' (*SE*, 25).

However, impersonality can also be construed not as 'more-than-personal' but as 'less-than-personal' or 'person-less'. Hare dismisses the thought that the negative morpheme 'im' should suggest that an impersonal judgment could be construed as one of a 'non-person' or 'no person', since he fails to see what sense could be attached to the idea of such a judgment, believing as he does that all judgments, including divine ones, must be made by persons, even if the 'persons' are not human.[28] But the notion of impersonality does indeed suggest the idea (unacceptable as it may ultimately prove to be) of a viewpoint not only beyond the narrowly individual person and free from his particular prejudices, but also beyond the still arguably over-narrow vista of any group of persons who agree to a more-than-personal outlook which would satisfy the consensual notion of objectivity. For just as particular persons suffer from distortive bias, so groups of persons may similarly suffer from such bias, which, though agreed to by the group and hence more than narrowly personal, can none the less be regarded as essentially governed by personal needs, interests, or proclivities shared by the persons in the group, and therefore as potentially (if not actually) distorting an objective, disinterested outlook. To overcome such distortive bias in the aim of impersonal objectivity, the individual (or group) may be urged to suppress or extinguish all personal factors in perception, and the surest way to try to do this is by sacrificing personality altogether. Once personality's distortive gloss has been removed, impersonal perception can neutrally and accurately reflect things as they really are, independent of narrowly personal or interpersonal habits or conventions of perception. Here we see how objectivity as impersonality can easily collapse into and be construed as objectivity of the realist-correspondence variety.

Moreover, it may already be clear that Eliot's 'Impersonal theory of poetry' is very much steeped in this conception of impersonality as well, where 'the progress of the artist is a continual self-sacrifice, a continual extinction of personality', a 'process of depersonalization', so that he can serve as a 'neutral', non-distortive, 'finely perfected medium' for sundry things and images to be accurately recorded, stored, and allowed to form themselves into 'new combinations' (*SE*, 17-19). Similarly, this sort of impersonality is central to Eliot's objectivist theory of criticism, where the

[28] Hare, 211.

critic's personality is to be so suppressed that 'he should have no emotions except those immediately provoked by a work of art – and these ... are, when valid, perhaps not to be called emotions at all' (*SW*, 12-13). And Eliot goes on to claim, in a fashion which explicitly links critical impersonality to the objectivity of correspondence, that 'the end of the enjoyment of poetry is a pure contemplation from which all the accidents of personal emotion are removed; thus we aim to see the object as it really is and find a meaning for the words of Arnold' (*SW*, 14-15).

Thus it is gainless for students of Eliot's objectivism to try to avoid the problematic tension between objectivity as correspondence and objectivity as agreement by neutrally treating his conception of objectivity as synonymous with impersonality. For the very same duality and tension arises in this latter notion. We must therefore accept the presence of this basic duality in Eliot's objectivist theory, and indeed at the core of probably his most famous and seminal essay, 'Tradition and the Individual Talent' (1919). Let us turn, then, to this essay and to a closer examination of Eliot's use of these different notions of objectivity and of his purposes and problems in using them.

VII

Eliot's treatment of objectivity in 'Tradition and the Individual Talent', which centers on 'the Impersonal theory of poetry', begins with an attempt to base poetic objectivity and impersonality on the idea of a living tradition, which we have seen to be essentially a matter of consensual objectivity. Tradition, Eliot insists, is not a mere collection of past practices, 'monuments', beliefs, or standards. It is rather a live 'current' or living practice, continuing and developing from the past into the present and future, a current to which the participant poets of various ages must cohere and conform, and yet also modify and develop. This historical sense of tradition which Eliot requires of a poet is thus a consciousness 'not of what is dead, but of what is already living' (*SE*, 22). Eliot therefore maintains that the poet cannot 'take the past as a lump, an indiscriminate bolus', but 'must be very conscious of the main current', which is not fixed but rather 'changes' and develops (*SE*, 16). The current of living tradition might, at a given juncture, admit of external representation in terms of 'an ideal order of existing monuments' of poetry, or perhaps even in a set of poetic canons. Yet such a set of canons or order of canonical works cannot constitute a fixed and absolute standard, but only serves as an essentially heuristic device for trying to grasp the living tradition and to help both to maintain it and at the same time to project or develop it. For this reason, though it is necessary for the poet who aims at objective excellence to conform to the tradition, 'the necessity that he shall conform, that he shall cohere, is not onesided' (*SE*, 15):

what happens when a new work of art is created is something that happens simultaneously to all the works of art which preceded it. The existing monuments form an ideal order among themselves, which is modified by the introduction of the new (the really new) work of art among them. The existing order is complete before the new work arrives; for order to persist after the supervention of novelty, the *whole* existing order must be, if ever so slightly, altered; and so the relations, proportions, values of each work of art toward the whole are readjusted; and this is conformity between the old and the new. Whoever has approved this idea of order, of the form of European, of English literature will not find it preposterous that the past should be altered by the present as much as the present is directed by the past. And the poet who is aware of this will be aware of great difficulties and responsibilities. (*SE*, 15)

Possessing a tradition and conforming to it is not, therefore, slavishly adhering to fixed rules and models, but instead involves what Wittgenstein calls knowing 'how to go on', even when this means going beyond the rules or even breaking or changing some of them.[29] Hence, 'to conform merely would be for the new work not really to conform at all' (*SE*, 15). The principles, canons, etc. that the tradition has endorsed have no transcendental objective status, for they may be and should be modified by the tradition's development, which could indeed develop in more than one direction, and not necesarily the best – hence the great responsibility of the participant artist.

Such principles, canons, or ideal orders are what Margolis (after Wittgenstein) describes as 'synchronically idealized regularities [of a practice] best projected by participants within a given society's form of life', which are 'provisionally predictive, ... openended, and subject to revision'. And 'objective understanding of such a practice includes a sense of continuous, diachronic, even multiply divergent lines of development for which, correspondingly, shifting idealized rules could (perhaps) be provided'.[30] But clearly long before Wittgenstein, the idea of a participatory model of consensual objectivity was cogently presented by Eliot, in whose theory of tradition the community of competent participants included also 'the dead poets and artists' without whom no artist can be objectively appreciated (since 'his appreciation is the appreciation of his relation to the dead poets and artists') nor any work of art objectively valued (since 'its fitting in is a test of its value') (*SE*, 15).

But, whatever the cogency of the participatory model of consensual objectivity that his theory of tradition provided, Eliot evidently felt that it was inadequate to his needs. For midway through the essay, Eliot tries to bolster it by introducing 'the other aspect of this Impersonal theory of poetry', the 'depersonalization' of poetic perception, which, as I have

[29] See L. Wittgenstein, *Philosophical Investigations* (Oxford: Blackwell, 1968), 59, 72, 81-86.
[30] Margolis, 14, 9.

argued, is demanded by the scientific, realist ideal of objectivity as mirroring correspondence, and in which, according to Eliot, 'art may be said to approach the condition of science' (*SE*, 17-18).

Why was the consensual felt inadequate? Three problems most likely troubled Eliot. First, there was the fear that exclusive dependence on tradition-grounded consensuality to achieve objectivity could well degenerate into dogmatic conservatism; where, in the desire to cling to a tradition, we simply worship the past monuments, failing to distinguish the still vital from the inessential or outgrown; or where, in the desire to ensure consensus, we formulate and institute definite and fixed rules or standards to which participants are required to conform rigidly and one-sidedly. These dangers of dogmatic conservatism and slavish conventionalism, which threaten to transform tradition into something stagnant and immovable, present a fearful prospect for a poet like Eliot who wants to use the notion of tradition to develop and modernize English poetry, believing as he did that 'in the writing of verse one can only deal with actuality' (*ASG*, 30). Thus, though Eliot conceives of tradition as something living, dynamic, and open-ended, he reasonably fears that the ideal of objectivity as consensuality to tradition could all too easily generate rigid dogma and stagnation in the name of stability and preservation of tradition.[31]

The fear is a reasonable one because of a second problem of participatory consensual objectivity – the uncertain stability of objectivity as mere agreement in practice, devoid not only of an independent ontological base but even of a firm and clearly formulated standard to consent to and to compel consent. This is more than merely the problem adduced earlier – the possibility that something universally consented to by competent discussants could none the less prove wrong. It is rather the following. Though, on the one hand, we may want objectivity's consensuality to be purely *participatory*, that is, to flow from common inner-felt consent or agreement as to 'what is right' or 'how to go on', rather than require for its justification or preservation its external translation into formulated dogma (with the consequent threat of stagnant conservatism and sterile conventionalism); there is also the fear, on the other hand, that mere reliance on the consensuality and momentum of a living tradition will not suffice to ensure enough stability, direction, and force to preserve and develop the tradition and its consensuality. In this lies the temptation to affirm the use of dogma or orthodox standards, if only as an heuristic device. One is therefore aware of an intense need, at least in Eliot, to anchor the objectivity of consensuality in tradition onto something firmer and steadier than agreement *per se*.

It is surely not enough to assuage such anxiety with Margolis's probable

---

[31] Eliot discusses such dangers of conservatism for 'a living tradition' in *ASG*, 18-32. See my treatment of this matter in Chapter Seven below.

retort that this threat of loss of tradition, though logically possible, is implausibly remote, since a living tradition or practice (if it exists) will tend to take care of itself, being constantly bolstered by the reinforcing consent of its 'naturally groomed participants'. For however true this may be in principle, it seems more like a vague 'consolation of philosophy' than a viable solution to the dilemma facing Eliot. This is because of the third problem – the fact that (at least in Eliot's eyes) the tradition was no longer robustly and properly living, but was fractured, debilitated, and mis-guided. Eliot repeatedly bemoans his living in 'a formless age', after two centuries of dissociation from the main current of the Western literary tradition (e.g. SW, 61-64; SE, 287-290; ASG, 35-53; OPP, 184-192). How then, one wonders with Eliot, when tradition is in crisis, and consensuality to its forms is undermined and unstable, how can we rely on consensual tradition to support itself? We rather need something powerful, attractive, and compelling outside the weakening circle of traditional consensuality to support and reinforce it, some firm foundation which, by compelling consent, could recreate the strong consensuality needed to continue the tradition and revitalize it.

In this need, it was not surprising that Eliot turned to the scientific-realist model of objectivity as correspondence to the independently real. Apart from promising such a firm foundation, this strategy had additional attractions. First, it linked Eliot's poetic objectivism not only with the hallowed literary objectivism of Arnold, but also, more importantly, with the objectivism of modern science, which seemed (at least in Eliot's youthful eyes) the very paradigm of robust objectivity, commanding universal consent through correspondence to the real. Eliot's need to associate poetic objectivity with scientific objectivity is made pathetically obvious by his grotesque comparison of poetic creation to 'the action which takes place when a bit of finely filiated platinum is introduced into a chamber containing oxygen and sulphur dioxide' (SE, 17). The idea of speaking of poetry (and criticism) in terms of natural science was frequently employed by Eliot and his modernist cohorts,[32] and it seems more than a shallow rhetorical ploy to induce a guise of respectable objectivity by linguistic osmosis. The natural sciences were successfully progressing on the model of objectivity as correspondence to the external and independently real; and this attractive objectivity could perhaps provide the needed boost or basis to achieve literary objectivity (even if of an ultimately consensual kind) by compelling assent and thus recreating consensuality.

Moreover, the belief in an external, definite, and independent reality

---

[32] For discussion of Eliot's use of scientific terminology, see B.Lee, Theory and Personality (London: Athlone, 1979), 98-101; and for Pound's use of it, see I. Bell, Critic as Scientist: The Modernist Poetics of Ezra Pound (London: Methuen, 1981). Eliot apparently had little understanding of science, and no real education in it. See L. Gordon, Eliot's Early Years (Oxford: Oxford University Press, 1977), 21.

that could in principle be known had also formed the basis of Moore and Russell's successful modernist revolution in philosophy, which, by the time of Eliot's essay, was well on its way to overpowering its opponents and establishing a substantial consensuality which promised real cooperative progress. And this realist-correspondence philosophy was a natural ally for Eliot's poetic cause, since both were reacting against the solipsism of late-nineteenth-century idealism.[33]

The realist ontology and empirical epistemology of Moore and Russell could be supplemented by the (allegedly Symbolist inspired) imagism of Pound and Hulme to provide Eliot with the following case for poetic objectivity of inert reflective correspondence. There is an independently real world of objects outside us which may be perceived by sensation. However, this independently given sensible reality is, ordinarily, never perceived as it really is, since we typically never even see the pure 'objective' sensation as it really is. For sensation is typically present to our consciousness only after it has been interpreted or construed in terms of our conventional conceptual categories of perception. These conceptual categories are clearly additive structures of the human mind which shape and interpret experience, and do not allow the pure reflection of things as they really are or even as how they are immediately given to sensation. Our typical perceptions are thus clouded, if not distorted, by our conventional categories of seeing or the discursive conceptual framework which shapes and interprets the sensually given so that we no longer see it as the sense-datum it is. Thus Russell has to urge his audience to make the difficult effort to perceive a simple object or fact of sense-data (e.g. 'This is white') without its conventional conceptual interpretation: 'I do not want you to think about the piece of chalk I am holding, but of what you see when you look at the chalk.'[34] Similarly, Hulme insists on the arduous task of the poet (and 'visual philosopher') 'first ... to see things as they really are, and apart from the conventional ways in which you have been trained to see them ... [and] second, ... the actual expression of what one sees. To prevent one falling into the conventional curves' of human thought and language.[35]

Eliot's notorious advocacy of 'depersonalization' of the poet is an attempt to base poetic objectivity on correspondence with such basic and undeniable objects of perception which are maximally free from the conventions

---

[33] Moore and Russell had felt before Eliot the need to break out of the stifling solipsistic dream world of nineteenth-century idealism and to adopt instead a 'robust sense of reality' which would help to cope with and affirm the modern world and scientific advancement. Russell vividly describes the thrill of following Moore in rejecting idealism, 'I felt it, in fact, as a great liberation, as if I had escaped from a hothouse on to a windswept headland. I hated the stuffiness involved in supposing that space and time were only in my mind.' See B. Russell, *My Philosophical Development* (New York: Simon and Schuster, 1959), 54, 61-62.

[34] B. Russell, 'The Philosophy of Logical Atomism' (1918) in D. Pears (ed.), *Russell's Logical Atomism* (London: Fontana, 1972), 53.

[35] T.E. Hulme, *Speculations* (London: Routledge and Kegan Paul, 1960), 133. For poetry as 'visual philosophy', see T.E. Hulme, *Further Speculations* (Minneapolis: University of

of conceptual construal and the vagaries of human interpretation. The poet's mind should be a highly sensitive, accurate, but inertly uninterpret-ing mirror of perception, 'a more finely perfected medium' which remains 'inert, neutral' (*SE*, 18). But since Eliot recognizes that the poet cannot rest content with merely mirroring the real but must rather yield something new ('create' hardly seems the right word for the poet's passive role here as medium), a product of the funding, combinations and superimposition of his passively reflective perceptions, Eliot apparently realizes that the mirror is not the best image for the depersonalized poet's mind. He therefore likens it instead to 'a receptacle for seizing and storing up numberless feelings, phrases, images, which remain there until all the particles which can unite to form a compound are present together' (*SE*, 19). To insure that the poet's mind can faithfully receive and store its objects without contaminating them by human or personal interpretation, Eliot is virtually forced to claim that the poet *qua* poet is not a person at all or at least 'has not a "personality" to express, but ... is only a medium ... in which impressions and experiences combine' (*SE*, 19-20). And Eliot explicitly relates this theory of his to the denial of 'the metaphysical theory of the substantial unity of the soul' (*SE*, 19) and thus of the very possibility of personal identity or personhood.

This ideal of poetic objectivity as faithful correspondence to reality through depersonalization and consequent neutral uninterpreting absorp-tion of the real is obviously riddled with problems which Eliot could not long ignore. But despite these problems, soon to be discussed, it inspired enough initial enthusiasm to be carried over and applied to criticism. Thus, in 'The Perfect Critic' (1920), Eliot advances a correspondence theory of critical objectivism, anchored in an independent external 'object', the work of art. The ideal is 'to see the object as it really is', and in order to achieve this one must suppress all personal inclinations ('impure desires') and even one's 'sensibility [which] alters the object' (*SW*, 6, 11, 15). The perfect critic must be like a highly polished mirror of perception directed 'solely and steadfastly at the object' with nothing to distort its faithful reflection or impression. Thus, 'a literary critic should have no emotions except those immediately provoked by a work of art' (*SW*, 11, 12).

Eliot not surprisingly tries again to link this depersonalized correspond-ence notion of objectivity to scientific objectivity. He does this here by describing such 'disinterested exercise of intelligence' directed steadfastly at the object as the essence of 'the scientific mind'; by identifying the most perfect manifestation of this mind in Aristotle, who is also identified as the most perfect critic; and by (somewhat ludicrously) connecting Rémy de Gourmont's excellence as a critic with his being 'an excessively able amateur in physiology' (*SW*, 13, 14). However, we soon see quite clearly

---

Minnesota Press, 1955), 9-11. See also my 'Remembering Hulme', *Journal of the History of Ideas*, 46 (1986), 559-576.

what science ultimately meant here for Eliot (who indeed had no real grasp of it) – a magical, modern-day philosopher's stone whose invocation could conjure up objectivity in any field and could inspire a transcendental, almost mystical, ideal of a purely objective God-like perception, perfectly corresponding to the real. For the scientific mind, which Eliot also calls 'the intelligent mind', leads to the following goal in criticism.

> The end of the enjoyment of poetry is a pure contemplation from which all the accidents of personal emotion are removed; thus we aim to see the object as it really is and find a meaning for the words of Arnold. And without a labour which is largely a labour of the intelligence, we are unable to attain that stage of vision *amor intellectualis Dei*. (*SW*, 14-15)

But, even while propounding this ideal of objectivity as correspondence, Eliot seems rather uncomfortable with it and with the mystical transcendentalism to which it points. Thus, even in 'Tradition and the Individual Talent', he abruptly breaks off his increasingly problematic exposition of this ideal by suddenly starting a new (concluding) section of the essay, with the revealing assertion (*SE*, 21): 'This essay proposes to halt at the frontiers of metaphysics or mysticism' (both of which had negative coloring in Eliot's early criticism, which emphasized the scientific and the factual in their stead). And Eliot's discomfort with this ideal of objectivity as correspondence was justifiable for several reasons.

First, there are the sort of problems adduced earlier against the ideal of objectivity as accurate, uninterpreting, mirroring correspondence – an ideal which by definition seems beyond our possible realization and application, if not beyond the realm of understanding and meaning altogether. Secondly, there is the problem, already briefly suggested, that this notion of objectivity seems to undermine the poet's role and status as creator, limiting him to an inert, neutral recorder and storer of images, feelings, and phrases. This, of course, is in sharp contrast not only to the much more positive romantic conception of the poet as creator (essentially constituting not merely poetry but reality itself with his primary and secondary imagination) but also to the classical view of poet as maker [i.e. as engaged in *poiesis*]. Eliot's view of the poet as a passive, inert, even if 'finely perfected medium' through which poetry is formed is obviously an unsatisfactory account of the poet's creative role; and Eliot is just as obviously uncomfortable with it. He struggles at the end of Part II of 'Tradition and the Individual Talent' to give the poet some active role (that of 'concentration' of experience) in poetic creation, but, in doing so, gets himself helplessly caught up in paradox, asserting that poetic composition should not proceed 'consciously and of deliberation' and yet also 'must be conscious and deliberate' (*SE*, 21).

The third, and philosophically most serious, problem with Eliot's imagistic ideal of an impersonal poetic perception free from conceptual construction and personal interpretation and thus perfectly reflective or correspondent to external reality is that this ideal, rather than helping us to attain such objectivity, seems to throw us back into our own inner private world from which we so much wanted to escape. In the attempt to escape the confinement of the mind and reach objective reality by stripping our experience of reality from all conventional constructions of language and all interpretation of discursive thought that the mind allegedly has distortingly added, what we finally come to are immediate sensations, the images of sense-data, which paradoxically seem to thrust us back into subjectivity. For our uninterpreted sense-data, though undeniable, are also undeniably our own and not necessarily anyone else's. They seem firmly confined to the private, subjective domain, because the moment we try to communicate (or even think about) the sensually given, we must linguistically and hence discursively interpret or characterize it. Moreover, even when maximally stripped of the human mind's conceptual constructions, our impressions still remain human and mental, and their apparent lack of conventional linguistic discursivity only deprives them of precisely the public, intersubjectively objective dimension of our ordinary discursive perception of the world. Thus, to discipline our perception (poetic or otherwise) to give only the non-discursive, uninterpreted sense-data we experience seems not to lead us into the fresh air of the external world but to deliver us back to a reality of impressions and to the stifling prison of subjectivism and solipsism which Eliot so anxiously wished to avoid.

There is added cause for Eliot to be uncomfortable with such a phenomenalistic, sensation-orientated objectivism, since it seems all too close to the *fin-de-siècle* philosophy of impressionism, which tends to dissolve the integrity and unity of the mind or personality into a passive egoless medium of sensibility, as indeed we saw Eliot was tempted to. But impressionism in English letters was associated with Pater, Wilde, and *fin-de-siècle* decadence and subjectivism against which Eliot was in declared (if not essential) revolt. Thus we find him violently attacking impressionism as 'sick and sorry' in the very same essay ('The Perfect Critic', *SW*, 3) in which he presents as its alleged rival an ideal of objectivity in criticism which, we have seen, seems ineluctably to lead to an epistemological impressionism of some sort.[36]

Moreover, in this same essay Eliot raises (perhaps unwittingly) the basic problem of the foundationalist program of objectivity through reflection of

[36] For discussion of the epistemological underpinnings of literary impressionism and its links with egoless phenomenalism (e.g. in Mach), see W.M. Johnston, 'Viennese Impressionism: A Reappraisal of a Once Fashionable Category', in E. Nielsen (ed.), *Focus on Vienna 1900* (Munchen: Fink, 1983), 1-11. Eliot's suspicion that uninterpreting mirroring is too closely connected with personal (subjective) impressionism is evident in his use of Rémy de Gourmont's motto, 'ériger en lois ses impressions personelles', which is first cited in the introductory epigraph of 'The Perfect Critic'. But then in the body of the article the 'personal' is altogether omitted, and even the term 'impressions' is removed from focus; and we are merely urged to 'ériger en lois' rather than to use the work of art creatively to express the 'personal' (*SW*, 1, 5-7).

minimally interpreted sense-data. Though the immediately sensually given is undeniable, and in its lack of conceptual interpretation cannot misrepresent or be false; it cannot, by the same token, be true either. It is mere experience, and as such can be neither true nor false. In Eliot's own words: 'So far as you can isolate the impression, the pure feeling, it is, of course, neither true nor false' (*SW*, 5). Russell, who shared the same foundational problematic, had much earlier noted that 'the actual sense-data are neither true nor false', but simply exist as experience and are 'not the sort of thing that is true or false'.[37] And as Russell also suggests (though goes on to ignore), the undeniability of the sensually given is simply a psychological one and constitutes no epistemological guarantee of truth which can serve as an undubitable foundation for knowledge.[38] Furthermore, there is also the basic problem that since the alleged objectivity of the immediately sensually given is non-discursive, non-linguistic, and hence apparently ineffable and incommunicable, it can hardly serve as an adequate basis for empirical knowledge or for poetry, both of which seem to require clear and close communication and cooperative labor.

VIII

Thus the ideal of objectivity as uninterpreting, mirroring correspondence to an immediately given external object paradoxically seems to lead Eliot back into the solipsistic subjectivity of impressions and the isolation of incommunicability. It is therefore not at all surprising to find that Eliot soon abandons his advocacy of objectivity as correspondence and instead readopts the notion of objectivity as agreement within a community of competent practitioners engaged in a cooperative enterprise. This is precisely what we find in Eliot's essay of 1923, 'The Function of Criticism', which clearly is meant to supersede 'The Perfect Critic' as his theory of critical objectivity, since the earlier essay is significantly omitted from Eliot's *Selected Essays*. Since objectivity is only to be found in agreement, the critic is urged to curb his personal eccentricities and conform to accepted practices in order to promote what should be 'a quiet cooperative labour' of a Kuhnian 'normal-science' kind.

> The critic, one would suppose, if he is to justify his existence, should endeavour to discipline his personal prejudices and cranks – tares to which we are all subject – and compose his differences with as many as his fellows as possible, in the common pursuit of true judgment (*SE*, 25).

[37] B. Russell, *The Problems of Philosophy* (1912; repr. Oxford: Oxford University Press, 1959), 65.

[38] B. Russell, 'The Philosophy of Logical Atomism', 32. This important philosophical problem is discussed at great length in M. Williams, *Groundless Belief* (Oxford: Blackwell, 1977).

Objectivity here is so clearly in terms of consensus, community, and conformity that one is tempted to translate Eliot's famous phrase 'the common pursuit of true judgment' into 'the true pursuit of common judgment', or at least to regard 'true judgment' as necessarily founded on (though not always identified with) the 'common judgment' of the professionally competent. For Eliot seems to recognize that only community of consent can constitute objective truth in criticism, much as recent philosophers have argued that a certain community of beliefs and practices is necessary for a given language to have meaning.[39]

Eliot's problem, however, which he was too scrupulous to ignore, is that criticism, rather than being an 'orderly field' of 'quiet cooperative labour' 'from which imposters can be readily ejected, is no better than a Sunday park of contending and contentious orators, who have not even arrived at the articulation of their differences' (*SE*, 25). Here, as in poetry, we face the problem of 'a formless age' which lacks a firm sense of a common and still compelling tradition. And indeed, one of the most important points to be made about Eliot's advocacy of objectivity in 'The Function of Criticism' is its intimate connection with the idea of tradition and tradition's participatory model of consensual objectivity. Thus it is most crucial to note that Eliot begins this essay not only by mentioning, affirming, and even quoting from his early theory of tradition in 'Tradition and the Individual Talent', but by explicitly asserting (what Eliot scholars have largely ignored) that 'the present paper is an application of the [same] principle' transferred from poetry to criticism (*SE*, 23). Eliot continues:

> There is accordingly something outside of the artist to which he owes allegiance, a devotion to which he must surrender and sacrifice himself in order to earn and to obtain his unique position. A common inheritance and a common cause unite artists consciously or unconsciously: it must be admitted that the union is mostly unconscious. Between the true artists of any time there is, I believe, an unconscious community. And, ... our instincts of tidiness imperatively command us not to leave to the haphazard of unconsciousness what we can attempt to do consciously, ... what ... we could bring about, and form into a purpose, if we made a conscious attempt. ... If such views are held about art, it follows that *a fortiori* whoever holds them must hold similar views about criticism. (*SE*, 24)

These remarks should make it clear that tradition is being used as a principle to establish the community or consensus that is the necessary basis, if not the very essence, of objectivity. It should also be clear that this

[39] See, for example, S. Kripke, *Wittgenstein on Rules and Private Language* (Oxford: Blackwell, 1982); and D. Davidson, 'Thought and Talk' and 'On the Very Idea of a Conceptual Scheme' in *Inquiries into Truth and Interpretation* (Oxford: Clarendon, 1984). Here the shadow of an argument seems to emerge: If we have a consensual model of objectivity and meaning, and if we recognize that thought is essentially linguistic and language essentially consensual, then the fear that subjectivity must inevitably lead to solipsism should evaporate; for all human thought, as we know it, rests on the shared and social. The subjective self can

tradition, 'common inheritance', or 'common cause' not only has a uniting, consensus-creating function, but also an external anchoring one. Eliot's quest for objectivity was, we noted, much motivated by the need to escape solipsism and to find something outside the self that could be confirmed as real and could command assent and allegiance. The ideal of depersonalized reflective correspondence to external reality was engendered by this need, but unfortunately issued in the impressionistic subjectivity from which it was supposed to free us. Instead of an independent, non-human reality, Eliot therefore turns back to the community and consensus of tradition as that 'something outside of the artist to which he owes allegiance'.

However, as Eliot recognizes, the *critical* community or tradition is not limited to artists alone – nor should we want it to be, since it would seem that the wider the circle of community and cooperation, the greater the force, validity, or objectivity of its products. Moreover, critics might seem more docile than artists about curbing their vanity and individualism to create conformity in the name of progress. Thus one can explain Eliot's new grudging acceptance of critics who are not also poets as an attempt to establish a wider and thus stronger community of consensus or tradition. And one cannot help but admire the deftness with which he simultaneously both locates the community between artist and critic, and demonstrates their common objectivity by maintaining that they share a 'highly developed sense of fact' that is all too rarely found (*SE*, 31).[40]

Eliot's talk of facts here cannot be construed as a return to the purely mirroring, transcendental realism of 'The Perfect Critic' and the second part of 'Tradition and the Individual Talent'. For they are not foundationalist atomic facts like 'This is white' but rather the ordinary sort of historical 'facts about a work – its conditions, its setting, its genesis' (*SE*, 32) – that the community of scholars would regard as potentially useful or relevant in understanding or appreciating the work. Aware of the solipsistic or else transcendentally mystical *cul de sac* of objectivity as correspondence to the independent, uninterpreted real, Eliot ends 'The Function of Criticism' (and with it his sustained and explicit advocacy of objectivism) by suggesting a very modest consensual model of objectivity, which, though claiming to get at something outside our subjective selves, makes no pretence to guarantee the achieving (or even the understanding or existence) of truth, fact, or external reality.

> For the kinds of critical work which we have admitted, there is the possibility of cooperative activity, with the further possibility of arriving at something outside of ourselves, which may provisionally be called the truth. But if

itself be seen as a social construct. For more on this see my discussion of consensus and language in Chapter Seven, 171-174.

[40] Eliot writes: 'At one time I was inclined to take the extreme position that the *only* critics worth reading were the critics who practised, and practised well, the art of which they wrote. But I had to stretch this frame to make some important inclusions; and I have since been in search of a formula which should cover everything I wished to include, even if it included more

anyone complains that I have not defined truth, or fact, or reality, I can only
say apologetically that it was not part of my purpose to do so, but only to find a
scheme into which, whatever they are, they will fit, if they exist (*SE*, 34).

Thus we see Eliot's desire to put aside the whole question of realist truth
of correspondence, and to let objectivity simply reside in the consensus of a
cooperative community maintaining a common tradition which can serve
as that 'something outside of ourselves'.[41] Without such a something
outside the poet or critic to serve as an anchor against the natural pull of
personality, there can be, Eliot believes, no hope of objectivity of even the
consensual sort, and we shall be condemned to the prison of subjectivity, to
be governed by 'the Inner Voice' which Eliot so fiercely dreads that he
devotes two entire sections of the essay to its vituperation and ridicule (*SE*,
25-29).

It is not hard to see why Eliot protests so much about this meta-critical
notion advocated by Middleton Murry. Of course, the very term 'inner'
evokes associations of the subjective and personal. But I think that much of
the extreme (and sometimes excessive) vehemence of Eliot's criticism of the
inner voice stems from his desire to distinguish it by polemical opposition
from his own cherished notion of tradition. For it does not seem particularly
clear how one is to distinguish (so as to ignore) the inner voice from the
internalized voice of tradition. We must recall that tradition is not a thing
with physical extension, nor is it even externally codified in any definite
formulation; it is rather a vaguely sensed 'main current', 'inheritance', or
'common cause' uniting the many generations of Western culture. As Eliot
himself already remarks in 'The Function of Criticism' (and as he would
later increasingly emphasize), tradition's community or consensus is one of
which we are largely unaware and unconscious, involving attitudes which
we unreflectively take for granted: 'it must be admitted that the union is
mostly unconscious..., an unconscious community' (*SE*, 24). Since our

than I wanted. And the most important qualification which I have been able to find, which
accounts for the peculiar importance of the criticism of practitioners, is that a critic must have
a very highly developed sense of fact. This is by no means a trifling or frequent gift' (*SE*, 31).

[41] Eliot's concern that his emphasis on facts should not be construed as necessarily
requiring a realist-correspondence account of facts is given further testimony by the following
bibliographical curiosity which it helps explain. When reprinting 'The Function of Criticism',
Eliot deleted the following remarks which are found in the original *Criterion* version of the
essay: 'So important [the sense of fact] seems to me, that I am inclined to make one distinction
between Classicism and Romanticism of this, that the romantic is deficient or undeveloped in
his ability to distinguish between fact and fancy, whereas the classicist, or adult mind, is
thoroughly realist – without illusions, without day-dreams, without hope, without bitterness,
and with an abundant resignation' (*Criterion* 2 (1923), 39-40). The realism Eliot demands in
this essay is that which distinguishes commonly established facts from private fancies, *not* the
philosophical realism which construes and seeks to capture facts as totally unmediated
representations or configurations of a completely independent reality. The expression
'thoroughly realist' could well generate confusion here and was understandably deleted, as
was the whole sentence in which it centrally figures. In any case, by the time the essay was
reprinted in 1932, Eliot had become much less interested in the romantic/classic distinction
and the polemics which surrounded it.

grasp of tradition seems mainly an inner, not fully conscious one, how are we to distinguish the objective voice of internalized tradition from the arbitrary inner voice of the individual personality, for both issue or are felt from within?

This problem explains why Eliot feels obliged 'not to leave to the haphazard of unconsciousness' what we can achieve deliberately, and therefore is ready to suggest that we make 'a conscious attempt' to elucidate and formulate ('form into a purpose') the principles of our tradition. But then he suddenly seems confronted by the doubt that perhaps there is no real and substantial consensual community of critical tradition which would allow the formulation of 'a common cause' and shared standards or principles. For, as Eliot sees, criticism resembles less an orderly cooperative community than a chaotic jungle of contention.

Again we have the problem of 'a formless age' (*SW*, 64) where the consensuality of tradition has broken down and there is no solid community of practice or principle upon which to rely for consent. Eliot's sole apparent (and but vaguely suggested) proposal here is that by recalling and classifying the critical works that 'have been useful to us' we may 'establish ... principles ... and [determine] what aims and methods of criticism should be followed' (*SE*, 25). But this hardly seems a viable solution, for how can there be any real hope 'to find any common principles for the pursuit of criticism' (*SE*, 29) amidst the chaos of sharply conflicting critical practices and aims that Eliot cannot help but recognize as dominating contemporary criticism?[42] Nor does there seem to be anything transcendentally objective beyond consensuality to which Eliot can appeal to compel consent and arbitrate decisively between conflicting practices. This, then, is Eliot's frustrating problem of objectivity, and I believe it is also, to a great measure, our own. Let us conclude by briefly collecting and summarizing some of its diverse strands.

IX

The quest for objectivity may be pursued under the ideal of accurate, uninterpreting, mirroring correspondence to an external object or reality independent of human cognition. However, this ideal of objectivity is not only unworkable as a standard for judging objectivity but also seems difficult to attach a clear sense to. Moreover, the attempt to approach this ideal of objectivity by stripping our perception of objects from all conceptual interpretation added by the human mind to the sensually

---

[42] As Eliot seems to realize, it is not enough simply to have agreement on certain paradigms of critical excellence: 'certain books, certain essays, certain sentences, certain men, who have been useful to us'. In order to secure a truly effective critical consensus there must also be agreement on how these paradigms are to be interpreted and applied, so that 'our next step' must be to attempt to derive from them 'principles ... and aims and methods' that can command general assent (*SE*, 25).

given only issues in unsatisfying, impressionistic subjectivity, ineffability, and isolation.

An apparently superior alternative is the notion of objectivity as consensus or agreement of participants in a practice or, for Eliot, a tradition. The problem here, however, is how this consensus of tradition is to be recognized and preserved. One possible means is to formulate and codify the practice in explicit principles or canons. But this runs the risk of stunting and ossifying a living and developing tradition into dogmatic conservatism and sterile conventionalism. In the creative field of literature this is particularly pernicious. If, however, tradition is left unformulated but simply felt from within, internalized from our commerce with the great literature and criticism of the past, how can we distinguish the allegedly objective verdicts issuing from our sense of tradition from the dreaded subjective verdicts issuing from the abominated 'inner voice'? For the immediate source of both verdicts is within the individual, and hence both are potentially subjective.

We therefore seem obliged to try, as does Eliot, to externalize or objectify the common tradition, however partially and imperfectly, in order to ensure the consensual objectivity of current practice by formulating it into 'common principles for the pursuit of criticism', even at the risk of dogmatism and conventionalism. But here we see that in the chaotic hotch-potch of conflicting critical aims and practices we can uncover no significant set of principles that command common assent. We then face perhaps the hardest problem of all. How can we trust in a common tradition to guarantee or reinforce the (consensual) objectivity of practice, when such a tradition seems to have broken down and there simply is no substantial community of practice or principles that command general consent. There is no clear and solid consensus to appeal to as a basis for objectivity. But to seek a foundational objectivity beyond human consensus and in terms of an independent external reality has been seen to be an unviable option.

Eliot apparently could find no philosophically adequate solution to this complex problem of objectivity, and came increasingly to affirm and emphasize the subjective and personal in his critical theorizing. This move is arguably overhasty, for perhaps deeper or more careful scrutiny of tradition's paradigms and the variety of established poetic and critical practices will emerge with a substantial body of commonly accepted critical canons. Yet such a prospect, we must confess, hardly seems likely. Perhaps, however, we can at least get a substantial consensus on principles within a particular poetic or critical 'language-game' or project-type, while debate continues to rage as to which game (and consequent set of principles) is the right one to practice.[43]

However, one could also say that Eliot does indeed suggest some sort of

---

[43] In a series of articles I have shown that established critical practices display not only a plurality of aims and methods, but a fundamental plurality of variant logics. See the works cited in n. 10.

solution for achieving consensual objectivity, though not a standardly theoretical one. Seeing that no 'philosophical' solution seemed available, Eliot tried instead, with significant success, a *practical* solution to the loss of a strongly felt consensus: by compelling and creating such consensus through the power and authority of his own critical judgment and poetic practice, reinforced by his institutional power as the editor of *The Criterion* and his authoritative status as regent-protector of Western culture and spokesman for Christianity. Here theory does not simply emerge from some established traditional practice but beseechingly looks to present and future practice for its own resolution, which theory itself was too impotent to achieve. Eliot reveals here the essential pragmatism of his philosophy of criticism, his perception of the primacy of practice over theory. He seems to recognize that not only is the justification, criticism, and improvement of practice the major aim of theory, but that for all theory's ability to mold and alter practice, it itself is not only generated, shaped, and changed but also validated or confounded by practice.

It is perhaps not so surprising that the consensual model of objectivity should be found quite convincing and appealing in periods of perceived conflict and lack of consensus. For disagreement is apt to disturb us from a naive realist sense of transparent correspondence which full consensus could well induce and foster. Acceptance of the consensual model in a period of perceived division can lead in two rather different directions.

The first is the attempt to create greater or maximal consensus in the name of objectivity. If there is ultimately no more to objectivity than consensuality, and if there is not sufficient consensuality to be found, the ideal of objectivity demands that it be created. And its creation would seem to demand that we be far less disinterested, pluralistic, and tolerant than we might like to be and have been trained to be in the liberal tradition. We instead seem to be urged to endorse prescriptively a particular shared practice (or consistent set of practices, judgments, and principles) and to reject and denounce conflicting practices in order to achieve and preserve strong consensuality. The quest for objectivity in a formless age thus might seem, in a sense, to demand that we be *less* objective or at least more strongly partisan, pragmatically directing our suasive efforts to compel critical conformity. And since criticism is deeply embedded and influenced by more general cultural attitudes, conformity is to be established and upheld in the social sphere as well.

This is the direction which Eliot pursued for a while, occasionally with appallingly ferocious severity. It led in the early 1930s to the bigoted extremism of *After Strange Gods* (a book Eliot himself later described as that of 'a very sick man',[44]) in which the aesthetic aims of originality and expression of personality were violently denounced and a number of great writers were harshly condemned as 'heretical' and dangerous because they

[44] Quoted in H. Gardner, *The Composition of 'Four Quartets'* (London: Faber, 1978), 55.

express 'their own personal view of life'. The same passion for unifying conformity similarly inspires his attack on that 'spirit of excessive tolerance' which fails to recognize that the aim of cultural homogeneity makes the presence of 'any large number of free-thinking Jews undesirable' (*ASG*, 24-25, 34, 57, 20). Such one-sided uncompromising passion for comformity is but a short step away from racist fascism; and Eliot's apparent subsequent perception of this and of the horrors of Nazism best explain his prohibiting the book from being republished. In any case, with the growing awareness of the evils of Nazism, Eliot's concept of cultural consensus and unity moves increasingly toward acceptance of diversity as productive of a valuable and satisfying cultural richness.

This leads to the other path which follows from taking consensus as the only basis and model of objectivity that is feasible for us. If objectivity is no longer an absolute God's-eye view of things, then much of its traditional appeal and claim to exclusive rightness, which depends on its putative absolute status, would seem to disappear. For if the value of objectivity could no longer be explained in terms of its communion with absolute truth and the divine point of view, it would have to derive from its service to man, its pragmatic value in understanding and coping with our experience, including our social experience with other individuals. But if the value of the consensually objective is pragmatically explained in terms of the satisfaction of human needs, is there not room then for a similar justification of the subjective or personal? For their expression also answers to important and acceptable human needs. Is maximal consensus in every aspect of life, total conformity and uniformity, the highest ideal of human existence? Is there not a superior ideal of unity, applied not only to human life and society but most frequently to works of art, an ideal of unity embracing rich diversity?

This is the direction and ideal that Eliot ultimately pursued in his later writings on culture and tradition (discussed in Chapter Seven), and it is also evident in his growing acceptance of the subjective factor in criticism which we demonstrated at the beginning of this chapter. Eliot recognized that diversity and disagreement are not necessarily evils that must be overcome. They can provide a more satisfying variety and richness of experience, and can moreover serve as a productive tension to stimulate thought and progress, provided they have enough common background to make themselves mutually intelligible. Hence even if a given critical judgment is subjective and divergent, this does not necessarily mean it is worthlessly wrong and unjustified.

It is interesting to note that some important analytic philosophers are today following Eliot's movement away from a uniform scientistic objectivism to a pluralism which tries to embrace the values of objectivity and consensus with those of subjectivity and divergence. As Eliot maintained that the cultural ideal is 'variety in unity' where 'the variety is as essential as the unity' (*NDC*, 120, *OPP*, 23), so Hilary Putnam has recently advocated a 'pluralistic ideal' of 'human flourishing' according to which even in an ideal world we would want differences of view, for 'diversity is part of the ideal'.[45]

It is, however, only part of the ideal, and apparently the easier part. Certainly in the field of aesthetics, both critics and philosophers have worried more about maintaining adequate unity and convergence of outlook in the face of a manifest diversity of judgments. Moreover, doubts may be raised about how practicable, innocently open, and tolerantly free such pluralistic ideals really are. Terry Eagleton[46] is not alone in criticizing pluralism as impracticably incoherent, since it tolerates procedures that are 'mutually incompatible' and therefore cannot produce potently convergent and uncontested results. Pluralistically divided, criticism becomes ineffectual, unable to work man's redemption whether this be through its revelation of beauty or authorial truth, or through its advocacy of 'the socialist transformation of society'.

This charge, however, begs the question by presuming that systematic compatibility and unity of mission or direction are just what we want from criticism, rather than wanting the expression of differences, not only about methods but about final aims. Secondly, much of the putative incompatibility is more apparent than real. Certainly one cannot coherently interpret a poem by simultaneously employing intentionalist and deconstructive methods, any more than one can simultaneously eat and sleep. But this does not mean that such conflicting practices cannot be kept together in a wider whole, a life or literary tradition, which embraces and connects such differences even through the bond of conflict. This possibility of unity in conflict will be explored and related to narrative unity in Chapters Four and Seven.

Moreover, it often seems that beneath the surface of pluralism's differences there lurks a solid core or range of consensus, which would insure some unity. This, however, does not render the pluralistic ideal immune from criticism. For precisely this consensus is seized upon by pluralism's critics as evidence that its gesture of liberal, humanist tolerance is only feigned. True, humanist pluralism is open to a number of diverging practices and attitudes, and allows the critic to choose freely among them. But clearly it will not tolerate any practice whatever, and will tend to reject as worthless or illegitimate those methods which do not fall within its particular pluralistic alliance. Pluralism's guise of tolerance and freedom masks its repressive intolerance of what lies outside its institutionally authorized practices and forms of discourse. Further, this deception only

---

[45] See H. Putnam, *Reason, Truth and History* (Cambridge: Cambridge University Press, 1981), 148. See also B. Williams, *Ethics and the Limit of Philosophy* (London: Fontana, 1985), 133-134, 170-173; and Nagel, 213.

[46] See T. Eagleton, *Literary Theory: An Introduction* (Oxford: Blackwell, 1983), 198-211. Readers interested in exploring further the contemporary debate on pluralism should consult the recent issue on 'Pluralism and its Discontents', *Critical Inquiry*, 12 (1986).

strengthens the grip that these repressive discursive structures and institutions have on us, and these critical institutions are closely tied up with and in service of academic and political institutions which are more obviously oppressive. Affirmation of humanistic pluralism in the appreciation of art is tantamount to complicity in a constraining status-quo conservatism which will tolerate a variety of already institutionally accepted views so long as this serves to diffuse rather than incite the threat of any really radical change or divergence.

Any convincing response to this serious challenge must begin by conceding that even a tolerant pluralism involves the policing of discourse to repress or banish threateningly deviant modes as absurd or nonsensical. But this Foucauldian point must be balanced with his related insight that any knowledge-producing discourse requires some such repression; and one could go on to urge that pluralism's constraints are less narrow and severe than any of the monistic doctrines it embraces. The question whether the pluralistic appropriation of our artistic tradition is necessarily wedded to socio-political conservatism and cannot equally serve the cause of liberation will be considered at the end of Chapter Six.

One traditional way to establish the substantial unity of the apparently plural and diverse is by the strategy of essentialism: the idea that underlying the diversity of things that we think somehow belong together, there exists an identical unchanging common core, an essence which is shared by and peculiar to the diverse things in question and which holds them together and individuates them as a kind from other kinds of things. One way of seeking some unity in literary and critical theory would be to establish some permanent essence of literature or of criticism. But history, unfolding the diversity and change of literary and critical forms, threatens to subvert the essentialist strategy for unity. Eliot's treatment of this strategy and threat forms the substance of the next chapter.

Chapter 4

History and Essence,
Pluralism and Critical Reasoning

... History may be servitude,
History may be freedom.

'Little Gidding'

Time the destroyer is time the preserver.

'The Dry Salvages'

I

Eliot's was a mind passionately longing for unity but penetratingly perceptive to plurality and difference. His critical theory, no less than his poetry, is greatly motivated by this productive but often very taxing tension. In this chapter we shall first study it as a tension between historicist pluralism and essentialism as to the nature of poetry. But Eliot struggled with much the same problem in criticism, and we must assess his attempts to balance the recognition of criticism's very different and changing forms against the equally recognized need for some sort of unity or structuring order and focus in this field.

In his drift to historicist pluralism, Eliot this time anticipated rather than followed analytic philosophy. Some of the important themes shaping his pluralistic views on poetry and criticism will here be shown to have similarly motivated Wittgenstein's later aesthetic theory and engendered his influential account of aesthetic reasons. This account has been widely endorsed by analytic aestheticians and developed by them into a general theory of critical reasoning, which deserves our scrutiny and assessment. Eliot's more radical and consistent historicism will be seen to provide needed therapy for some of that theory's distortive one-sidedness.

II

The fundamental tension in Eliot's theory between the firm recognition or advocacy of a pluralistic approach to poetry, and, on the other hand, the drive to maintain unity by persistent sliding towards assumptions and assertions of a kind of essentialistic or monistic view of poetry is best exemplified in *The Use of Poetry and The Use of Criticism*. This book, based on Eliot's Norton lectures at Harvard in 1932-33, provides his most extensive and definitive treatise on poetry and its criticism. Eliot himself, on republishing it in 1964, expressed the wish that *it* (rather than his earlier theoretical essays) be taken as representative of his work, and he re-endorsed it as the 'statement of [his] critical position' (*TUP*, 9-10).

There is no doubt that the book's main thrust is towards critical pluralism.[1] Indeed it might have been more accurately (though perhaps less attractively) entitled 'The Uses of Poetry and the Uses of Criticism'. For Eliot repeatedly asserts that poetry and criticism have, over the years, been fruitfully employed in a wide variety of uses which do not seem reducible to a single underlying use.

Early in the book Eliot advances his contention that there have been (and will be) changes in the form and function of poetry as a result of social changes, since literature cannot be isolated 'from the circumstances of life'. 'Such changes as that from the epic poem composed to be recited to the epic poem composed to be read, or those which put an end to the popular ballad, are inseparable from social changes on a vast scale, such changes as have always taken place and always will' (*TUP*, 21). More generally, as 'the development of poetry is itself a symptom of social change', we should therefore also expect 'changes in the function of poetry, as society alters' (*TUP*, 22, 23).

And with these changes in poetry and its function inevitably come changes in the nature and function of criticism. 'Each age demands different things from its poetry. ... So our criticism, from age to age, will reflect the things that the age demands; and the criticism of no one man and of no one age can be expected to embrace the whole nature of poetry or exhaust all of its uses' (*TUP*, 141). But not only does Eliot assert and argue abstractly for the irreducible variety of different kinds of poetry and criticism, his actual examination of the different periods of English poetry and criticism clearly demonstrates just 'how various are the kinds of poetry, and how variously poetry may appeal to different minds and generations equally qualified to appreciate it' (*TUP*, 149).

From the great variety of kinds of poetry and criticism, Eliot draws an important conclusion for poetic theory and meta-criticism: the impossibility of accurate and yet significant (i.e. non-empty) generalizations about poetry as a whole or about the essence of poetry which would be common and special to all poetry.

> A perfectly satisfactory theory which applied to all poetry would do so only at
> the cost of being voided of all content; the more usual reason for the

---

[1] Wellek and Warren attest to the work's dominant pluralism, though they argue against it. See R. Wellek and A. Warren, *Theory of Literature* (Harmondsworth, U.K.: Penguin, 1970), 31.

unsatisfactoriness of our theories and general statements about poetry is that while professing to apply to all poetry, they are really theories about, or generalisations from, a limited range of poetry. (*TUP*, 141)

Yet despite these clear and uncompromising assertions of fundamental plurality, and indeed alongside them, we find occasional declarations of essentialism, that there is something special that is common to and permanent in all poetry. For example, early in the book, having just completed his initial argument for pluralism, Eliot tries to justify his incipient survey of English literary criticism on the grounds that 'the study of criticism ... may also help us draw some conclusions as to what is permanent or eternal in poetry, ... [for] by discovering what does change, and how, and why, we may become able to apprehend what does not change' (*TUP*, 27).

Eliot goes on to assert that despite the great variance in the creative processes of different poets (and even of the same poet in different poems), 'there must also be something in common in the poetic process of all poets' minds' (*TUP*, 83). Still later in the book, after challenging the idea 'that there is just some one essence of poetry ... and that poets can be ranged according to their possession of a greater or less quantity of this essence' (*TUP*, 98); and after his case for the fundamental plurality of poetry has been virtually and, I think, successfully concluded, Eliot again seems to retreat to a view of underlying monism or essentialism. For he claims that behind all the types and uses of poetry there is some permanent, uniting common element or essence.

> Amongst all these demands from poetry and responses to it there is always some permanent element in common, just as there are standards of good and bad writing independent of what any one of us happens to like and dislike; but every effort to formulate the common element is limited by the limitations of particular men in particular places and at particular times; and these limitations become manifest in the perspective of history. (*TUP*, 141-2).

In asserting the presence of this common element in all poetry, Eliot clearly departs from the view he asserted earlier on the very same page – that any accurate theory of all poetry would be 'void of all content'. For this common element would guarantee some significant content. Eliot seems strangely unaware of this apparent contradiction, perhaps because he continues to maintain the impossibility of a satisfactory theory of all poetry. But in the passage just quoted it is merely an epistemological impossibility owing to man's finite nature and limited scope; while in the earlier quotation it was a logical impossibility owing to a lack of common content for which a general theory could account.

It is worth noting that Eliot's pluralist/essentialist vacillation is never decisively resolved in *The Use of Poetry and the Use of Criticism*. Unable to commit himself wholly and uncompromisingly to either position in this

tension, Eliot concludes the book by assigning the resolution of this conflict
to aestheticians, arguing that it is beyond his role as a critic and poet: 'The
extreme of theorising about the nature of poetry, the essence of poetry if
there is any, belongs to the study of aesthetics and is no concern of the poet
or of a critic with my limited qualifications' (*TUP*, 149-150).[2]

III

The presence of a pluralist/essentialist tension in Eliot's poetics has been
made sufficiently clear. But can it be adequately justified? Why, when the
major thrust of his theory is strongly pluralistic, does Eliot still try to hold
on to some remnant of essentialism, 'some permanent element in common'?
Let us consider and assess some of Eliot's possible reasons.

Eliot's first motive may simply be a basic psychological predisposition
towards monism rather than pluralism. Such a basic bias, easily linkable to
Eliot's deep concern for unity, could account for his grasping for some
vestige of essentialism in his overridingly pluralistic position. But such a
subjective motive of psychological predisposition is more on the level of
causal explanation than logical justification.

There are, however, additional reasons which Eliot (and others) may
think logically justify adherence to some type of essentialist or monistic
view of poetry. First, it may be thought that without some essential
function of its own, a special use common to all poetry, no real value or
worth could be attributed to poetry itself. This argument is put forward by
Wellek and Warren, who explicitly discount the fact that poetry serves a
wide variety of functions and instead posit an essential literary function,
simply on the grounds that 'to take art or literature or poetry seriously is,
ordinarily at least, to attribute to it some use proper to itself'.[3] But such
reasoning is hardly persuasive, since the value or 'seriousness' of poetry
might well derive from the many different functions that different works of
poetry perform at different times. Having no special use proper to itself
does not imply being useless or valueless. The positing of an essential use or
function to ensure the value of poetry is thus unnecessary and unjustified.

Another reason for Eliot to profess some sort of essentialism may have
been a belief that without any underlying essence of poetry there could be
no basis for the existence of objective standards of evaluation and
consequent objective evaluative judgments. Indeed, we may recall that one
of Eliot's declarations of essentialism was immediately connected with the
assertion of objective 'standards of good and bad writing independent of ...
like and dislike'. It is a characteristic move for aestheticians to derive
standards of aesthetic evaluation from the alleged nature or essence of the

---

[2] It is worth noting that Eliot subsequently expressed his anti-essentialism more
emphatically and less equivocally, decrying what he called 'the Essence of Poetry fantasy'. See
Eliot's review of Housman's *The Name and Nature of Poetry*, *Criterion*, 13 (Oct. 1933), 153.

[3] Wellek and Warren, 31.

art evaluated or indeed from the alleged essence of art in general. Expression, representation, and form, for example, have functioned both as definitions of art and as standards for evaluating art. This close connection between defining essence and evaluative standards reflects, I think, the basic classificatory/ evaluative ambiguity of 'art' and its sub-concepts like 'poetry'.

However, though evaluative standards may often be derived from or based on an alleged essence, it does not follow that without such an essence of poetry there can be no objective standards. Moreover, there can be a plurality of objective standards reflecting and serving the plurality of kinds and uses of poetry. The standards of epic poetry are surely different from those of lyric poetry, but that does not mean that only one of these sets of standards can be objective. Nor does it mean that judgments of epic poetry based on 'epic standards' cannot be absolutely (and not merely relatively) true. Logic at least allows the possibility of a plurality of absolute standards: different genres may have different absolute standards, where such standards, though absolute within the given genre, may be invalid or irrelevant outside the genre. Objectivity and absoluteness of standards in poetry does not require total uniformity and universality of standards.

Moreover, it must be further maintained that objective evaluation does not require absolute standards. As E.D. Hirsch has noted, 'objectivity and accuracy' of literary evaluation may 'reside entirely in the judged relationship between literature and the criteria we choose to apply to it'.[4] Thus, not only are absolute judgments of works of poetry compatible with a plurality of standards but also objective judgments of such works are compatible with relativity of standards. There is, then, no need to assume or posit a common essence from which to derive absolute standards uniformly applicable to all poetry in order to maintain the possibility of objective evaluations of poetry. This third possible reason for Eliot's adherence to some sort of essentialism in the face of obvious pluralism has therefore been shown to be inadequate and unjustified.

Perhaps there is still one more consideration which may have convinced Eliot of the need to maintain that in all poetry 'there is always some permanent element in common', some permanent or eternal essence. Eliot maintains that one of the two major aims of criticism is 'to find out what poetry is, what its use is' (*TUP*, 16); and he may well think that with no common element or essence of poetry the question 'what is poetry?' cannot be meaningfully asked, let alone answered. Eliot, writing here in the early 1930s, may have made the traditional philosophical assumption: *unum nomen, unum nominatum*, i.e. that for every meaningful substantive there must be something specific named. With a general term like 'poetry' this specific something could only be a particular essence or element common to

---

[4] E.D. Hirsch, 'Privileged Criteria in Literary Evaluation' in *The Aims of Interpretation* (Chicago: Univ. of Chicago Press, 1976), 123.

all poetry. This essence, by the traditional assumption, was held necessary for explaining and maintaining any shared meaning of 'poetry' and for justifying the application of the term 'poetry' to different poems and types of poetry. Eliot may have asserted that there is 'some permanent element in common' in all poetry in order to ensure that 'poetry' could have a shared meaning, and thus that the question 'what is poetry?' could be meaningfully asked, even if not perfectly answered.

However, it is surely clear now, after Wittgenstein, Ryle and several decades of philosophical argument too familiar to warrant repitition here, that the assumption *unum nomen, unum nominatum* is false. General terms (e.g. 'games', 'food', 'fish', or 'poetry') do not need to denote a common essential property (or set of properties) in order to be meaningful, though we may wish to reserve the logical possibility that general terms could (and some perhaps do) designate things sharing a common essence.[5]

Once this questionable assumption is rejected, the question 'what is poetry?' need not be seen as a demand for a shared poetic essence, but can be intelligibly asked and answered as a question about the many varieties of poetry, its many different uses and the different ways in which it is created and appreciated. In short, Eliot's crucial question 'what is poetry?' may be interpreted pluralistically and historically rather than essentialistically. Here again, his retreat to token essentialism is unnecessary. Indeed, as already noted, *The Use of Poetry and the Use of Criticism* is in fact such a pluralistic, historical answer to this question, a very substantive and well documented answer. Poetry's historicity, its history of diversity and change which remains unchangingly open to future change, is what ultimately vitiates the idea of any permanent, distinctive essence of all poetry.

None the less, one might still challenge the view that mere presentation of poetry's plurality and history could constitute a satisfactory explanation of what poetry is. May we not rightly demand of such an explanation more than a list of types, styles, and dates, but the discovery or organization of some satisfying order and unity in its explanatory field? Here the issue of unity re-emerges and stubbornly refuses to be dismissed as an irrelevant psychological bias. And yet how can we achieve any significant unity in the diverse poetic field without some unifying essentialist hypothesis?

An historicist pluralist like Eliot is not without an answer. Though

---

[5] My rejection of the *unum nomen, unum nominatum* assumption is what Diffey identifies as the weaker version of the anti-essentialist thesis. It is worth noting that aestheticians like Diffey and Wollheim who have resisted anti-essentialist extremist views denying any substantive unity or content to the general concept of art nevertheless deny art a permanent constitutive essence because of art's fundamental historicity – its having been contingently formed and greatly modified by the past and its being still open to further shaping in the future. As Diffey puts it, 'art has no real essence because art has a history'. This, I submit, is precisely what Eliot's historical study shows with respect to poetry. See T.J. Diffey, 'Essentialism and the Definition of "Art" ', *British Journal of Aesthetics*, 13 (1973), 116, and R. Wollheim, *Art and its Objects* (New York: Harper and Row, 1968), 160-167.

typically understood as achieved through the constant presence of some common crucial element in the various things so unified, unity is not narrowly confined to such a static model. An alternative model of unity can be found in the literary theorist's own backyard – in the unity of narrative. A satisfyingly unified story can be told without requiring that any one (i.e. essential) character or place be constantly present or essentially unchanged; and satisfying narratives seem not only to tolerate but to thrive on the variety and conflicts of their characters' aims and motives. What we need for narrative unity is a coherently told tale starting from some pragmatically chosen beginning and developing through intelligible transitions and intermediary situations to a pragmatically designated concluding situation which (like the intermediary ones) can best be understood in terms of its development from earlier stages and its formation through forces or events which have similarly emerged from some past and currently impinge on the given situation. Such a complexly coherent narrative is what Eliot offers in his genealogical account of the growth and varieties of poetic theory from Elizabethan to modern times, in which the growth and variety both emerge from and are united around a longstanding, continuing debate about the nature of poetry. Eliot's own effort both relates and further extends this story of controversy as to the nature and function of poetry.

What we have been calling the narrative unity of poetics and what we have described as the narrative, genealogical mode of explaining poetry were very obvious and crucial to Eliot, though he never so labelled them. Instead of talk of narrative, he speaks of tradition – the need for some unity of tradition and the fact that tradition provides the necessary explanatory structure for understanding the meaning and importance of any literary achievement. ('No poet ... has his complete meaning alone' but needs to be placed in the context of the tradition for his proper appreciation, 'the appreciation of his relation to the dead poets and artists', *SE*, 15.) It is worth noting that MacIntyre, who has recently advanced the idea of explanation as narrative, explicitly insists on the intimate connection of narrative and tradition, and even defines tradition as the narrative of an argument over the tradition's most important features and goods and over its proper maintenance in the present and future.[6] Eliot's notable views on tradition are sadly neglected by MacIntyre whose own currently influential account of this concept is remarkably Eliotic.

In understanding the idea of unity of narrative or tradition, and the idea of tradition or narrative as explanation, two points must be emphasized. First, an historical narrative or tradition is not a mere list of facts or neutrally reflective chronology. It is a structure which incorporates and structures facts, giving them their meaning and importance. Without the

[6] See A. MacIntyre, 'Epistemological Crises, Dramatic Narrative and the Philosophy of Science', *Monist*, 60 (1977), 453-472; and *After Virtue: A Study in Moral Theory* (London: Duckworth, 1981), 190-209.

prior Hebraic narrative structure of the messianic coming, the alleged facts about the birth and life of Jesus would not have had their significance. Without the subsequent narrative structure of the birth and growth of a mighty nation proclaiming democracy, liberal tolerance, and welcoming freedom to refugees of foreign oppression, the landing of some Pilgrims (the term itself presupposing a narrative) on Plymouth Rock would be an irrelevancy. Similarly, without the narrative of literary history, we cannot speak of such facts as the birth of literary genres (like the novel) and the decline of others (like the long poem or ballad). It follows, moreover, that when we belong to a tradition, our present situation is structured in large part by the shape of tradition's past narrative from which it emerges. Whatever order and unity in diversity we find in the present is constituted by categories or customs of classification evolving from past tradition. Hence, as Eliot insists, we cannot properly understand our present without understanding our past, and in losing hold of our past we lose our hold on our present and future. The unity of tradition, the coherence and continuity of the past developing into the present, is therefore a crucial achievement which must be maintained no matter how arduous the task of holding things together may be. Eliot regarded this the supreme and undeniable duty of the critic and man of letters, but we must postpone the detailed discussion of these matters.

For now the second point must be broached. Not only are the meaningful facts entering a narrative structure of tradition not given or selected independently of that structure, but the structure itself is not an independently and indisputably given, nor is it immutable. The structure of a tradition is not constituted by necessary, universal, and eternally valid principles but is itself something that has been contingently and continuously structured and refashioned over time. It is a product of historical circumstances, choices, and achievements (including previous structures on which it builds), and is in large part a product of conflict and experiment over how best to understand, maintain, and apply it in the face of present needs and experience.

From this it follows that we cannot simply rely on tradition to be there, well-preserved and unequivocally defined, when we need it. Tradition is only alive when embodied in a practice or perception of it as a continuing story. But since the proper understanding of a tradition is essentially contested, rival understandings will differently shape its narrative, and since we have no omniscient or omnipotent view to rule out deviant versions, the unity of tradition and hence its preservation is always threatened. As MacIntyre notes, 'every tradition therefore is always in danger of lapsing into incoherence and when a tradition does so lapse it sometimes can only be recovered by a revolutionary reconstitution'.[7] Deeply troubled by the sense of living in a formless age where tradition's

---

[7] 'Epistemological Crises ...', 461.

vitality and coherence were severely debilitated, Eliot attempted precisely such a revolutionary reconstitution of the tradition of English poetry. Reconstituting the tradition and restoring its unity meant significantly reshaping it; not only by reforming its canon (elevating the Elizabethans, Jacobeans, and metaphysicals and devaluing Milton, the Romantics, and the Victorians) but by creating a new narrative of the history of English poetry which coherently explains the development of the 'bad' as well as the good, which brings us up to the present situation of poetry and projectively points to the poetic direction which should afford greater and more productive unity with what is most important and valuable in the poetry of the past.

This, of course, is what Eliot provides in his famous doctrine of 'the dissociation of sensibility', which Eliot calls a theory but which is more obviously an explanatory narrative of English literature. It tells the story of poetry before and after the alleged radical dissociation of thought and feeling which took hold after the seventeenth-century metaphysical poets, thereby plaguing more than two centuries of verse and requiring in the twentieth century a radical return to something very much like the metaphysical sensibility which had been in the direct line of literary tradition until the seventeenth-century crisis set in.[8] Thus, as Eliot seems close to realizing, although the unity of poetry may indeed be threatened or lost through history, it is also to be understood and re-established in terms of history by means of a complexly coherent narrative. The unity of such a narrative is not one of essentialist uniformity since the narrative itself embodies conflict and division. Essentialism is thus unnecessary (and unable) to hold poetry, or any tradition of achievement, together.

IV

What has been said about pluralism, historicism, and unity can be carried over from poetry to criticism. Since literary criticism is concerned with works of literature, changes in literature (frequently generated by social change) will similarly issue in changes of criticism. As 'each age demands different things from its poetry ... so our criticism from age to age will reflect the things that the age demands' (*TUP*, 141). But Eliot's critical pluralism was not confined to historical pluralism, for he stresses that even the particular situation in which he finds himself theorizing is characterized by fundamental and irreducible plurality: 'Criticism seems to have separated into several diverse kinds' (*TUP*, 27).

Eliot's troubled awareness of the plurality of critical modes is displayed in his repeated attempts to classify varieties or types of criticism. Such classification, which involved recognizing the legitimacy of more than one type, had begun by 1918 and was still going on in Eliot's final essay on

---

[8] See 'The Metaphysical Poets', *SE*, 281-291.

criticism in 1961.[9] The varieties of critics he identified include the reviewer, the biographer, the literary historian, the academic scholar, the theoretical or philosophical critic, the moral critic, the advocatory (versus judgmental) 'Critic with Gusto', and the poet-critic who criticizes literature in order better to create it and who is consequently much concerned with technique.[10]

Critical plurality presents at least two problems for Eliot. First, simply on the practical level, since it seems impossible for us properly to practice and synthesize all the varieties (for they tend to pull in different directions), we have the problem of choosing which to practice. Yet, on the other hand, the alleged different types are not all that clearly demarcated from each other, and often seem to interact and merge in the work of a critic. ('Coleridge ... wrote both philosophical and poetic criticism'.)[11] Thus, though apparently compelled to choose, we are hardly offered any well-defined or clearly distinct choices.

Eliot's personal resolution of the problem was to insist on his status as poet-critic. Part of his motive (for identifying the category as well as for placing himself in it) was surely to give greater authority to his own critical pronouncements, since he well knew that traditionally the most authoritative critics were famous poets. Yet Eliot's self-representation as poet-critic was also needed to control (though not to repress) his irresistable attraction toward philosophical and moral criticism, and yet simultaneously to bestow on his efforts at the latter an authority borrowed from his poet-critic status. But whatever the personal success of Eliot's strategy, it will not work for the rest of us non-poets.

However, perhaps choice of critical mode is the least distressing problem of critical plurality, since our particular background, knowledge, and interests together with the salient features of the work and the critical situation in question might conspire in most cases to determine the choice for us. More serious may be plurality's threat to the status of literary criticism as a proper coherent field of its own, whose unity (of approach, aims, or objects) marks it off from neighboring fields as an autonomous (though not self-sufficiently independent) discipline. In admitting critical pluralism, the unity and hence integrity of criticism is at stake. For once you admit the legitimacy of philosophical, historical, and moral literary criticism, it appears problematic to distinguish such literary criticism from philosophy, history, and ethics. How, for example, do we clearly distinguish philosophical literary criticism or literary theory from philosophy proper using literary material or styles, remembering as we should that numerous

[9] See, for example, T.S. Eliot, 'Studies in Contemporary Criticism', *Egoist*, 5 (1918), 113-114, 131-133; 'A Brief Treatise on the Criticism of Poetry', *Chapbook*, 2 (1920), 1-9; and 'To Criticize the Critic', in *TC*, 11-26.

[10] In *The Use of Poetry and the Use of Criticism* Eliot further notes psychological and sociological literary criticism, claiming them to be 'probably the most advertised' of critical modes at that time (*TUP*, 27).

[11] 'A Brief Treatise ...', 3.

philosophical works (e.g. of Plato, Montaigne, Nietzsche, etc.) have long been considered *literary* works as well? This problem of the integrity of criticism is not to be dismissed as idle and hypothetical, since the currently potent and prolific deconstructionist school is committed in both theory and practice to challenging precisely the distinction between literary criticism and philosophy.[12]

Realizing that 'it is impossible to fence off *literary* criticism from criticism on other grounds' (*TC*, 25) and yet committed to maintaining its integrity so that not any discussion of a text by another text would constitute literary criticism, how could Eliot represent literary criticism as a coherent and distinctive field? What principle could unify the motley variety of literary critical texts and distinguish them from others? The common-sense solution that literary criticism can be defined by its object, i.e. by being distinctively focused on literature, seems inadequate. This is not so much because other fields often focus on literary works while literary criticism can also be directed at non-literary texts, but because the whole strategy circularly begs the question. It presupposes that we already know exactly what literature is, what makes a textual object a literary work. But the answer to the question 'what is literature?' is, as Eliot noted, a fundamental question of literary criticism itself, to which it has no adequate answer (*TUP*, 16). Literature cannot be used to explain criticism, since criticism itself needs to explain literature (though conversely requiring literature, at least as a posited object, in order to account for itself).

Without a distinctive essential group of objects or underlying essential property of 'literariness' to constitute the unity of literary criticism, one is tempted to seek unity by finding some generally shared and distinctive critical standards, methods, or aims. But here, as Eliot recognized, there was no substantial common ground to be found. Far from being a unified 'simple and orderly field ... from which imposters can be readily ejected' criticism 'is no better than a Sunday park of contending and contentious orators' who cannot even unite in 'the articulation of their differences' (*SE*, 25). Criticism today is no less contentiously contested and disorderly, displaying not only a variety of rival methods and aims but different logics.[13]

[12] See, for example, C. Norris, *Deconstruction: Theory and Practice* (London: Methuen, 1982) especially x-xiii, 18-41, 90-108. For some criticism of deconstructionist logic with respect to distinctions, see my 'Analytic Aesthetics, Literary Theory, and Deconstruction', *Monist*, 69, 22-38; and 'Deconstruction and Analysis: Confrontation and Convergence', *British Journal of Aesthetics*, 26 (1986), 311-327.

[13] For a detailed classificatory analysis of these different logics, see my *The Object of Literary Criticism* (Amsterdam: Rodopi, 1984) chapters five and six; and 'The Logic of Interpretation', *Philosophical Quarterly*, 28 (1978), 310-324; 'The Logic of Evaluation', *Philosophical Quarterly*, 30 (1980), 327-341; and 'Evaluative Reasoning in Criticism', *Ratio*, 23 (1981), 141-157. For reasons that will soon emerge, it is, however, premature to argue (as does Terry Eagleton) that from literary criticism's lack of a unifying object or essence or unitary methodology it follows that literature, literary criticism, and literary theory do not

As with poetry, Eliot located the source of criticism's plurality in history. His genealogy of critical pluralism, expressed in a number of places, is given concise and cogent formulation in his 'Experiment in Criticism', a fugitive essay which deserves to be incorporated in his collected works.[14] It is not only that history brought changes in criticism by providing it with new ideas and disciplines to draw upon. (Thus, just as Coleridge drew on German idealist philosophy, so Richards drew on philosophical semantics, Frye on the anthropology of myth, the structuralists on Saussurian linguistics, etc.) It is also more than the fact that history generated social changes requiring criticism to address different audiences with different needs. It is further and perhaps primarily that critical plurality is inexhaustibly nourished by the growth through history of 'the historical attitude' to literature and criticism. This attitude with its active temporal consciousness, involving 'the notion that literary values are relative to literary periods, that the literature of a period is primarily an expression of the time', was not, according to Eliot, an attitude of which pre-nineteenth-century criticism was aware, let alone embraced (*EC*, 227-228).

However, once criticism (through the ground-breaking work of the first modern literary historian, Sainte-Beuve) became alive to the idea that literature existed 'not only as a body of writing to be enjoyed, but as a process of change in history, and as a part of the study of history' (*EC*, 228), the assumption that there was one permanent critical mode for understanding literature was thoroughly shaken. The idea that we need to understand literature as a product of its particular age, culture, or author, whose perception of life and literature may be enormously different from our own, revealed a gap whose bridging constitutes the central hermeneutic enterprise of modern criticism. This crucial enterprise of understanding calls for the work of a variety of specialist critics: historical, philological, anthropological, philosophical, etc. (Thus, as Eliot here remarks, 'The awareness of the presence of time has obscured the frontiers between literature and everything else', *EC*, 228.)

Moreover, awareness of the changing, temporal character of the literary and critical past incites a similar consciousness of the present, thus raising the question of what *should* be the nature and function of literature and criticism at the present time – a question which irresistibly leads into questions of philosophy, ethics, and social theory. Similarly, if the nature of literature and criticism is perceived as not intrinsically and permanently fixed but rather continuously made and remade, the critic, like the artist, is incited to create new modes in order to make his mark. Given this historicism, why should rival critical factions ever be shamed into abandoning their differences and converging in common recognition and

'really' exist or are 'non-subjects'. See T. Eagleton, *Literary Theory: An Introduction* (Oxford: Blackwell, 1983), 197.

[14] T.S. Eliot, 'Experiment in Criticism', *Bookman*, 70 (1929), 225-233. Future references to it in this chapter will be designated in the body of the text with the abbreviation *EC*.

obeisance to the alleged 'true nature' of criticism? For criticism is only what it has been made to be and the rival critical schools largely determine the form it will come to be.

There is no escaping the plurality of contesting forms of criticism; and Eliot is troubled by the fear that without some distinctive unity or consensus to unite them as a distinctive field, literary criticism would lose the right to remain a discipline in its own right. 'As the number of sciences multiply, of sciences, that is, which have a bearing upon criticism, so we ask ourselves first whether there is still any justification for literary criticism at all, or whether we should not merely allow the subject to be absorbed gently into exacter sciences which will each annex some side of criticism' (*EC*, 231).

To avert such loss of criticism's integrity through the disintegrating disunity of its plurality of modes, Eliot employs two strategies. One is to advocate the achievement of future unifying consensus through 'the collaboration of critics of various special trainings' and the pooling synthesis of their contributions by neutral arbiters 'who will be neither specialists nor amateurs' (*EC*, 233). But after several decades of such intense specialist critical activity and dialogue, there is no reason to believe that such collaboration will issue in general critical agreement, since there is no reason to believe that rival factions will prefer to agree in compromise than to differ in championing pursuit of their own preferred critical modes. Nor is there any chance that partisan specialists will abide by the judgment of the neutral, non-specialist, non-amateur arbiter, whatever such an arbiter might be, if indeed he could exist and be genuinely interested in the future of literature and criticism. Finally, the whole idea of collaborative effort seems rather empty if no sense is given of what common aim collaboration is directed at. For surely we don't want to say that collaboration or agreement are to be sought simply for their own sake as the ultimate or essential aim of criticism.

Eliot's second unificatory strategy then is to suggest such an underlying essential aim by hearkening back to what he regards as the pre-nineteenth-century view that the primary function of literature (and hence ultimately of criticism) is to provide a refined form of pleasure. Conceding that we cannot reinstate the pre-hermeneutic hedonistic innocence of our early critical past, Eliot still insists that 'we should return again and again to the critical writings of the seventeenth and eighteenth centuries to remind ourselves of that simple truth that literature is primarily litera-ture, a means of refined and intellectual pleasure' (*EC*, 227). If the argument is that the variant legitimate modes of criticism should be unified and collectively distinguished by the aim of enhancing literary pleasure because the aim of literature and criticism was originally so conceived, this is far from logically compelling. In the first place, it seems guilty of the genetic fallacy, projecting from a putative originally essential aim the conclusion that this aim must or should remain primary or

essential. Moreover, the historical premise which generates the argument
– pre-nineteenth-century unanimity on the primacy of pleasure in literature – might also be challenged. Long before Coleridge (who, for Eliot,
inaugurated with Sainte-Beuve the modern critical era) literature was
treated philosophically and appreciated in terms of the knowledge rather
than simply the pleasure it affords. This can be seen in Sidney's 'Apologie
for Poetry'; and the contesting claims of pleasure and edification in the
appreciation of literature can be traced back at least as far as Horace's
formula for literature as *dulce et utile*, if not still further to Plato and
Aristotle's debate over the cognitive dimension of art. Thus, rather than
appealing to a unifying shared principle beyond all debate, Eliot is actually
joining a longstanding, continuing debate over the most important function
of literature and criticism, taking sides to redress what he sees as the
romantic-modernist critical heritage of imbalance toward the cognitive
and edificational.

    Though failing to retrieve from history a permanently paramount and
unifying critical essence, Eliot's search for critical unity in history is not too
far off the mark. For here, as in poetry, the distinctive unity of the discipline
can be seen *not* in terms of a uniquely shared, unchallengeable, and
unchanging presence, but in terms of the unity of a distinctive historical
narrative, a complexly coherent narrative of debate as to the proper way(s)
to write, understand, and evaluate literature. What most holds today's
diverse critical writings together and binds them to those of Arnold,
Coleridge, Johnson, Sidney, etc. is not a common essence or quality but a
common genealogy involving certain paradigm figures, questions, projects,
and achievements whose precise meaning and relative value is, however,
continuously debated. To express the point in more familiarly Eliotic
terms, the unity, integrity, and very existence of literature and literary
criticism depend on the existence of a literary and literary critical tradition.
Such traditions are what distinguish these fields from each other and from
others like philosophy, which too has its own special history or tradition of
projects and achievements. Disciplinary unity and distinction could not
derive from the presence of any peculiarly shared feature of the texts of the
given field, for sometimes the same text may count as a work of literature, of
literary criticism, or of philosophy. What thus determines the distinction
between the fields and determines our attribution of a text to one or more of
them is in key part the different networks of genealogical connections or
narrative links that can be established between the texts of a given field.
Though we surely can see synchronic networks of similarities between the
diverse elements of the particular field at a given present which gives some
measure or sense of structural unity to the field, these networks make
sense only on a background of genealogical connections which are
established and sustained by narrative and can be modified by it. Thus in
order to help maintain the unity and integrity of literary criticism, we need
to provide or sustain a coherent story of the tradition of debate over the

form that literature and criticism should take; and by joining and developing that debate we continue and extend that tradition and discipline. Eliot had done this well enough not to need to search for a nostrum of unifying essence, but his fear that the continuity and coherence of tradition's debate would disintegrate with the accelerated divisiveness of our modern 'formless age' (as indeed it could) made him hanker for such a strong unifying remedy.

V

It is time to relate our discussion of Eliot's critical pluralism to a topic that has greatly preoccupied contemporary analytic aesthetics – the nature of critical reasoning. Having noted Eliot's insistence on the variable and fundamentally contested character of critical concepts like 'poetry', on the irreducible diversity of critical modes and aims, and on the fundamental historicity of critical appreciation, we shall see how very similar ideas led Wittgenstein to an extremely seminal account of critical reasoning. This account, which can be linked to some of Wittgenstein's most important aesthetic and philosophical doctrines, has seemed so powerful and attractive to many contemporary aestheticians that they have interpreted it as providing an adequate global theory of critical reasoning, despite Wittgenstein's own notorious injunction against philosophy's advancing any kind of a theory (*PI*, 109).[15]

In what follows, I first trace three important (and Eliotic) themes of Wittgenstein's aesthetics which impelled him to seek a new account of critical reasoning, and then I examine his account and the general theory it allegedly provides. But, finally, I shall argue that this general theory seems inconsistent with the very doctrines which engendered it, and that if Wittgenstein really held such a theory, he has ironically fallen victim to the very dangers of which he and Eliot so fervently warn us, and which Eliot seems to escape.

(1) The first of the three themes that induced Wittgenstein to offer a new account of critical reasoning might be called the *radical indeterminacy of aesthetic concepts*. This all too familiar theme is a straightforward application in aesthetics of Wittgenstein's general doctrine of the indeterminacy of many ordinary concepts, and his insistence that despite their

---

[15] We find discussion of aesthetics in both the early and later phase of Wittgenstein's philosophy. There are very pointed remarks presenting a mystical, transcendental aesthetic in the early *Notebooks: 1914-1916* (Oxford: Blackwell, 1961) and the *Tractatus Logico-Philosophicus* (London: Routledge, 1922). But it is Wittgenstein's later philosophy which has been influential in aesthetics and literary theory. My discussion will therefore concentrate on his later phase and will be based chiefly on his *Philosophical Investigations*, 2nd ed. (Oxford: Blackwell, 1958), hereafter *PI*, and on his lectures on aesthetics in 1932-33 and in the summer of 1938. A report of the former lectures can be found in G. E. Moore, 'Wittgenstein's Lectures in 1930-33', repr. in Moore's *Philosophical Papers* (London: Allen and Unwin, 1959), 252-324. The 1938 lectures have been transcribed from students' notes and published as part of

blurred edges, vague and flexible boundaries and lack of determinate essences, these concepts are none the less usable, adequate, and legitimate.[16] But Wittgenstein further asserts that it is particularly wrongheaded to seek or expect precise definitions for the especially blurred concepts of aesthetics, since such precise definition cannot by its very nature be faithful to the vagueness of the concept it is supposed to represent. 'Won't it become a hopeless task to draw a sharp picture corresponding to the blurred one? ... And this is the position you are in if you look for definitions corresponding to our concepts in aesthetics or ethics' (*PI*, 77).

The thesis of the radical indeterminacy of aesthetic concepts induces one to seek a new account of critical reasoning since it severely threatens the adequacy of the most standard traditional form of critical reasoning, deductive argument based on universal premises supplied by essentialist definitions of aesthetic concepts. To illustrate this more clearly we can roughly distinguish aesthetic concepts into two general kinds, both of which have traditionally generated critical arguments of a deductive form. First there are artistic genre concepts, such as 'tragedy', 'comedy', 'epic', 'symphony', 'sonnet'; and we may include with them also artistic style or period concepts, such as 'Gothic', 'Mannerist', 'Baroque', 'Cubist'; and finally in this same group we may also include the granddaddy of all artistic concepts – the concept of art itself – and its sub-concepts of 'poetry', 'painting', 'music' and the other arts.

We may distinguish this group of concepts (let us call them genre concepts) from another fundamental kind of aesthetic concept, which cuts across genre, period, and style distinctions, and applies not only to art but to other realms of aesthetic appreciation. The second group of concepts, sometimes called aesthetic predicates, includes such terms as 'vivid', 'elegant', 'unified', 'awkward', 'lifeless', and, of course, the paradigmatically aesthetic binary opposites – 'beautiful' and 'ugly'.[17] Another trait which distinguishes this second variety of aesthetic concepts from the first is their characteristic evaluative coloring. For all our love of the novel and the Gothic, the description of a work as a Gothic novel has very little evaluative import compared to its description as vivid and unified.

However, this is not to say that what we have called genre concepts do not function in evaluation. Indeed, one of criticism's oldest and most widely accepted forms of evaluative argument, one which goes back to Aristotle, is criticism by defining essence or rules of genre. The argument is of a

---

Wittgenstein's *Lectures and Conversations on Aesthetics, Psychology, and Religious Belief*, edited by C. Barret (Oxford: Blackwell, 1970), 1-40.

[16] See *PI*, 66-71. Wittgenstein indeed suggests that a concept's vagueness and flexibility often make it *more* useful (*PI*, 71) and that exactness is not only not an end in itself but makes no sense in itself, for it always depends pragmatically on the goal or aim in question (*PI*, 88).

[17] The special logic of this second group of aesthetic concepts has been very much discussed since F. Sibley's seminal treatment of them in 'Aesthetic Concepts', repr. in J. Margolis (ed.), *Philosophy Looks at the Arts*, 2nd ed. (Philadelphia: Temple Univ. Press, 1978), 64-87.

deductive form, based on the definition of the given genre. The necessary elements or properties which define the genre (e.g. those of Aristotle's definition of tragedy) also define what is required for a paradigmatic or excellent example of the genre and thus become necessary and sufficient criteria which define success or excellence in the genre. The basic underlying idea here, as Collingwood later articulated it, is that 'the definition of any given kind of thing is also the definition of a good thing of that kind'.[18] Thus, if a proper (or good exemplar) of tragedy requires properties P_1-P_n, and if work W achieves these properties, then it would follow that work W is a good tragedy.

Morris Weitz has shown that this model of evaluative argument underlies much of the evaluation of Shakespearean tragedy, especially in Johnson and Coleridge; and I have shown elsewhere that this sort of argument is even used when there is some uncertainty about ascribing genre.[19] Addison, for example, waives the controversial question of whether *Paradise Lost* is an epic poem, arguing that 'it will be sufficient to its perfection' if it satisfies 'the rules of epic poetry' and has all 'the beauties which are essential to that kind of writing'.[20] Addison then shows that *Paradise Lost* has all the properties or 'beauties' required by Aristotle's definition of the epic, and thus he concludes that whether or not we choose to call it epic poetry, it is certainly good poetry.

Since so much evaluative argument in criticism has been regarded as having this deductive form, relying ultimately on the definition of genre concepts, the correct definition of such concepts (including that of art itself) has naturally been assumed to be of vital importance. This helps to explain why there has been so much heated debate as to the proper definition of tragedy, poetry, or art in general, why such concepts are essentially contested. For depending on which persuasive definition of the relevant genre is embraced as the proper one, many works would be upgraded as being more congruent with the definition, while others would be down-graded as departing from it, or at least could no longer justify their value by appeal to genre.

Since the definition of genre concepts was thought to supply ultimate premises for deductive evaluative argument, one of the major aims and interests of aestheticians has been the proper definition of these concepts, concepts like 'poetry', 'tragedy', and 'art' itself. The assumption had always been, of course, that there must be a determinate essence of each genre concept, for otherwise how could we use and understand our genre terms? However, Wittgenstein, by showing that our concepts need not have clear, fixed, and definite essences in order to be usable and adequate, and by

[18] R.G. Collingwood, *The Principles of Art* (Oxford: Oxford Univ. Press, 1958), 280.

[19] M. Weitz, *'Hamlet' and the Philosophy of Literary Criticism* (London: Faber, 1972), 156-186, 272-275; and R. Shusterman, *The Object of Literary Criticism*, 204-205.

[20] J. Addison, 'Criticisms on *Paradise Lost*', repr. in E.D. Jones (ed.), *English Critical Essays (Sixteenth, Seventeenth, and Eighteenth Centuries)* (London: Oxford Univ. Press, 1943), 280.

further insisting that aesthetic concepts are especially vague and flexible and thus inherently resistant and unsuitable to essentialist definition, has shaken this assumption and with it much of the promise and attraction of deductive critical argument based on essentialist genre definitions. This in turn has undermined much of the urgent critical interest in defining art and its genre concepts, and it is therefore not surprising that after Wittgenstein's doctrine of the indeterminacy of aesthetic concepts was first applied to art (and its sub-concepts) in the mid-1950s, there has been a tremendous loss of interest in traditional attempts to define art and its genre sub-concepts.[21]

Wittgenstein's theme of the radical indeterminacy of aesthetic concepts has had much the same effect with respect to concepts of the second kind, such as 'beauty', 'sublimity', etc. The concept of beauty, like that of art, has since ancient times been the target of countless attempts at definition. Again, as with art and many of its genre concepts, these definitions were often sought and thought to provide criteria for evaluation, to provide the categorical, universal premise in a deductive argument justifying particular judgments of aesthetic value. If beauty is defined as constituted by property B, then whatever has B is beautiful; and thus, if a particular artwork or natural phenomenon possesses B, we can conclude that it is beautiful. However, definitions of beauty have been no more successful than definitions of art; for beauty too is a concept whose content, borders, and application are not only vague and flexible, but are essentially contested by its many users. Wittgenstein realized this and, according to Moore, 'seemed to hold definitely that there is nothing in common in our different uses of the word "beautiful", saying that we use it "in a hundred different games" – that, e.g. the beauty of a face is something different from the beauty of a chair or a flower or the binding of a book'.[22] Thus, by challenging the assumption that concepts need clear boundaries and common essences to be functional, and by pointing to the apparent lack of these features in the concept of beauty, Wittgenstein destroyed the aesthetician's faith that there must be a correct definition of beauty, somewhere at the end of the rainbow, which once found could serve as a touchstone for critical evaluation and as an ultimate justificatory premise for evaluative argument. With this loss of faith that there must be an essence of beauty to be defined, there has been considerable loss of interest in attempts at definition.[23] Another traditionally central problem of aesthetics had been rendered marginal if not mistaken through the agency of Wittgenstein. But

[21] The only notable recent attempt to define art – Dickie's institutional definition – differs sharply from pre-Wittgensteinian definitions of art in that it sees no inherent essence in works of art, but rather defines art in terms of external social behavior, which as we shall see, is a Wittgensteinian idea. See G. Dickie, *Art and the Aesthetic* (Ithaca: Cornell Univ. Press, 1974) and *The Art Circle* (New York: Haven, 1984).

[22] Moore, 313.

[23] One notable recent exception has been Mary Mothersill's attempt to restore beauty as a central topic for aesthetic theory in her *Beauty Restored* (Oxford: Oxford Univ. Press, 1984).

another account of critical reasoning would have to be offered.

(2) The second important Wittgensteinian theme which helped to change the field of aesthetics and generate a new account of critical reasoning is the *logical plurality of critical discourse*. This theme has two aspects: (a) recognition of the logical variety of critical statements and (b) recognition of the plurality of critical frameworks. Both these ideas are saliently present in Wittgenstein's 1938 lectures on aesthetics, and at least the first is a straightforward application in aesthetics of his famous doctrine that language performs a variety of logically different tasks. It is not a monolithic, uniform instrument, but, in Wittgenstein's image, more of a tool-box. The functions of sentences and indeed the functions of words are at least as different as the functions of different tools. 'Think of the tools in a tool-box: there is a hammer, pliers, a saw, a screw-driver, a rule, a glue-pot, glue, nails and screws. The functions of words are as diverse as the functions of these objects' (*PI*, 11).

According to Wittgenstein, one of the major sources of errors in philosophy is the assimilation of the many different functions of diverse words into one single paradigmatic type. It is an altogether natural but altogether pernicious tendency to concentrate one's attention wholly on one or on one type of word and to see it as representing all words of a certain kind or area of inquiry, and thus to assume that by determining the meaning of this word we can essentially resolve the entire area of inquiry. In aesthetic theory of evaluation this error is often manifested by the aesthetician's excessive and narrow attention to the predicate 'beautiful'. As we noted earlier, intense concentration had been directed at the definition of the beautiful, on the assumption that an adequate definition or understanding of it would solve all important questions of critical evaluation.

However, Wittgenstein insists, this could not be further from the truth. For, in the first place, if we look at our evaluative judgments in criticism, we find what we hardly use the word 'beautiful' at all, but more often words like 'right' and 'wrong'. Indeed, we use a variety of kinds of predicates and expressions:

> It is remarkable that in real life, when aesthetic judgements are made, aesthetic adjectives such as 'beautiful', 'fine', etc., play hardly any role at all. Are aesthetic adjectives used in a musical criticism? You say: 'Look at this transition', or ... 'The passage here is incoherent'. Or you say, in a poetical criticism, ... 'His use of images is precise'. The words you use are more akin to 'right' and 'correct' (as these words are used in ordinary speech) than to 'beautiful' and 'lovely'.[24]

The explanatory poverty, if not vacuousness, of her definition of beauty is discussed in my 'Poetics and Recent Analytic Aesthetics', *Poetics Today* 7 (1986), 323-329.
[24] *Lectures and Conversations*, 3.

Secondly, not only are there different kinds of critical predicates, but often the very same critical predicate can be used in logically different ways. For instance, though 'beautiful' and 'lovely' are most often used as interjections and expressions of approval, they can also be used descriptively. We can describe the *character* (as opposed to the value) of a picture as beautiful or lovely. We might even describe certain works of art, e.g. Kitsch, as too beautiful or too lovely. Here these aesthetic predicates are surely functioning very differently from their typical use as (non-descriptive) expressions of approval, e.g. 'How beautiful!', 'Lovely.', etc.

Thirdly, and this is central to Wittgenstein's thought, whatever words we use in evaluating art, the main thing that gives meaning to our judgments is not the words themselves but the complex cultural and critical context, the occasions and activities in which these words are used. To understand what an aesthetic judgment is or means, says Wittgenstein, requires 'concentrating, not on the words "good" or "beautiful", which are entirely uncharacteristic, ... but on the occasions on which they are said – on the enormously complicated situation in which the aesthetic expression has a place, in which the expression itself has almost a negligible place'.[25] Thus, not only are there many different terms of judgment in criticism, having logically different functions, but even the very same term can have different functions; and hence the significance of an aesthetic judgment is not so much in the words uttered but more in the cultural and critical context in which it appears, in its role in our 'ways of living' with art, which so centrally involve our ways of talking about art.

These very points (as indeed the indeterminacy of such terms as 'poetry' and 'criticism') were repeatedly inculcated by Eliot, who insisted that we cannot properly appraise or understand a critic's judgment without taking account of the cultural and critical context or circumstances in which it was made; and who incessantly warned of the dangers of confusion arising from the fact that our terms have 'different senses in different contexts', because of the virtually 'inevitable shifts of meaning in context' (*TC*, 16, 66; *ASG*, 27).[26]

However, if the meaning of critical statements is so substantially context-dependent, we then face the second aspect of this theme of pluralism: there is in our culture a variety of critical contexts or frameworks, which often have different aims. Recognizing that a note is wrong is not like recognizing that a particular movement is triumphant; appreciating the right length of a sonnet (or of a dress) is something very different from appreciating the sublimity of a tragedy. And, to turn from evaluation to interpretation, the literal explanation of, say, a religious

[25] *Ibid.*, 2. See also 11.

[26] For examples of Eliot's emphasis on the contextual meaning and appraisal of critical judgments, see his 'Introduction' in *The Literary Essays of Ezra Pound* (London: Faber, 1960), xi-xii and *TC*, 14-17. Eliot was perhaps most acutely aware of the problems of context and terminology with regard to the terms 'romantic' and 'classic'.

poem is something very different from a psychoanalytic interpretation of it. As Wittgenstein says, 'The games played ... are utterly different. The explanations could in a sense be contradictory and yet both be correct.'[27]

(3) Moreover, as both Wittgenstein and Eliot emphasize, plurality abounds not only synchronically but diachronically. Different periods produce different cultures and thus the aesthetic judgments of, say, the Middle Ages would be very different in meaning from those of today, even if the very same words were used. As Wittgenstein insists:

> The words we call expressions of aesthetic judgement play a very complicated role, but a very definite role in what we call a culture of a period. To describe their use or to describe what you mean by a cultured taste, you have to describe a culture. What we now call a cultured taste perhaps didn't exist in the Middle Ages. An entirely different game is played in different ages.[28]

This historical pluralism or contextualism directly involves us in the third Wittgensteinian doctrine I wish to treat as motivating his new account of critical reasoning: the essential cultural *historicity of art and art-appreciation*. As the previous quotation indicates, Wittgenstein regarded the notions of beauty, art, and aesthetic appreciation not as things necessary, unchanging, and independent of social change and human history, but rather as products of human culture and history which could have been otherwise (e.g. could have had different standards, used different media, etc.) and which change as society changes, even if sometimes imperceptibly. Our aesthetic concepts are inextricably bound up in our forms of life, in ways of living which change over history through social, technical, and even theoretical developments. In this aspect of his aesthetics, Wittgenstein paved the way for the historical, social, and institutional theories of art which dominate contemporary analytic aesthetics in the work of Wollheim, Danto, and Dickie.[29]

But how do these second and third Wittgensteinian themes lead to a new account of the nature of critical reasoning? First, recognition that the meaning of an aesthetic predicate is not some fixed and autonomous essence, but rather changes significantly according to culture and context, has made the prospect of infallibly deriving or justifying our evaluative judgments deductively from firm unchanging definitions of such predicates seem hopelessly quixotic and misguided, since such predicates seem to have no firm or fixed meaning to be defined. The old hope of establishing critical reasoning on a firmly fixed and certain deductive model was thus immeasurably dimmed, if not altogether extinguished.

[27] *Lectures and Conversations*, 23.

[28] *Ibid.*, 8. Eliot makes the very same point concerning religious statements, whose meaning greatly differs in different historical periods even though they are 'expressed in substantially the same words'. See 'A Note on Poetry and Belief', *Enemy* 1 (1927), 15-17.

[29] See, for example, *Art and its Objects*, 160-169; A. Danto, 'The Artworld', repr. in Margolis, 132-144; and Dickie in works cited in n. 21 above.

Secondly, the flexibility and historical change of aesthetic concepts that Wittgenstein insists upon can be taken even further to question also the validity of much inductive argument in criticism. For, if the very meaning of an aesthetic predicate or expression changes with changing critical, cultural, or historical context, how can we confidently use its past applications to justify its present one? An entirely different game may be played with the expression; it may have changed its meaning and become inapplicable. If the concept of unity changes from context to context, age to age, the fact that poems lacking property *P* were formerly correctly described as disunified gives little confidence that whatever now lacks this property will also be lacking in unity. We may be in a new context, a new game. The creative artist with his new poem may have added a new dimension to the notion of poetic unity. In the light of the challenge that his pluralistic and contextualistic views pose for comprehensive inductionism, it is not surprising that Wittgenstein vehemently rejects the idea that all aesthetic reasons could be reduced to causal, statistical inductive explanation. One does not demonstrate the unity of a symphony by the evidence that fifty million Frenchmen can't be wrong.[30]

VI

If Wittgenstein's doctrines of the radical indeterminacy of aesthetic concepts and the logical plurality and essential historicity of aesthetic judgment work to undermine the charm and credibility of both deductive and inductive models of critical reasoning, what account of critical reasoning does Wittgenstein himself offer? Surely this cultured Viennese devotee of the arts did not wish to conclude that the domain of aesthetics and critical evaluation was altogether barren of reasoning and rational justification, though in his early *Tractatus* phase he did consign aesthetics to the realm of *das Mystische*.[31]

In point of fact, Wittgenstein's lecture remarks on aesthetics do suggest an intriguingly original account of the nature of critical reasoning. G.E. Moore recounts these remarks as follows:

> *Reasons*, he said, in Aesthetics are 'of the nature of further descriptions': e.g. you can make a person see what Brahms was driving at by showing him lots of different pieces by Brahms, or by comparing him with a contemporary author;

[30] Wittgenstein could hardly be more derisive about the idea (once suggested by I. A. Richards) that aesthetics could be profitably pursued simply as a psychological science: 'People often say that aesthetics is a branch of psychology. The idea is that once we are more advanced, everything – all the mysteries of Art – will be understood by psychological experiments. Exceedingly stupid as the idea is, this is roughly it. (*Lectures and Conversations*, 17); 'People still have the idea that psychology is one day going to explain all our aesthetic judgements, and they mean experimental psychology. This is very funny – very funny indeed. There doesn't seem any connection between what psychologists do and any judgement about a work of art' (ibid., 19).

[31] See paragraphs 6.41-7 in the *Tractatus*; and *Notebooks*, 74-86.

and that all Aesthetics does is 'to draw your attention to a thing', to 'place things side by side'. He said that if, by giving 'reasons' of this sort, you make another person 'see what you see' but it still doesn't appeal to him, that is 'an end' of the discussion.[32]

As I have argued elsewhere, Wittgenstein's view of critical reasoning may be characterized as perceptualist rather than logical or causal.[33] In other words, the critic's reasons are regarded not as logically justifying his judgment in terms of principles or evidence in a deductive or inductive argument; nor as causally explaining or recommending it in terms of the motives or causes which engendered it. Rather the critic's reasons function as devices for focussing the reader's perception in such a way that he will see the work as the critic sees it. Perception is the proof. The critic, both in interpretation and in evaluation, is trying to get his reader to perceive the work in a certain way, and the reasons he gives are devices to induce in the reader the desired perception of the work.

Moreover, it is only the giving of these reasons, and not the reasons themselves, which may be the cause of the reader's accepting the critic's judgment; for following the reasons given may help the reader to focus on the work so that he sees it as the critic does. This difference between the citing of reasons and the reasons cited can be explained by the following example. Suppose that in justifying his judgment of a love poem as harsh and crude, a critic cites the predominance of voiced plosives and the similarity of its imagery to some bawdy song. Neither the plosives nor the similarity may themselves be what causes the reader to perceive the poem as harsh and crude; but the act of citing these reasons may focus attention on the work in such a way that the perception of harshness and crudity is induced, and the critical judgment is thus accepted.

This Wittgensteinian idea of the fundamentally perceptual nature of critical reasoning has been adopted and developed by the majority of analytic aestheticians, and also gains support from the frequent inadequacy of reading criticism without having the work of art perceptually before us. Moreover, certainly much good criticism suits this perceptualist model of reasoning.

Wittgenstein not only presents critical reasoning as typically perceptual in nature, but also as neither deductive nor inductive in form. Critical arguments, it is suggested, are rather of a complex, open, and flexibly structured form, consisting of comparisons, associations, leading questions, and focussing instructions directed at an often hypothetical interlocutor, the reader. I have called this form of argument 'dialectic', John

---

[32] Moore, 315.

[33] For a discussion of the perceptualist, logical, and causal theories of critical reasons, see *The Object of Literary Criticism*, 160-165, 191-201; and 'The Logic of Interpretation', and 'Evaluative Reasoning in Criticism'. These works also contain analyses of examples of perceptualist reasoning in criticism, as well as other forms.

Wisdom has called it 'rhetoric';[34] both terms have unfortunate associations. But whatever we call such argument, the main question is how its
validity is to be assessed.

Wittgenstein's apparent answer is an extremely simple and pragmatic
one: validity is success, success in inducing the desired perception of the
work, if not also the desired critical verdict. He held that 'aesthetic
discussions were like discussions in a court of law', where the goal and
criterion of success is that 'what you say will appeal to the judge'.[35]
Elsewhere, Wittgenstein suggests that the criterion for adequacy of
argument and correctness of explanation is acceptance or satisfaction of
some sort. 'The answer in these cases is the one that satisfied you.'[36] 'That
explanation is the right one which clicks' and is accepted by one's
interlocutor; 'if he didn't agree, this wouldn't be the explanation'.[37]

There is no doubt that much critical argument has this dialectical or
rhetorically persuasive form and is evaluated not by principles of deductive or inductive validity but rather by its power in convincing or
satisfying its readers. Yet what is especially important here is that
Wittgenstein does not present this form of reasoning as an inferior,
degenerate departure from rational reasoning, which reflects, as it were,
the inherent irrationality of aesthetics itself. Wittgenstein rather regards
this style of reasoning as perfectly legitimate and reasonable, and as not
at all limited to the domain of aesthetics. It may also be found in the law
courts and even in philosophy, and indeed in some areas of science.
Wittgenstein confessed that much of his own philosophical argumentation is just persuading his audience or readers to see a particular
phenomenon in a particular way, much as the critic tries to persuade his
readers to see a work of art in a particular way. 'What I'm doing is also
persuasion. If someone says "There is not a difference", and I say "There
is a difference", I am persuading; I am saying I don't want you to look at it
like that'.[38] Wittgenstein in fact suggests that such persuasion is also
present in science. For instance, it underlies our firm and ready acceptance of the theories of Darwin and Freud, even when the grounds for
their doctrines were, in strictly logical terms of confirmation, 'extremely
thin'. We have been largely persuaded by the attraction of looking at
things the way these theories present them.[39]

---

[34] See J. Wisdom, 'A Note of Ayer's *Language, Truth, and Logic*', in *Philosophy and Psycho-Analysis* (Oxford: Blackwell, 1957), 247.
[35] Moore, 315.
[36] *Lectures and Conversation*, 18.
[37] *Ibid.*, 19, 21.
[38] *Ibid.*, 27.
[39] *Ibid.*, 26-27.

VII

The liberating effect of Wittgenstein's account of critical reasoning and its apparent philosophical legitimation of critical *laissez-faire* and persuasion make it seem very attractive in these days of plurality and controversy as to the practice and methodology of criticism. But some, on the contrary, might object that precisely this radical libertarianism makes Wittgenstein's account very unattractive as a theory of critical reasoning, for it seems to render such reasoning too free and unprincipled to be considered an acceptable form of reasoning at all. One could argue that the very notion of a rational form of argument requires some constraints on the manner of reasoning, on the way it may be conducted. For if successful persuasion were indeed the sole constraint on reasoning, there would be no way of distinguishing the illocutionary act of reasoning from the perlocutionary act of persuading.

Moreover, on many occasions, both in aesthetics and elsewhere, although we are not convinced by a given argument, we can recognize it as reasonable or legitimate, and assess it as superior to other, perhaps frivolous or irrational, arguments which might be advanced for the same conclusion of which the given reasonable argument failed to convince us. In other words, we seem able to assess the reasonableness or rationality of a piece of critical reasoning apart from its success in perceptually convincing us of its conclusion; and this again suggests that some principles or constraints seem to govern critical reasoning, however vague, liberal, and flexible these constraints may be. This might also be made clear by imagining ways in which a critic might succeed in getting an interlocutor to see something his way but which would not be regarded as constituting good or even legitimate argument for his view, e.g. hypnosis, threats, or suggestion through drugs. To put it more generally, we want to allow for cases where persuasion is achieved improperly or illegitimately, where one could be but should *not* be persuaded.

Thus, the extreme libertarian view that in critical reasoning anything goes provided that it evokes perceptual assent is fundamentally problematic, and Wittgenstein's apparent acceptance of such freedom would seem to vitiate his account of critical reasoning. However, I believe this difficulty may be avoided by arguing that the Wittgensteinian account's apparent acceptance of total freedom is only apparent and not real. First, though Wittgenstein seems to suggest that successful persuasion or induced satisfaction is a criterion of an *adequate* critical argument (or a correct aesthetic explanation), he never explicitly maintains that satisfaction or success is the only constraint on the *legitimacy* of a critical argument. In other words, the Wittgensteinian could maintain that simply to qualify as a legitimate critical argument certain constraints or requirements must be observed, and only then would satisfaction or successful persuasion entail *adequacy* of argument. One might put this another way by reading such constraints into the very notion of a critical argument's satisfying or persuading, i.e. that such satisfaction or persuasion is not mere assent, but assent under certain constraints, through certain acceptable means.

Moreover, Wittgenstein's remarks not only allow the possibility of constraints on how perceptual persuasion is to be achieved, but they also give a definite indication as to how these constraints or requirements should be conceived. They are to be construed as the diverse, vague, flexible, and largely unformulated rules and principles which govern the various language-games and procedures that are entrenched in our forms of living with art. Critical arguments of perceptual persuasion involve a great many conventional procedures which are shared by those competent in aesthetic appreciation within the given culture. Wittgenstein, characteristically, does not try to enumerate or classify these procedures for perceptual persuasion, but he does indicate by his examples of perceptual reasons that they fall centrally in the domain of conventional critical practices which Eliot has conceived under the two general principles of comparison and analysis.

Critical reasoning is thus limited by the language-games which constitute our aesthetic forms of life. The freedom that Wittgenstein allows the critic is only within these limits. But this is not to say that critical reasoning is fixedly limited to any *particular* given boundaries, for that would be to assume that our critical language-games or forms of life are fixed and cannot be modified or supplemented. This, by Wittgenstein's own historicist account, is patently wrong. Our forms of aesthetic appreciation can change (and have changed) with time, and so can the forms and constraints of critical reasoning.

However, Wittgenstein's recognition of the flexible, historicist, and conventional character of critical reasoning should not be interpreted (as it sometimes is)[40] as an aesthetic subjectivism where reasons are given but cannot 'establish conclusions' since their coercive power rests only on conventional practices which are contingent rather than necessary and have no further metaphysical grounding. Here we must reply that for Wittgenstein there need not be (nor perhaps is there) anything deeper and metaphysical on which to base human conventional practices and ways of life. Conventions (or, as Eliot would prefer to say, traditions) constitute the bedrock of our language and of our world and experience that language informs. As Wittgenstein remarks in *The Blue Book*: 'here we strike rock bottom, that is we have come down to conventions.'[41]

Though we can free Wittgenstein's position from the charge of vitiating radical anomie, other problems must be faced. For whether or not he so

40 See H. Slater, 'Wittgenstein's Aesthetics', *British Journal of Aesthetics*, 23 (1983), 34-37.
41 L. Wittgenstein, *The Blue and Brown Books* (New York: Harper, 1958), 24. For discussion of the depth, complexity, and variety of convention, see my paper 'Convention: Variations on a Theme', *Philosophical Investigations*, 9 (1986), 36-55.

intended it, his account of (some) critical reasoning as perceptual and persuasive in nature has been adopted by many analytic aestheticians and transformed into a theory of what all critical reasoning essentially is or should be, a theory that all valid or effective critical reasoning ultimately is and must be of this perceptually persuasive kind. In other words, not only does it maintain that (good) critical reasoning *need not* be deductive or inductive in form and that critical reasons *need not* function as general principles or evidence logically supporting a critical judgment, but also and more radically that (good) critical reasoning *cannot be* of such inductive or deductive character nor can its reasons be seen as having a logical, evidential, or even strictly causal role. Critical reasoning can be nothing else than perceptual persuasion.

Thus Stuart Hampshire rejects the idea of any 'general principles' in critical reasoning and insists that the critic's role is only 'to direct attention'; 'the point is to bring people to see these features, and not simply to lead them to say: "That's good".'[42] Again, as with Wittgenstein, the criterion of success is getting someone to see: 'if one has been brought to see what there is to be seen in the object, the purpose of discussion is achieved'.[43] Margaret Macdonald likewise asserts that reasoning about critical judgments is 'unlike ... deductive and inductive inference' and that 'to justify such a verdict is not to give general criteria as "reasons" but to ... "show" the value'.[44] For her, as for Frank Sibley, the critic's reasons serve as 'a kind of key to grasping or seeing', where the goal is to get 'his audience to see what he sees'.[45] In a similar vein, Arnold Isenberg comes out against deductive and inductive justifications of critical judgments and maintains that the critic's reasons not only function perceptually but that their very meaning is perceptual in character: 'the critic's *meaning* is "filled in", "rounded out", or "completed" by the act of perception', which is necessary for the simple understanding of the reason he cites. Again, also with Isenberg, the goal of critical reasoning is 'to induce a sameness of vision, of experienced content', which 'may or may not be followed by agreement ... in identical value judgements'.[46]

It thus seems that Wittgenstein's portrayal of critical reasoning as perceptually persuasive and not necessarily deductively or inductively logical has evolved into a theory asserting that all valid critical reasoning is

[42] S. Hampshire, 'Logic and Appreciation', repr. in W. Elton (ed.), *Aesthetics and Language* (Oxford: Blackwell, 1954), 169, 166.

[43] *Ibid.*, 165.

[44] M. Macdonald, 'Some Distinctive Features of Arguments Used in Criticism of the Arts', repr. in Elton, 121, 129.

[45] 'Aesthetic Concepts', 79, 80.

[46] A. Isenberg, 'Critical Communication', repr. in Elton, 137-138. John Casey, who draws heavily on Wittgenstein and describes critical reasoning as 'persuading ... to see ... in a particular way', goes even further than Isenberg (and Wittgenstein) by maintaining that sameness of vision entails identical value judgments. See J.Casey, *The Language of Criticism* (London: Methuen, 1966), 172-173.

of this perceptually persuasive kind and that deductive and inductive models of critical reasoning are simply wrong (i.e. not reflective of accepted critical practice) and fundamentally wrongheaded. And though the first view is clearly correct, the second seems rather dubious. Yet it is very natural and dangerously easy to slide from one view to the other.[47] For when one is intent upon insisting that critical arguments need not be deductively or inductively logical but can be instead (and often are quite effectively) perceptually persuasive, one is naturally preoccupied with the presence and merit of this latter form of criticism, and thus one is apt to ignore the claims and even existence of other kinds of critical reasoning. One falls victim to what Wittgenstein diagnosed as 'a main cause of philosophical disease – a one-sided diet: one nourishes one's thinking with only one kind of example' (*PI*, 593).

Perhaps we shall never be certain whether Wittgenstein himself held the more extreme doctrine that all critical reasoning is or should be of the perceptually persuasive kind, for we have only transcriptions and reports of his remarks on this subject. But I am reluctant to impute to him this strongly essentialistic theory of critical reasoning, since it seems not only wrong but also quite inconsistent with the three themes which I have shown to have engendered his perceptual-persuasive account of critical reasoning. Let us consider the second charge first.

The three Wittgensteinian (and Eliotic) themes we earlier considered all reflect and indeed insist upon critical pluralism. First, critical concepts cannot all be clearly and precisely defined because many have a plurality of different uses and are governed by flexible and changing conditions of application. Secondly, the diverse expressions used in criticism are made to perform a variety of logically different roles and indeed may change their roles and meaning in different contexts. Finally, since the whole notion of critical appreciation and judgment depends on our complex forms of life which can and do change over time, the fact that at a particular time and in a particular context critical concepts are applied in a particular way and critical judgments are made or supported in a particular way does not mean that they always are or need be applied, made, or supported in these particular ways.

If we take this pluralism seriously, as I think we should, we cannot simply rule out deductive and inductive models of critical reasoning as intrinsically wrong and illegitimate. We cannot argue, from our contemporary critical standpoint with its confusion, controversy, and lack of faith

---

[47] We can see this slide quite clearly in the following passage from Casey: 'The idea that particular judgements, if they are to be objective, *have to* be deduced from general principles, or entailed by general descriptions, is the fundamental fallacy. To defend a judgement of a poem one *has to* go on describing it, relating it to other poems and so on, until the person one is trying to convince is satisfied. There are no general laws which will take the place of this' (ibid., 138, my italics). In opposing the fallacy that objective critical reasoning must be deductive, Casey falls into the fallacy that such reasoning cannot be deductive or non-perceptually persuasive.

as to general principles and definitions, that deductive argument from general principles or shared definitions is never possible in criticism nor could ever have been successfully practiced since such principles or definitions are impossible to formulate or agree upon. For though they may be so today, they may not have been so in the past and may not be so again in the future. In Aristotle's time there may well have been a shared essence of tragedy to define. In Johnson's time, as Eliot argues, there seem to have been general principles and standards of criticism which were commonly held and firmly established.[48] We cannot simply deny this on the basis of the state of criticism today.

There is thus no justification for asserting (as some theorists have) that although certain critics claim to be and seem to be arguing deductively from general principles and definitions, they cannot really be doing so since 'critical evaluation ... cannot be true (or false) deductive argument', their being no satisfactory definitions or irresistibly conclusive standards on which to base such argument.[49] For even if the definitions and standards on which critics have based their deductions seem wrong to us (in fact even if they are and were wrong), this cannot negate the fact that their arguments were deductive and indeed deductively valid. To claim that critical reasoning never was nor could be deductive is to deny that different critical games may be played at different times, which is precisely what Wittgenstein labored so hard to establish. The same considerations hold against ruling out the possibility of inductive critical reasoning, and we can point to critics of the past who seem to reason inductively.[50]

Moreover, even if we consider only contemporary criticism but make ourselves aware of the variety of differently functioning predicates it employs, we should realize that the theory that (good) critical reasoning can only be of the perceptually persuasive kind is far from convincing. Let us remember that criticism ascribes not only predicates like 'lovely', 'unified', and 'powerful', but also predicates like 'important' and 'original', which clearly can be and often are justified inductively through confirmatory evidence. As Graham Hough maintains:

> It is not really open to anyone to say 'Yes, Dante's works exist, but they are not of any importance'. This is contradicted by a large body of indisputable

[48] See T.S. Eliot, 'Johnson as Critic and Poet', *OPP*, 162-193.

[49] Weitz, *'Hamlet' and the Philosophy of Literary Criticism*, 275. Casey (138) also argues that adequate general 'standards ... neither can exist, nor can have the function' of cogent premises in a deductive argument. Weitz, besides questioning the conclusiveness of evaluative principles in criticism, also rules out evaluative deduction on the basis of an argument which commits a 'speech act' fallacy of denying the compatibility of description and praise. For criticism of Weitz's argument, see 'Evaluative Reasoning in Criticism', 152. For a general discussion of such fallacies, see J. Searle, *Speech Acts* (Cambridge: University Press, 1969), 131-156.

[50] See *The Object of Literary Criticism*, 191-193, 202-203; and for deductive reasoning, 204-205.

evidence. And it would be a very strange position to hold that Dante's fame and influence were no evidence of literary merit.[51]

Here we should remember that not only ascription of merit but also the very ascription of importance itself can constitute critical evaluation.

Thus, the fact that arguments of a deductive or inductive form have been or are successfully employed by established critics clearly seems to render untenable the theory that all valid critical reasoning is or must be that of perceptual persuasion. To maintain that these other arguments cannot be valid or effective, despite their entrenched acceptance in critical practice (which perhaps in itself constitutes their justification), merely on the grounds that they are *not* perceptual persuasion and that perceptual persuasion *is* the only valid or truly effective form of critical argument is simply to beg the whole question, and to do so in a way wholly inconsistent with the pluralism inherent in Wittgenstein's aesthetics and Eliot's critical theory.

Finally, embracing this pluralism allows us to accept Wittgenstein's account of critical reasoning as perceptual persuasion, while rejecting the erroneous general theory which evolved from it. Wittgenstein's account is to be taken as describing one form of critical argument or explanation, highlighting one of many language-games in aesthetic appreciation, one which is today extremely widespread and important but which had until then escaped philosophical attention. His attention to this one game should not blind us to the existence and efficacy of other games involved in the justification and explanation of critical judgments. And as both Wittgenstein and Eliot persistently remind us, these games are extremely numerous and diverse, serving as they do a variety of critical aims whose comparative importance has been and should continue to be debated over the course of history.

[51] G. Hough, *An Essay on Criticism* (New York: Norton, 1966), 176.

Chapter 5

Historicism, Interpretation, and Hermeneutics

The restless demon in us drives us to 'interpret' whether we would or not; and the question of the meaning of 'interpretation' is a very pretty problem ...

'Introduction' to G.W. Knight's *The Wheel of Fire*

I

In an important recent book on philosophical aesthetics, Anthony Savile attacks Eliot as representative of the radically historicist theory of the 'autonomy of interpretation' which holds that once created a literary work of art has 'its own life' and can, over history, change and develop in meaning. In trying to refute this view Savile seeks to establish in its place what he calls 'the historicist alternative': the theory that every work of art has its 'canonical interpretation which does not change over time'. According to Savile, such a canonical interpretation is permanently fixed and determined historically and intentionalistically as 'what the artist must expect his intentions to be taken to be' by 'his contemporaries, the only audience he can knowingly work for'. Without such a canonical interpretation, Savile argues, works of art can have no identity and therefore cannot admit of proper understanding and evaluation.[1]

Savile's views are demonstrably wrong and misleading on several counts, some of which I discuss elsewhere.[2] Here I shall only challenge his attack on Eliot's theory of interpretation and more particularly his charge that it stands in fundamental contradiction to Eliot's crucial theory of tradition. This will provide a convenient and topical point of departure for the main project of this chapter – analysis of Eliot's historicist stance on literary understanding and interpretation, in terms of the philosophical

[1] See A. Savile, *The Test of Time: An Essay in Philosophical Aesthetics* (Oxford: Oxford University Press, 1982), 40-85. Citations here are from pp. 61, 64.

[2] See R. Shusterman, 'On Knowing the Value of a Work of Art', in P. McCormick (ed.), *The Reasons of Art* (Ottawa: University of Ottawa Press, 1985), 368-374; and 'Poetics and Analytic Aesthetics', *Poetics Today*, 7 (1986), 323-329.

underpinnings and themes it shares with contemporary continental hermeneutic philosophy. Here Eliot may most profitably be compared to the German philosopher Hans-Georg Gadamer, many of whose central ideas Eliot clearly prefigures. Two of these are historicism and tradition, so it is apposite to begin with Savile's charge that Eliot's historicism regarding the meaning and understanding of literary works is inconsistent with his commitment to the idea of tradition.

Historicism points to the inexorable change of beliefs, aims, methods, vocabularies, and standards over the course of time. In recognizing the inevitability of change, it thus recognizes the necessity of novelty, and similarly the possibility of very different, non-converging, standards and practices which may find rational justification in their respective temporally different communities. How can such views be reconciled with Eliot's emphasis on the preponderant importance of tradition – with his claim, for example, that poetry 'must inevitably be judged by the standards of the past' (*SE*, 15) and his not infrequent condemnations of the rapt pursuit of novelty?

One way to reconcile Eliot's historicism and 'traditionalism' is in terms of a distinction between *praxis* and philosophical theory; that is, between a theory for practice (a theory of what needs to be done or emphasized at a certain time) and, on the other hand, a meta-theoretical or philosophical theory which accounts for or helps to justify the pragmatically advocated theory. In Eliot's case, one might argue, that it is precisely because he was so philosophically aware of historical change (and especially of the dizzyingly rapid rate of change in modern times) that he so strongly emphasized tradition in his pragmatic theorizing and polemics. In other words, Eliot inculcated the indispensability and value of tradition in order that tradition might be better maintained, strengthened, and used to achieve greater cultural stability and unity at a time when these seemed greatly threatened. Thus Eliot's appeal to tradition need not be inconsistent with historicism, but rather can be seen as a pragmatic corollary of it.

Savile, however, advances a different and more sophisticated argument to show that Eliot's historicism must be inconsistent with his emphasis on tradition. Savile argues that the historicist tenet that our understanding of art is inevitably conditioned and limited by our present historical situation and conceptual set must make any putative appeal to tradition empty and invalid. For if we are so conditioned and limited by our *present* mental set, then the tradition of the past is not really available to us; we cannot see it as it really is, and thus cannot appeal to it or use it as a standard. If historicism 'makes us creatures of our present mental state, ... it denies us access to the tradition'.[3]

The rejoinder to Savile's argument concerns an important dimension of

3 Savile, 44.

Eliot's (and Gadamer's) historicist philosophy. To put the point briefly for the moment (pending further elaboration in our chapter on tradition), Savile's argument makes two basic wrong assumptions. First, though tradition is indeed a product of the past, it is not a thing of the past. On the contrary, a healthy tradition is a living force and presence in the present, something which informs our current language, thought, and action. We do not need any special 'access' to it, for in a sense it already belongs to us or is open to us, because we exist in its ambience.

Secondly, Savile's complaint that historicism cannot allow us to see tradition (or any object in it) as it really and unchangingly is rests on the questionable assumption (challenged both by Eliot and Gadamer) that tradition (or every cultural entity it transmits) exists as an independent intact object whose autonomous, inviolate nature might in principle be perceived as it really is, wholly independent of changing human interpretation and appropriation. This assumption not only begs the question against historicism, it also relies on an unconvincing unstated assimilation of tradition and its cultural components to the sort of ordinary physical objects (mordantly characterized by Austin as 'middle-sized dry goods') which philosophers are all too prone to take as the exclusive model of all being, the form of whatever can be said to exist.

No intelligibility can be attached to such a notion of tradition. A tradition may grow, flourish, branch out, rot, and die like a tree but it is obviously not individuated like one (unlike trees, traditions are typically embedded in larger ones) and not grasped as a clearly bounded object. Traditions cannot be perceived apart from the appropriating interpretation of them, because they do not exist without such interpretation. A tradition continues to exist only in and through the community's interpretative understanding and practice of it, which may change over the course of history in response to historical exigencies and struggles, thus not only changing the present and future form of tradition but also to some extent its past outline.

Having disposed of Savile's charge of inconsistency, let us consider the underlying ideas motivating Eliot's historicist view of literary understanding and note their striking affinity to the more recent and fashionable hermeneutic philosophy of criticism expressed most systematically in the work of Gadamer. Eliot, already acknowledged as a leader of modernist criticism and father of the New Criticism, may then be seen also as a precursor of certain positions in postmodernist theory.

II

We may begin with three basic and closely related ideas which individually seem innocuously obvious, but taken together impel one toward an historicist pluralism regarding literary understanding. The first two concern human finitude and situatedness as fundamental and inalienable features which condition understanding, while the third concerns the mutability over time of man's situation, and his perception of this mutability and temporality. Together they threaten the possibility of any uniquely and immutably valid understanding of the literary work and thus lead to critical pluralism.

(1) The term 'situatedness' refers to the view that man is essentially and irremediably located in (some part of) the spatio-temporal world and that his perception or point of view is consequently structured or conditioned by and contingent upon his particular situation. The way we see, judge, and describe things (if not also sometimes the things themselves described) are largely determined by the place, period, and culture which we inhabit, by the particular concepts and language in which we think and speak. Differences in such factors will determine whether we see a carved figure as a divine presence or a mere work of art, or whether we judge something to be a flower or a weed, an antique or a piece of junk. The fact that our actual concrete situation fundamentally informs and conditions our understanding and experience of the world should not be belabored, having been established by anthropological and linguistic research and independently urged by both existential and hermeneutical philosophies which build on Heidegger's central notion of *Dasein* – human beings' 'there-being' or 'being-there', i.e. being in the midst of the world, situated in a concrete historical situation.[4]

Gadamer, a student of Heidegger, makes this historical situatedness and its ineluctable pervasiveness in human thinking the cornerstone of his philosophy.[5] For him all human understanding, even the allegedly transcendental reason, can exist 'only in concrete historical terms, i.e. it is not its own master, but remains constantly dependent on the given circumstances in which it operates' (*TM*, 245). There is no escaping situatedness by self-awareness or appeal to logical consistency. 'Even if, as historically enlightened people, we are fundamentally aware of the historical contingency of all human thought concerning the world, and thus of our own contingency, we still have not taken up an absolute position. The consciousness of contingency does not do away with contingency', nor does the reflexive argument that this view's own claim to truth is self-refutingly contingent (*TM*, 406-407).

4 The term 'Dasein', literally 'There-being', is used by Heidegger to characterize what he regards as uniquely human being, and in later writings is inscribed as 'Da-sein' to emphasize further that man's being is ineluctably there, in the midst of the concrete historical world. For a concise and intelligible account of Dasein and Heidegger's philosophy, see G. Steiner, *Heidegger* (Glasgow: Fontana, 1978).

5 I shall be using the following texts of Hans-Georg Gadamer, referring to them with the following abbreviations: *Truth and Method* (New York: Crossroad, 1982), *TM*; *Philosophical Hermeneutics* (Berkeley: University of California Press, 1976), *PH*; *Reason in the Age of Science* (Cambridge, Mass.: MIT Press, 1983), *RAS*; 'The Hermeneutics of Suspicion', in G. Shapiro and A. Sica (eds.), *Hermeneutics* (Amherst: University of Massachusetts Press, 1984), 54-65, *HS*; 'Replik', in K-O. Apel *et al.* (ed.), *Hermeneutik und Ideologiekritik* (Frankfurt: Suhrkamp, 1976), 283-317, *R*; *Kleine Schriften* (Tübingen: Mohr, 1967), *KS*.

That understanding is always historically conditioned does not mean that it is always fully determined and that we have no choice or freedom in the way we interpret a text or a phenomenon. Historical situatedness determines, as it were, a limiting framework with certain possibilities of logical-linguistic space for understanding to work in, but it does not determine precisely which of these possibilities must be actualized or chosen.[6] We should not want to assert a determinism precluding the possibility of choosing between alternative ways of understanding (or misunderstanding) literary texts which is an undeniable part of critical experience. Nor should Gadamer want to, since choice seems essential to his concept of application which he regards as an integral part of understanding.

Noting this crucial distinction between historical dependence and determinism, we can go on to show Eliot's similar emphatic recognition of the situatedly conditional character of human understanding. Apart from his early, short-lived, but very important advocacy of the ideal of 'neutral' perception of 'the object as it really is', Eliot stressed that our understanding is always conditioned and limited by our concrete historical situation. 'We are all limited, by circumstances if not by capacities'; 'limited by the limitations of particular men in particular places and at particular times' (*TC*, 104; *TUP*, 141-142). Art can never be created or appreciated in an historical vacuum. Obviously the artist is and should be influenced by his historical situation and his perception of its needs. But Eliot also asserts the same of criticism, that 'each generation, like each individual, brings to the contemplation of art its own categories of appreciation, makes its own demands upon art, and has its own uses for art' (*TUP*, 109). For this reason, Eliot dryly notes, contemporary criticism will always be in some sense experimental and new, since it will always be criticism from a new historical situation, involving 'a new point of view'.[7]

Eliot's insistence on the situatedness of critical understanding should not be construed as merely the trivial negative reminder of human fallibility and cognitive limitation. It surely includes this but further suggests the positive pragmatist point that being shaped by and serving the needs of a situation is not a bad thing for human understanding, since its very role is to promote the welfare of a being whose needs in this world are overwhelmingly situational and pragmatic. Recognition of this leads both Eliot and Gadamer to elevate the status of contextual thinking and

[6] The principle of choice, the logical possibility of understanding (or misunderstanding) something differently seems necessary to our very notion of understanding, and is an analogue of what semanticists call the principle of choice from the point of view of the communicator: 'the possibility of selection between alternatives, is a necessary, though not sufficient, condition of meaningfulness'. See J. Lyons, *Semantics* (Cambridge: Cambridge University Press, 1977), vol. 1, 33.

[7] See T.S. Eliot, 'Experiment in Criticism', *Bookman*, 70 (1929), 225. Eliot sometimes takes care to distinguish a general and reasonably motivated point of view from mere personal bias or prejudice, *SE*, 109.

practical wisdom over scientific method with its rigid, universalizable character.

(2) The idea of finitude, so close as to be hardly separable from situatedness, includes but goes beyond the simple matter of man's temporal finitude or mortality. Yet even this limitation of life span is not without cognitive consequences. It denies the hope that through trial and error we can eventually overcome all our misunderstandings so that the truth will finally emerge; for our time on earth for such experimentation is all too limited. Moreover, despite their emphasis on the valuable funding and transmission of experience through community and tradition, Eliot and Gadamer recognize that this transmission is never total and that what is transmitted may anyway prove inapplicable because of the mutability of our world. As Eliot remarks, it is not as 'if we were always the same generation upon the earth' or as if people always 'learned much from the experience of their elders' (*EAM*, 106); and even 'a good tradition might, in changing circumstances, become out of date' and thus hinder understanding (*ASG*, 31).[8]

More important, then, than the finitude of mortality is the finitude implied in situatedness. For even if historical research enables us cognitively to transcend the temporal limits of our actual experience and learn of and from the situations of others in the past, we still remain, as does our historical thinking, located in a particular finite present situation and conditioned by its particular interests, needs, vocabularies, etc. From this principle of situated finitude Gadamer rejects Dilthey's assumption of a transcendental, absolutely objective historical understanding (*TM*, 192-204). From the same standpoint, Eliot rejects the possibility of an absolutely pure and incorrigible appreciation of art.

> 'Pure' artistic appreciation is to my mind only an ideal, when not merely a figment, and must be, so long as the appreciation of art is an affair of limited and transient human beings existing in space and time. Both artist and audience are limited. ... Hence each new master of criticism performs a useful service merely by the fact that his errors are of a different kind from the last; and the longer the sequence of critics we have, the greater amount of correction. (*TUP*, 109)

This sequence of 'correction', however, implies no hope of reaching an absolute vision, for human (and hence literary) understanding must always be from some limited and limiting situation. 'Our contemporary critics, like their predecessors, are making particular responses to particular situations'; and as such their views, like all critics' views, are

---

[8] Eliot therefore realizes that human understanding always to some extent 'must submit to the pressure of circumstances. We have to adopt our minds to a new age'. 'Commentary', *Criterion*, 6 (1927), 386-387.

necessarily 'limited by the limitations of particular men in particular places and at particular times' (*TUP*, 140-141).[9]

But why does situation entail the limitation of human understanding? Gadamer tries to clarify the connection by noting that as 'every finite present has its limitations' so every situation 'represents a standpoint that limits the possibility of vision. Hence an essential part of the concept of situation is the concept of "horizon", ... the range of vision that includes everything that can be seen from a particular vantage point' (*TM*, 269). Apart from the likely constraints placed on perception by one's situational interests and actual cognitive resources, the crucial point seems to be temporal. Any present perception or understanding is limited in not seeing the future; and since the future will reveal aspects of things past and present, our situational understanding of these, as well as future things, must be limited.[10]

The theme of the situated finitude and perspectivism of human understanding is not only present in Eliot's later historicist phase, but was in fact a central element in his early, pre-objectivist doctoral philosophy. His thesis systematically treats the idea of perspective or horizon as a key notion, referring to it by the technical terms 'finite centre' (borrowed from Bradley) and 'point of view' (Eliot's own). Like Gadamer, who recognized that situations and horizons inevitably change as we move through life and that understanding requires 'the fusion of these horizons' (*TM*, 273), Eliot was much concerned with the problem of the change and multiplicity of different horizons and the threat it posed to meaning and understanding which demand a certain unity or coherence of experienced points of view (*KE*, 140-142). Since throughout our life 'we vary by passing from one point of view to another', we face 'the painful task of unifying (to a greater or less extent) jarring and incompatible ones, and passing, when possible, from two or more discordant viewpoints to a higher which shall somehow include and transmute them' (*KE*, 147-148).

Eliot's account of how understanding merges perspectives not only prefigures Gadamer's idea of the fusion of horizons but seems superior to it. For Eliot avoids Gadamer's dubious transcendental device for fusion: 'the one great horizon that moves from within and, beyond the frontiers of the present, ... is, in fact, a single horizon that embraces everything contained

[9] Eliot insists that since limitation is necessary for any critical perspective at all, it in itself implies no derogation. As he claims in a later essay on Pound's criticism, 'To say that any kind of criticism has its limitations is not to belittle it but to contribute towards its definition and understanding'. Pound's limitation of focus to the craft of writing is essential to his success and penetration. See T.S. Eliot, 'Introduction', in *The Literary Essays of Ezra Pound* (London: Faber, 1960), xiii.

[10] To say that one's understanding of something must always be limited is not, however, to declare that it is necessarily always erroneous or inadequate but merely that it could be augmented or deepened in some way. Unlimited or unenhanceable understanding would, on this view, mean the end of inquiry, and what we ordinarily or rightly call complete understanding or full or perfect knowledge of some thing is itself contextually or pragmatically determined according to our different needs and purposes.

in historical consciousness' (*TM*, 271). This all-embracing horizon (which may recall Bradley's Absolute, for they both perform the same explanatory function of unifying divergent and narrower points of view) is not only of very questionable existence, but seems to contradict the very notion of a horizon, which necessarily implies finitude and limitation, i.e. that there is something beyond and not embraced by the horizon. As Eliot remarks, 'There could be no such thing ... as a single finite centre, for every experience implies the existence of something independent of the experience, something capable, therefore, of being experienced differently, and the recognition of this fact is already the transition to another point of view' (*KE*, 148-149). Eliot more bravely admits that the unification of points of view or horizons is not assured by any absolute horizon but must be pragmatically welded and hammered out by our efforts to understand ourselves and others.

Though Eliot later came to find his thesis incomprehensible, he did not long forget the idea of the finite point of view, even if he briefly hoped (in early objectivist enthusiasm) to transcend it in an absolute, God's-eye vision of 'the object as it really is'. With growing critical maturity came an increasing emphasis on the inevitability and productivity of the situated, limited point of view. The limiting directedness and pre-structuring of a point of view, informed by the interests, conceptual tools, and presuppositions of one's situation, may obstruct some things from understanding, but is more importantly a necessary condition for understanding anything at all. As Eliot maintained, 'if it be objected that this is a prejudice ... I can only reply that one must criticize from some point of view and that it is better to know what one's point of view is' (*SE*, 114). And he later continued to maintain that 'we have to see literature through our own temperament in order to see it at all, though our vision is always partial and our judgement always prejudiced'.[11]

Thus, for Eliot, prejudice and point of view provide not only the limits but the necessary direction and structure of understanding; and though we can and should be conscious of them and their limitation, we can never escape all prejudice and point of view to achieve a vision without horizon and a complete catholicity of taste. For such a vision would be a vast emptiness, and such a taste would be tantamount to no taste at all. 'Genuine taste is always imperfect taste – but we are all, as a matter of fact, imperfect people.' 'A catholic taste ... would be indistinguishable from no taste at all.'[12]

Gadamer's famous 'rehabilitation of the concept of prejudice' (TM, 246) is thus only following Eliot in insisting that 'all understanding inevitably involves some prejudice' and that the prejudices we bring with us help constitute the situation and horizon of a particular present, not only

[11] 'Experiment in Criticism', 225.
[12] See *TUP*, 35 and Eliot's review of E.E. Kellett, *Fashion in Literature: A Study of Changing Taste*, in *English Review*, 53 (1931), 635.

representing the present limits of our understanding but constituting 'the initial directedness of our whole ability to experience' (*TM*, 239, 245-247, 272; *PH*, 9). Gadamer similarly follows Eliot in drawing the conclusion that since there is no hope (or reason) to escape all prejudice and point of view, the main thing is to be aware of our own and its limits and to be flexibly open to entertain different views which challenge our prejudices and may enlarge our scope of understanding. 'The important thing is to be aware of one's own bias, so that the text may present itself in all its newness and thus be able to assert its own truth against one's own fore-meanings' (*TM*, 238).

With the aim of promoting flexible openness and enlargement of point of view, both Eliot and Gadamer stress the enormous importance of testing our prejudices through encounter with the unfamiliar – both with foreign languages and cultures and, no less importantly, with the past history of our own tradition. They are therefore extremely critical of the smug assumption that the attitudes of the present are always superior to those of the past, an assumption which they condemn as 'temporal provincialism' and 'naive historicism' (*OPP*, 69; *TM*, 484). Their recognition of the rich resources of the past for present and future understanding explains their common preoccupation with the idea of tradition. Yet they also scrupulously admit that their own views are limited and informed by situational interests and prejudices and may therefore be superseded as new situations present themselves over time (*TUP*, 143; *TM*, 483).

(3) This raises the third fundamental theme which joins with those of human finitude and situatedness to create the case for historicist pluralism of literary understanding: the essential mutability of man's situation in time. Given that our understanding of a literary text (or anything) is conditioned to some extent by our situation – by our present interests, circumstances, and accumulated experience, then as these must change through time, so must our understanding. We have seen how Eliot emphasizes and illustrates the relentless change through history of poetic understanding. Since each generation brings different 'assumptions', 'demands', 'uses', and 'categories of appreciation' (which are both the product and a constitutive part of its historical situation), 'our criticism, from age to age, will reflect the things that the age demands' (*TUP*, 27, 64, 109, 141). And even within the same age critics will differ somewhat in their understanding of texts, since their interpretations must be 'particular responses to particular situations' which may differ not only in precise historical coordinates but in terms of the 'divers interests' which the interpreters bring to literature and from which literary appreciation cannot be fruitfully separated.[13]

Gadamer echoes these very ideas in connection with his thesis that application is an integral part of understanding, and not a mere subsequent external appendage: 'understanding always involves something like

---

[13] See *TUP*, 141, and 'Poetry and Propaganda', *Bookman*, 70 (1930), 8.

the application of the text to be understood to the present situation of the interpreter' (*TM*, 274).[14] Hence: 'Every age has to understand a transmitted text in its own way', for 'the real meaning of a text as it speaks to its interpreter' is not limited to what it meant to 'the author and whom he originally wrote for' but 'is always partly determined also by the historical situation of the interpreter and hence by the totality of the objective course of history' (*TM*, 263). Given the inevitable change of situation, Gadamer therefore draws the paradoxical conclusion that in some strict sense 'a text is understood only if it is understood in a different way every time' (*TM*, 276). But the difference may be so slight that pragmatically we may speak of sharing the same understanding.

Recognizing the correlative status of meaning and understanding, Gadamer takes the different situational understandings of the literary work, its applicational meanings to its different interpreters, as belonging to the work's meaning which is consequently seen not as permanently fixed by the author but developing through its interpretative history of meaning to others. For Gadamer, since 'all reading involves application ... a person reading a text is himself part of the meaning he apprehends. He belongs to the text he is reading.' And though certain established critical readings exert a very powerful influence on the continuing history of the work's interpretative reception, every reader 'must accept the fact that future generations will understand differently what he has read in the text' (*TM*, 304). New times bring new situations generating new applicational understandings of old texts.

Gadamer's bold incorporation of the interpreter's response into the meaning of the text he is interpreting, and the related idea that 'the understanding of ... texts ... is ultimately a self-understanding' (*TM*, 231) should not be regarded as augmentations of Eliot's historicist theory of interpretation. For they are already saliently present there, and are arguably a natural (through belatedly drawn) consequence of his early separation of the literary work from its author, which meant that its meaning could develop over time by embracing the meaning it had for others as well. 'What a poem means is as much what it means to others as what it means to the author; and indeed, in the course of time a poet may become merely a reader in respect to his own works, forgetting his original meaning – or without forgetting, merely changing' (*TUP*, 130). This view of literary meaning and understanding explains why Eliot insists on sharply distinguishing between the understanding or interpretation of a work and its mere explanation through origins, philological exegesis, and close textual analysis, and why he challenges the assumption 'that there must be just one interpretation of the poem as a whole that must be right'. 'The meaning of the poem as a whole ... is not exhausted by any explanation, for

---

[14] Gadamer regards 'not only understanding and interpretation, but also application as comprising one unified process' (*TM*, 274-275).

the meaning is what the poem means to different sensitive readers' (*OPP*, 113).

Moreover, since what a text means to a reader is reflective not only of the text but of the reader, understanding this meaning provides the reader with an invaluable means of self-understanding. Eliot thus insists that 'a valid interpretation [of a poem] ... must be at the same time an interpretation of my own feelings when I read it' and that 'a good deal of the value of an interpretation is – that it should be my own interpretation' (*OPP*, 114). The ambiguity of phrase here (as often with Eliot) is pointed and productive: 'my own interpretation' economically conveying both 'my interpretation of the text' and 'an interpretation of myself'. This view of literary meaning and understanding as positively involving one's own situation as reader and thus demanding an effort not simply to understand a text but 'to understand oneself in relation to it' (*OPP*, 209) is frequently echoed in Eliot's later theorizing, and we shall subsequently consider the kind of interaction between text and reader he finds most fruitful for understanding.

III

First we must face an objection to what has been said so far. For one might argue that we have already gone much too far and too fast in dismissing the common-sense interpretational project of grasping the literary work itself as it really is or (as this is construed by Savile and many others) as it is understood by its author and his contemporaries. Even if Eliot and Gadamer assert that each generation must reinterpret the texts of the past in its own way, and even if each generation actually does, why is this really necessary? Many literary intepreters are blessed with considerable power of imagination, and indeed sometimes chided for its excesses. Why then should we reject the possibility of imagining oneself so thoroughly into the Elizabethan world as to understand *Hamlet* as Shakespeare and his contemporaries did? Its meaning could then be identified with this particular, uniquely authentic understanding (assuming that Shakespeare himself, if not his contemporaries, had only one) which could serve as a fixed and determinate standard to measure (complete or approximate) accuracy of interpretation.

Eliot and Gadamer's repudiation of this project does not depend on the obviously enormous difficulties which led many to reject it as unworkable. One could grant the remote possibility that with sufficient historical research, imagination, and luck we might see what Shakespeare saw when first contemplating his completed *Hamlet*, and even grant what seems impossible, that we could know that such coincidence of understanding obtained. All this would not blunt the principal point of the Eliot-Gadamer rejection, which is more normative and pragmatic than epistemological. For the main reason we understand and should understand the works of past masters differently from the way they and their contemporaries understood their works is that we necessarily see them as the works of *past* masters, while obviously they could not understand them as such. As Eliot incisively puts it:

> the difference between the present and the past is that the conscious present is an awareness of the past in a way and to an extent which the past's awareness of itself cannot show.
>   Someone said: 'The dead writers are remote from us because we *know* so much more than they did'. Precisely, and they are that which we know. (*SE*, 16)

This point may be clarified and elaborated by noting that we wish to understand the literary works in our tradition not only because of but in terms of the role they have played in a past history which leads up to our present situation. For it is their relation to this situation which originally prompts us to try to understand them. Therefore, to seek a purified understanding of Shakespeare as he understood himself by totally forgetting both his posthumous meaning and our own situation would be to forget why we wanted to understand Shakespeare in the first place. Whether or not such total historical and self-effacement can be sanely achieved, it seems clear that it cannot be reasonably desired as the prime goal of interpretation. And the same holds not only for our understanding of works of more contemporary authors but for an author's retrospective understanding of his own work. For he will tend to and wish to understand his past work in the light of his development and present situation; to understand one's past is not to indulge in an impossible escapist fantasy of reliving it, but to bring it to bear in coping with the present to which it led or contributed.[15]

The passage of time, our consciousness of it, and the effects that history and our consciousness of it have on our understanding: these factors are also at the heart of Gadamer's hermeneutic philosophy and generate his central notions of 'effective history' and 'the effective historical consciousness'. This consciousness seeks to maximize awareness of both the history and the historicity of our understanding of the past, 'at once the consciousness obtained in the course of history and determined by history, and the very consciousness of this gaining and determining' (*TM*, xxi-xxii). Gadamer's 'principle of effective history' concerns 'the effectivity of history within understanding itself'. Our understanding of literature is never

---

[15] Eliot is far from dismissing the value of historical research and the attempt to understand the historical context and point of view of past authors and their original readers; indeed he often insists on it (e.g. *TC*, 17). His radical historicism simply maintains that the only way we can profitably do this is by our own collaborative reconstruction of that point of view and comparison of it to our contemporary viewpoint. For the only way that an author's viewpoint can be real for us, the only 'cash value' of the notion, is in terms of some (actual or possible) reconstruction of it which we can accept.

really directed at and controlled by texts as isolated, unrelated objects but as elements in a tradition extending and relating to us through 'their effect in history (which also includes the history of research)' and the accumulated meaning they have accrued through history. Any attempt to understand an historical text (or event) is 'always subject to the effect of effective history ... [which] determines in advance both what seems to us worth enquiring about and what will appear as an object of investigation' (*TM*, 267-268). Thus, again, the interpretative aim of imaginatively erasing all trace of such history to achieve a purely unmediated under-standing of a literary work as originally understood seems not only quixotic but perverse and impoverishing, since its understanding will be richer and more fruitful for us when seen as 'part of the whole of the tradition in which the [present] age takes an objective interest and in which it seeks to understand itself' (*TM*, 263).

Gadamer, then, clearly follows Eliot in inculcating that our primary interest in understanding the literature of the past is the better under-standing of our present which is a product of that past. The formative presence of the past in the present underlies the importance of what Eliot calls 'the historical sense' (a clear prefiguration of Gadamer's 'effective historical consciousness') which he deems 'indispensable' for a writer. This sense 'involves a perception, not only of the pastness of the past, but of its presence' and 'makes a writer most acutely conscious of his place in time' (*SE*, 14). It is no less crucial to the critic whose 'work is twofold: to interpret the past to the present, and to judge the present in the light of the past.'[16] 'The important critic is the person who is absorbed in the present problems of art, and who wishes to bring the forces of the past to bear upon the solution of these problems' (*SW*, 37-38). But we should not forget that our understanding of the past is itself conditioned by our present situation (to which the past, however, contributed), and thus in this sense we shall 'not find it preposterous that the past should be altered by the present as much as the present is directed by the past' (*SE*, 15). Such a view of historical and literary understanding does not entail that meanings must change radically and discontinuously in a way that precludes any *relatively* shared and stable transhistorical understanding. However, it does mean that we should abandon the idea that the proper understanding of a literary work is a pure perception and faithful reflection of an immutably fixed meaning given once and for all in a uniquely correct canonical understanding of the work (which might never be known to us or articulated in interpretation). Yet if this neutrally reflective model of understanding is rejected, how is valid interpretation to be understood?

[16] 'Experiment in Criticism', 225.

IV

Before pursuing this question in the direction of hermeneutic theory, there is perhaps a more puzzling question to ask if we refuse to forsake the reflective objectivist model. It is a question which Eliot apparently asked himself and boldly answered. If the meaning of a poem is fixed and determinate in itself, expressed in its particular language and independent of our subsequent interpretation, how can any articulated interpretation of it ever be true? Given that its precise meaning is only expressed in its particular words, to interpret the poem or expound its meaning by paraphrase or textual exegesis is to substitute or supplement other words which do not belong to the poem and thus go beyond the meaning of the poem as given in its specific words. Since any interpretation of the work must depart from its original words, if only by supplementation, and since to depart from its original worded statement would be to depart from its original meaning, how can any interpretation be true? Why indeed should interpretation be thought legitimate at all?

Eliot's answer, in his early objectivist days, was shockingly bold and simple. Interpretation, since it cannot be true, is rejected as an illegitimate pursuit. To induce the proper understanding of a literary work one may supply background facts and comparisons with other works, but one cannot accurately represent a work's meaning by trying to express its meaning in other words.

> *Qua* work of art, the work of art cannot be interpreted; there is nothing to interpret; we can only criticize it according to standards, in comparison to other works of art; and for 'interpretation' the chief task is the presentation of relevant historical facts which the reader is not assumed to know. (*SE*, 142)

> ... it is fairly certain that 'interpretation' ... is only legitimate when it is not interpretation at all, but merely putting the reader in possession of facts which he would otherwise have missed. (*SE*, 32)

And the same objectivist anti-interpretative message underlies Eliot's attack on impressionist critics who by trying to put their interpretative 'impressions into words ... begin to create something else' and thus distort the work's real meaning (*SW*, 5).[17]

In short, given that understanding is conceived as accurate reflection of a fixed and fully determinate meaning which the given literary work expresses better than any other text could, the whole idea of interpretation becomes questionable. The way lies open not only to abjural of interpreta-

_____

[17] These views from early objectivist essays of 1919-1923 are applied to interpretative theatrical performance, where Eliot objects to such interpretation and appeals for a drama 'which needs only to be completed [by performance] and cannot be altered by each interpretation' (*SE*, 115).

tion but to the radical deconstructionist argument that since all interpretative readings are necessarily misreadings, supplementing or covering the text, there can be no valid interpretation, and the work will mean whatever we make it mean. This argument may seem self-refutingly to rely on the contradictory premise that the work's meaning is something fixed which further articulated interpretations cannot help but misrepresent. But it can be defended as dialectically showing how the traditional assumptions and aims of interpretation – the mirroring of fixed meaning and its elaborative articulation – are radically aporetic. In any case, this deconstructive argument for the necessity of misreading, which Eliot's attack on interpretation clearly adumbrates, has proven very helpful in challenging criticism's dogmatic faith in the correspondence model of literary understanding. Unfortunately, it has sometimes induced a contrary sceptical dogmatism, certain that any form of valid literary understanding is impossible, that all reading is necessarily misreading.

Eliot apparently recognized that the reflective, correspondence model of understanding, when coupled with the undeniable human need to interpret literature, could easily engulf literary criticism in sceptical confusion, and this perhaps contributed to his eventually rejecting the correspondence ideal of objectivity for the notion of consensus. Moreover, for Eliot, consensus regarding literary interpretation need not be complete but should allow room for variety of individual response.

The realization that literary interpretation is an inalienable human impulse and the conception of the literary work's meaning as a function both of consensus and of individual response are prominent points in Eliot's self-conscious declaration of 1930 that he had changed his 'previous skepticism' for a new recognition of the importance of interpretation.[18] He now admits to seeing the interpretation of literature as Bradley saw metaphysics' interpretation of the universe – as 'the finding of bad reasons for what we believe upon instinct; but to find these reasons is no less an instinct'. Our 'impulse' to grasp and elucidate a work's meaning is 'fundamental' and 'imperative'; and as for the meaning of a work (even a work of one's own authorship): 'its meaning to others, at least so far as there is some consensus of interpretation among persons apparently qualified to interpret, is quite as much a part of it as what it means to oneself.'

However, though interpretative consensus may provide a 'solid and enduring' basis for interpretative legitimacy (a shared sense of the work's meaning or shared set of assumptions or conventions for determining it), Eliot does not see interpretation as ever yielding or requiring for its validity the universal agreement of all competent interpreters as to the entirety of the work's meaning. In a valid critical interpretation there will be 'some part that can be accepted' but also 'some part which other readers can

---

[18] See T.S. Eliot, 'Introduction', in G. W. Knight, *The Wheel of Fire* (1930, London: Methuen, 1962). Quotations in this paragraph are from pages xiii and xvi-xvii.

reject'.[19] This is because, as Eliot later insisted, our interpretation will and should relate not only to the community of shared meanings and responses but to our particular situation and interests. The real aim of interpretation could not be simply maximum consensus, since such an aim could easily be achieved by proposing interpretative statements vague and general enough to command virtually universal assent (especially if we allow interpretative disjunctives like 'The work is *I* or not-*I*').

What then does interpretation seek if not the accurate reflection of an already fixed meaning or a set of interpretative statements to which all would assent? The truth is probably that the basic aims of interpretation are irreducibly plural and that consequently criteria of interpretative validity vary in relation to these different aims and to the different pragmatic contexts and constraints of the interpreter and his audience. To try to avoid this plurality by insisting that literary interpretation always aims at revealing the work's meaning is not simply unhelpful as abysmally vague (meaning of what sort and to whom?). It is also misleading in suggesting that there exists some determinate object 'the work's meaning' which already autonomously exists as the target of our understanding. Meaning, as Wittgenstein maintained, is not a separate object but simply the correlate of understanding something; and therefore, as Eliot realized, the interpreter's aim is better conceived as providing understanding of the work than as discussing or expounding its meaning (*OPP*, 113-115).[20] This more perspicuous formulation, however, does not dissolve interpretative plurality, for there surely seem to be more than one mode or standard of understanding in the interpretative practices we find fruitful. The understanding sought by the textual critic piously reconstructing his text is hardly that of the post-structuralist playfully deconstructing it. Contemporary criticism is indeed torn by the division between reading with and against the text, between the hermeneutics of acceptance and of demystificatory suspicion. Moreover, even within a given mode, standards of interpretative validity will vary with context: what is adequate for the Sunday paper may not do for the lecture hall or the academic journals, whose standards are themselves hardly uniform and consistent. The attempt to weed out interpretative variety by appeal to the concepts of literature and criticism is gainless, since they themselves are essentially contested with respect to these very issues of 'literary meaning' and 'critical interpretation'.

However, having recognized the stubborn variety of aims and standards, we can point to a twofold principle of literary interpretation which seems to underlie most established interpretative practices and seems widely endorsed by critics of very different persuasions. It could be

[19] *Ibid.*, xviii.
[20] For elaboration of this view of Wittgenstein, see G. P. Baker and P.M.S. Hacker, *Wittgenstein: Meaning and Understanding* (Oxford: Blackwell, 1984), 29-45.

called 'coherent comprehensiveness of understanding', for it aims at connectively constituting a greater wealth of meaningful features into a more coherent whole.[21] This principle dominantly informs Eliot's account of literary meaning and interpretation, making it strikingly holistic. From the beginning of his critical career, the holistic inclination is evident in his famous emphasis on the meaning that the literary tradition as an organic whole affords the individual works and authors who belong to it (*SE*, 15-17; 23-24); and holistic chords are also heard in his defense of Jonson's drama (1919) as requiring us to be 'alert to the whole before we apprehend the significance of any part' (*SE*, 156). However, at this stage interpretative holism is restrained by the explicit rejection of interpretation inspired by his regard for an alternative model of meaning – correspondence to the independently real.

By the time Eliot lifted this restraint in his 1930 'Introduction' to Knight's interpretation of Shakespearean tragedy, holism had become and remained the supreme and unchallenged principle of literary meaning and interpretation. Eliot does not merely concur with Knight that the interpreter's 'first duty must be to grasp the whole design' of the play; he takes holism further to seek a unified design or pattern in an author's entire corpus, the entire 'work of one artist as a whole', which he

[21] Considerations of coherence and comprehensiveness obviously direct the theory and practice of New Criticism with its emphasis on organic form and ambiguity-rich unity, and are clearly reflected in Beardsley's interpretative 'Principles of Congruence and Plenitude' [M.C. Beardsley, *Aesthetics* (New York: Harcourt Brace, 1958), 144-147]. They are similarly at work in the attempts of historical or intentionalist critics to explain as much of the text as they can in terms of its coherence with the historical circumstances, outlook, or authorial intention which generated it. Thus, even the arch-intentionalist E.D. Hirsch emphasizes that 'the reading must account for each linguistic component in the text' and that when faced with alternative readings that do so, 'the interpreter chooses the reading which best meets the criterion of coherence', which for Hirsch ultimately means coherence with the 'reconstruction of relevant aspects in the author's outlook' [E.D. Hirsch, *Validity in Interpretation* (New Haven: Yale University Press, 1967), 236-237].

Roland Barthes expresses structuralism's commitment to the twofold principle of coherent comprehensiveness while abandoning the goal of reflective truth for that of validity. The function of criticism is not to discover the truth of an author like Proust, but 'to evolve its own language and to make it as coherent and logical, that is as systematic, as possible, so that it can render an account of, or better still "integrate" (in the mathematical sense) the greatest possible quantity of Proust's language' [R. Barthes, 'Criticism as Language', in D. Lodge (ed.), *Twentieth Century Criticism: A Reader* (London: Longman, 1977), 650]. Similarly eschewing the notion of truth (if not also validity), post-structuralist Derrida resorts to the principle of comprehensiveness to define the most 'powerful' interpretations. 'There are interpretations which account for more meaning and this is the criterion.' ['An Interview with Jacques Derrida', *The Literary Review* (Edinburgh), 14 (1980), 21].

Even theorists who emphasize the institutional factors governing our judgments of interpretative validity would have to admit that a principle of coherent-comprehensiveness is at work here as well: the most acceptable or powerful interpretations being generally those which successfully combine, balance, and coherently hold together the most institutionally valued interpretative perspectives and strategies. For an interesting discussion of comprehensiveness and institutional acceptance as factors governing the validity of interpretation, see K.M. Newton, 'Validity in Interpretation', *British Journal of Aesthetics*, 25 (1985), 207-219.

declares to be 'a work of art' as well.[22] Two years later Eliot has followed his holistic principle of literary meaning to very radical conclusions about Shakespearean interpretation: 'we may say confidently that the full meaning of any one of his plays is not in itself alone, but ... in its relation to all of Shakespeare's plays, earlier and later; we must know all of Shakespeare's work in order to know any of it' (*SE*, 193).[23]

To avoid difficulties attaching to the problematic notion of 'full meaning', the first assertion may be construed convincingly as the idea that the better we understand Shakespeare's work as a whole, the better we shall be able to understand his individual plays. But the second assertion seems too extreme. For not only do we apparently understand or 'know' individual plays without knowing the entire corpus, it seems impossible to come to understand or know the entire corpus without first understanding or knowing the individual works which constitute it. This problem concerns the famous hermeneutic circle, and Eliot's holistic account of literary meaning needs to be seen within its ambit.

V

There are two aspects or versions of the hermeneutic circle. The most familiar and first formulated concerns the circular interdependence of parts and whole. For example, our understanding of the whole of a drama obviously depends on understanding its parts: its characters, actions, speeches, etc. But, on the other hand, we cannot properly understand the individual parts without understanding their place and function in the whole to which they contribute. This apparent circularity extends beyond the organic unities of art and arguably pervades virtually all linguistic meaning. For the meaning of a sentence obviously depends on the meaning of its component words, but the precise meaning of these words here may be said to depend on their context and role within the whole sentence. Not only hermeneutic philosophers have maintained that 'a word has meaning only in the context of a sentence'.[24]

---

[22] See Eliot's 'Introduction', in Knight, xix, xvii. Knight himself claims that each of the Shakespearean tragedies he treats needs to be interpreted 'in its totality' as 'a visionary whole' with both 'spatial and temporal unity' (2, 3, 11).

[23] Eliot seemed to be moving towards a similar view with respect to Dante in his 1929 essay, but it is never so explicitly or extremely stated. See *SE*, 262, 271.

[24] This dictum is central to Frege's and the early Wittgenstein's views of language, but also important for the later Wittgenstein's anti-Fregean, anti-Tractarian approach. It can serve these conflicting views because it can be very differently interpreted: either as a formal or structural principle where the meaning of a sub-sentential expression is actually fixed only by its structural relations with the rest of the sentence and where individual words are therefore denied any meaning at all outside of actual sentences; or, on the other hand, it can be interpreted as a principle of background use. Without a background of sentences used to say things, i.e. without a background of language-use, words could not have their meaning. This second interpretation can therefore nicely account for the later Wittgenstein's apparent sentence-language contextualism, 'to understand a sentence means to understand a

Disregarding such larger philosophical claims, we can certainly say that for Eliot the meaning and beauty of the parts of a literary whole depend on their context within that whole, which itself depends, of course, on its constituent parts. He notes that Shakespeare's line 'Never, never, never, never, never', so thrillingly meaningful in *King Lear*, would seem senseless babble 'apart from a knowledge of the context'. We cannot really say 'whether the lines give grandeur to the drama or whether it is the drama which turns the words into poetry', since the meaning of parts and whole are so interdependent (*OPP*, 260). But the meaning and music of poetry's words (the two for Eliot being 'indissoluble') depend not only on their immediate context within the whole poem, but also on their place in the context of their uses and assocations outside the work (*OPP*, 32-33). Nor should we forget the important dimension of meaning that the literary work (or author's corpus) derives from its particular context within the literary tradition. Finally, to all these contextual factors we must add the context of interpretation – the interpreter's situation and his aims of understanding. Recognizing that the meaning of any piece of literature is largely determined by context, Eliot also recognized that the contexts which determine literary meaning extend in different and ever widening ways: from line to work to corpus to period or genre to literary tradition, to literary-critical-cultural tradition. Moreover, given the continuing development of literary and critical traditions and the inevitable change of interpretative situations, the context of a text has in principle no fixed limit; and if meaning depends on context, it follows that a text in principle has no fixed meaning.

Having rejected the standard of authorial intention, can we find another way to escape the changing circles of context and guarantee some fixed meaning for a text? One traditional way out of the contextual circle is to base all meaning ultimately on certain foundational meaning units whose meaning is firmly fixed by reference to the independently, extra-linguistically real. The meaning of these linguistic elements would be independent of the wholes they form, and that of the wholes could be reduced to functions of the elementary parts. This was the strategy of logical atomism, which Eliot came to reject with his rejection of its correspondence model and which anyway proved itself unworkable by the mid-1930s, failing to generate adequate constructions from its more elementary parts. Another strategy for neutralizing the effect of context

---

language' (*PI*, 199), which would be hard to explain by the first. For surely we do not need to know the actual relations of a particular sentence with all the other sentences of the language in order to know its meaning. These different interpretations of linguistic contextualism are discussed in Baker and Hacker, 145-170.

Applying these two interpretative modes to Eliot's contextualism of tradition, one could say that if Eliot ever maintained that no work of art has *any* meaning (as opposed to its complete or proper meaning) alone and apart from tradition, he could only be right according to the second interpretation. That is, without the background of any tradition of art, we can attach no meaning to an individual work of art, for we could not distinguish it and understand it as art.

on linguistic meaning is by appeal to shared conventions of usage. But these are too flexible to determine meaning univocally, need to be supplemented by contextual factors for their proper application, and, moreover, vary in different historical or cultural contexts.

Finding contextualism unavoidable and realizing the need for literary understanding to move in repeated circles from parts to whole (often only an anticipated whole) and whole back to parts, Eliot sought to exploit contextualism as a principle which can afford greater meaning to whatever piece of literature is placed in context. He therefore refused to confine the contextual framework narrowly to the level of individual works, as New Criticism typically did, but instead advocated more comprehensive contexts which engaged not only wider literary dimensions but also extra-literary interests. One of the chief values of a literary tradition is its provision of a shared, comprehensive and coherent context which can afford richer meaning and understanding to its constituent works and participant interpreters. Indeed, it is only participation in a literary tradition which affords the practical knowledge of semantic strategies that enables an individual to make sense of a text; just as it is only such participation that provides an author with the same sort of linguistic knowledge and resources to create a meaningful text.

But a tradition and the network of structuring norms and practices which constitute it are not forever fixed, but rather continually challenged and refashioned by the changing needs of the present. A tradition is something essentially contested, the product not merely of cooperative consensus but of competitive conflict as to how it should be preserved and extended. Participant interpreters of a tradition are motivated by their somewhat different situations and consequent interests to understand its texts in different though mutually comprehensible ways, disagreement emerging from an assumed background of some agreement. It is, of course, wrong to demand or even hope for an understanding beyond all situation and interests. For even if, *per impossibile*, it were attainable, what situation or interest could it serve?

The upshot of these remarks is that the interpretative aim of coherent comprehensiveness cannot be erected into any fixed standard or terminal ideal of complete, absolute, unenhanceable understanding. For such an ideal presupposes a totalized, all-comprehensive context, but given the open-ended nature of tradition this totality is precluded. Eliot, therefore, realized the pragmatic truth that what we consider 'full understanding' merely counts as such 'only within a limited field of discourse, but unless you limit fields of discourse, you can have no discourse at all' (*SE*, 270-271).[25] Similarly untenable is the ideal or standard of an all-inclusive

[25] Eliot's recognition that the notion of full understanding is something pragmatically and contextually determined and thus extremely flexible can also be seen through his own quickly changing uses of it. After claiming that with Dante's *Divine Comedy* 'we cannot extract the full

understanding relative to time *t*, since the understandings of a text achieved from different perspectives or reading strategies within the global context of 'tradition at *t*' are often uncombinable, involving differences, conflicts, and incommensurabilities which defy integration into a satisfactorily coherent understanding. Nor can we even convincingly identify the most valid interpretation with that taken from the widest possible coherent perspective; for, as Eliot himself seems to realize, greatly enlarging the critical perspective will tend to block our appreciative awareness of valuable details which only emerge clearly from a narrower focus (*OPP*, 191).

Since logical considerations do not determine a particular holistic context as necessary or privileged for the proper understanding of literature, the acceptable contexts for interpreting literature are therefore pragmatically determined in a variety of ways which reflect our different literary interests. We may be formalist interpreters of individual poems or philosophical interpreters of nineteenth-century romanticism; though within such varying contexts or perspectives the principles of coherence and comprehensiveness still seem to govern interpretative cogency. Moreover, as an important aspect of interpretative strategy with great bearing on how interpretation will proceed, the notion of 'proper or appropriate context' is also essentially contested. Eliot's frequent claim that the author's corpus as a whole provides the most appropriate if not exclusively adequate context for literary understanding is not innocently advanced as a disinterested observation. It obviously reflects his own interests as a poet preoccupied with forming a coherently developing, comprehensive corpus of his own; and it pragmatically exhorts us to adopt the critical context in which he prefers both to understand and be understood.

As interpretative contexts are largely determined by our interests, by the things we want to understand and derive from literature, these in turn depend chiefly on what we expect we *can* understand and gain from literature. And such expectations are primarily formed by our literary critical tradition, our entrenched practices of interpreting texts. This is why we may feel deeply constrained and bound to our ways of interpreting, as if they were somehow more necessary or natural than the inherited product of pragmatic decisions of past interpreters, which can be overcome and supplanted by new ways of reading. However, as long as our (quite various) entrenched contexts and modes of interpretation are found rewarding, there is no reason to reject them for depending on

---

significance of any part without knowing the whole', Eliot immediately goes on to cite a part which 'we can read with full comprehension' before 'we come to fit the episode into its place in the whole Comedy' (*SE*, 244-246). The point is that the meaning, comprehension, or understanding of this part is full enough for the purpose at hand of providing the pleasurable stimulation to want to know more of the poem and know it better. This movement of understanding stimulating further understanding will be discussed below.

'arbitrary' [i.e. contingent] decisions rather than logical or natural necessity. *That* would be a very arbitrary decision in the vitiating sense of 'arbitrary' (i.e. 'unreasonable'). None the less, their proven value cannot render familiar critical contexts and strategies immune from criticism or neglect, for we are enjoined to advance or create those contexts and strategies we judge most rewarding. Such judgments will tend to change with changing circumstances, and so perhaps may the rewards we seek from understanding literature. Eliot, we recall, held literature's primary and most permanent reward to be enjoyment; he maintained that enjoyment is at once the preliminary stimulus and the consummatory aim of interpretation. Understanding stems from enjoyment and returns to issue in it. This temporal circuit of interpretative pleasure pertains to the hermeneutic circle's other dimension, which we shall now consider.

The second dimension of the hermeneutic circle concerns what might be called the relationship of fore-understanding to interpretation. It can be traced back to Heidegger's statement that 'any interpretation which is to contribute understanding, must already have understood what is to be interpreted'.[26] Elucidating this idea with respect to a literary text, we can say that before and while we try to interpret its meaning we must be struck and directed by some sense of what we are trying to interpret. It is our initial perception of the text as something meaningful and worth understanding more fully that generates our desire to interpret it. Moreover, our attempt to interpret is not only motivated but guided by this prior understanding, though it be vague and inchoate. For we form our interpretative hypothesis about the work (or accept or reject alternative interpretations) on the basis of what we already understand as properly belonging to the work rather than falsely foisted onto it. But how do we determine whether our guiding understanding is valid and not a misunderstanding? We might think we could do this by measuring it against the identity or meaning of the work. But since the work's meaning or constitutive identity is not self-evidently given but is precisely what is in question, we would first have to determine more clearly what this meaning or identity is. Yet to do this we must interpret, and thus we can only test our prior understanding by subsequent interpretation. In other words, though interpretation of the text must be based on our understanding of it; this understanding requires interpretation of the text for its own clarification and justification. But that interpretation, to continue the circular movement, depends again on the very understanding it has to sharpen or validate.

Considerations of this sort might induce assent to Gadamer's radical claim that 'all understanding is interpretation' (*TM*, 350). This claim, however, is misleading in suggesting that we can never understand anything without interpreting it. For if this were so, how could we

    [26] M. Heidegger, *Being and Time* (New York: Harper and Row, 1962), 194.

understand the interpretation itself? It too would have to be interpreted, and so would its interpretation, and so on *ad infinitum*. As Wittgenstein notes 'any interpretation still hangs in the air along with what it interprets'. Interpretation must ultimately depend on some prior understanding, some 'way of grasping ... which is *not* an interpretation' (*PI*, 198, 201).[27] This is simply a point of philosophical grammar about the way these two notions are related.

Gadamer's dictum also misleadingly suggests that no valid or useful distinction can be drawn between understanding and interpreting. I understand most utterances I hear in English without interpreting them; I interpret only those that strike me as somehow unclear or not sufficiently understood. To defend the conflation of understanding and interpretation by arguing that in simply understanding those alleged uninterpreted utterances I am in fact interpreting sounds as words (or perhaps further that my nervous system interprets vibrations as sounds) seems to stretch the use of 'interpretation' to no productive purpose and to confound a frequently helpful distinction between grasping or understanding something and interpreting that which is grasped or understood. Though it may often be unclear where simple understanding ends and interpretation begins, there are many contexts where the distinction is clear enough to be pragmatically justified. I can understand what someone said but need to interpret what he meant by saying it. I can understand a poem's words but need to interpret its point or message or underlying pattern.

What is correct in Gadamer's claim is that there is no rigid or absolute divide but an essential continuity and interdependence between understanding and interpretation. What is now immediately understood may once have been the product of a labored interpretation and may form the basis for further interpretation. Many things are felt to be insufficiently understood until they are interpreted by us or for us. We seek an interpretation because we are not satisfied with the understanding we already have – feeling it partial, obscure, shallow, fragmented or simply dull – and want to make it fuller or more adequate. Yet the superior interpretation sought must be guided by that inadequate understanding. We no longer feel the need to interpret further when the

---

[27] This prior understanding on which interpretation and further understanding depend need not be a self-conscious, explicit, or theoretical understanding, but can simply be an ability to perform or respond properly in conformity with certain rules whose mastery constitutes understanding, be they rules of language or of arithmetic. Wittgenstein thus maintains that 'to understand a language means to be master of a technique' (*PI*, 199), though not necessarily to have conscious, explicitly formulated knowledge of the rules governing this technique. He similarly emphasizes that brute training and drill form the foundation on which understanding can develop and eventually become explicit and self-conscious. See *PI*, 86; L.Wittgenstein, *Zettel* (Oxford: Blackwell, 1967), para. 419. For detailed discussion of Wittgenstein's idea of understanding as something akin to an ability and as relying on a foundation of prior training or inculcating drill, see Baker and Hacker, 29-45; 336-346.

new, fuller understanding that interpretation has supplied is felt to be satisfactory. Criteria of what is satisfactory obviously will vary with context and the sort of understanding sought. Wittgenstein put this pragmatic point effectively: 'What happens is not that this symbol cannot be further interpreted, but: I do no interpreting. I do not interpret, because I feel at home in the present picture.'[28]

Eliot is strongly committed to the idea of a fore-understanding, sometimes merely in the form of a primitive perception or anticipation of meaning, which prompts and guides the impulse to interpret literature. The importance of this preliminary apprehension is expressed in a number of places but most clearly in his famous 1929 essay on Dante, where Eliot elaborates on the fact that poetry can communicate or mean something before it is properly understood, and how the pleasurable promise of pleasure that this fore-understanding provides then spurs us on to seek deeper understanding and concommitant enjoyment. Remembering that for Eliot understanding and enjoyment of poetry are not at all sharply 'distinct activities' but intimately and inextricably interrelated,[29] consider the following passage:

> The enjoyment of the *Divine Comedy* is a continuous process. If you get nothing out of it at first, you probably never will; but if from your first deciphering of it there comes now and then some direct shock of poetic intensity, nothing but laziness can deaden the desire for fuller and fuller knowledge ... It is a test (a positive test, I do not assert that it is always valid negatively), that genuine poetry can communicate before it is understood. The impression can be verified on fuller knowledge. I have found ... that about such impressions there was nothing fanciful. They were not due, that is, to *mis*understanding the passage, or to reading into it something not there. (*SE*, 238)

The fore-understanding, initially a sense of communicated meaning before proper understanding is achieved, needs to be 'verified' (i.e. shown not to be simply a misunderstanding) by the fuller understanding achieved through interpretative deciphering which it both prompts and directs. If in trying to 'verify' or work it out we come to see that what was taken as poetry is really empty gibberish, we would conclude that we'd been deluded and that the initial fore-understanding was in fact a misunderstanding. Moreover, even a fuller, successfully worked-out interpretative understanding can serve in turn as a prompting, guiding fore-understanding for still further attempts to deepen or enrich our understanding, so long as it suggests that such attempts could be rewarding, that the work warrants further knowledge. Herein lies much of the reason for the inexhaustible

---

[28] *Zettel*, para. 234.
[29] See *OPP*, 115. This thesis will be fleshed out and closely examined in the following chapter. Other places where Eliot notes the phenomenon of poetic fore-understanding include 'The Social Function of Poetry' and 'The Music of Poetry' (*OPP*, 24, 30).

efforts to interpret and reinterpret great works of literature: it is not because such works are harder to understand, but because we want to understand and know them more deeply.[30]

Gadamer is much more explicit about this process where 'interpretation begins with fore-conceptions that are replaced by more suitable ones' through the interpretative clarification and working-out of these 'fore-meanings' (*TM*, 236).

> A person ... trying to understand a text ... projects before himself a meaning for the text as a whole as soon as some initial meaning emerges in the text ... The working out of this fore-project, which is constantly revised in terms of what emerges as he penetrates into the meaning, is understanding what is there ... The process ... is ... [such] that every revision of the fore-project is capable of projecting before itself a new project of meaning ... This constant process of new projection is the movement of understanding and interpretation ... The only 'objectivity' here is the confirmation of a fore-meaning in its being worked out. The only thing that characterizes the arbitratriness of inappropriate fore-meanings is that they come to nothing in the working-out. (*TM*, 236-237)

Gadamer makes two more important points about the fore-understanding or 'anticipation of meaning' that governs our understanding of texts, both of which were previously recognized by Eliot. First, our anticipations of meaning, fore-conceptions, and fore-understandings are largely a product of belonging to and being trained and educated by a tradition which forms our expectations of textual meaning and makes them more communal than private. Anticipating the recitation of a poem will immediately activate in members of our tradition certain shared expectations of meaning as well as shared strategies for working it out, anticipation of a news-report will evoke certain very different ones. (In Gadamer's words: 'The anticipation of meaning that governs our understanding of a text is not an act of subjectivity, but proceeds from the communality that binds us to the tradition ... in the constant process of education' (*TM*, 261)).

Secondly, crucial to our anticipation of meaning and our idea of working it out is the principle (called 'the fore-conception of completion') 'that only what really constitutes a unity of meaning is intelligible' (*TM*, 261). We expect the text we encounter to issue in some coherent whole when it is worked out and understood. Thus when the text seems incoherent, either in itself or in its relation to our views on the topic it treats, we need to interpret

---

[30] Eliot seems close to suggesting this idea in a passage which also evinces his view that poetic experience needs to be integrated into a larger unity or pattern of life-experience in order to be solidly and lastingly meaningful: 'The experience of a poem is the experience of a moment and of a lifetime. ... [Even an intense] moment which can never be forgotten ... would become destitute of significance if it did not survive in a larger whole of experience, which survives inside a deeper and a calmer feeling. The majority of poems one outgrows and outlives, as one outgrows and outlives the majority of human passions: Dante's is one of those which one can only just hope to grow up to at the end of life' (*SE*, 250-251).

it so that some 'unified meaning can be realized'. We do this either by interpreting the text as more coherent (with itself or with our beliefs) or by interpreting its incoherencies within a coherent explanatory account, e.g. historically or psychologically as the product of an age or mind with different experience, beliefs, or inclinations (*TM*, 262). Interpretation aims to make understanding and its unity of meaning more complete, with the ultimate 'task of revealing a totality of meaning in all its relations'. But since for Gadamer (and Eliot) the meaning relations of a text are never complete as long as the text continues to be read, 'interpretation ... is always a relative and uncompleted movement' toward completion; a movement in whose temporary resting places of satisfying unity 'understanding still finds ... its relative fulfillment' (*TM*, 428-429). These satisfying resting places are what we pragmatically designate as fully or completely understanding a text, and their precise locations and limits are continuously being contested and changed by the text's different interpreters.

Perhaps still more significant is Eliot and Gadamer's insistence that the unity of meaning that literary understanding seeks is not confined to the internal or formal unity of a detached aesthetic object. Instead it deeply engages our own need for unity and our own views about the world and topics treated by the text. Our attempt to understand a text relates the otherness or novelty of the text to the expectations and beliefs we bring to it, and seeks to integrate these dialectical factors into a richer unity of order which enlarges our self and self-understanding. Gadamer therefore claims that aesthetic experience 'is a mode of self-understanding', which by incorporating the radically different experience of art's 'strange universe' into 'the continuity of our existence' affords an enriched 'unity of self-understanding' (*TM*, 86-87). To satisfy man's immense need for meaningful unity and order by creating or inducing more satisfying and comprehensive perceptions of such order is also for Eliot an essential function of art: 'it is ultimately the function of art, in imposing a credible order upon ordinary reality, and thereby eliciting perception of an order *in* reality, to bring us to a condition of serenity, stillness, and reconciliation' (*OPP*, 87). Through our appreciation of art we ultimately aim at organizing our tastes, beliefs, and experiences 'into a whole' which will satisfy our 'need and craving for perfection and unity' and for self-realization:

> we aim in the end at a theory of life, or a view of life, ... to terminate our enjoyment of the arts in a philosophy, and our philosophy in a religion – in such a way that the personal to oneself is fused and completed in the impersonal and general, not extinguished but enriched, expanded, developed, and more itself by becoming more something not itself.[31]

---

[31] 'Poetry and Propaganda', 598-599.

The manner in which Eliot thinks self-understanding, self-enlargement, and perhaps even wisdom can be achieved through the reader's interactive encounter with works of literature will be presented in the next chapter. There we shall also consider how, for Eliot, this edifying encounter is, paradoxically, nothing other than a game of pleasure.

Chapter 6

Eliot on Reading:
Pleasure, Games, and Wisdom

> ... I searched all the ways
> That lead to pleasure, advancement and praise.
> Delight in sense, in learning and in thought,
> Music and philosophy, curiosity ...

> *Murder in the Cathedral*

I

Eliot frequently speaks of poetry as essentially a game or amusement whose first and foremost function is to give pleasure. The poet, says Eliot, 'would like to be something of a popular entertainer, ... would like to convey the pleasures of poetry ... As things are, and as fundamentally they must always be, poetry is not a career, but a mug's game' (*TUP*, 154). Surely much of the point and appeal of these remarks is their deflationary contrast to the over-lofty claims made for poetry since romanticism, claims which continue to be heard in Arnold's ideas of poetry as criticism of life and surrogate of religion and which extend to modernism with Richards' claim that 'poetry ... is capable of saving us'.[1] In mordant debunking of the poet's putative status as world legislator, prophet, and savior, Eliot says he would be pleased to secure for the poet 'a part to play in society as worthy as that of the music-hall comedian' (*TUP*, 154).

But Eliot's idea of poetry as an amusement or game is much more than an ironic rhetorical ploy against romantic attitudes. It contains a positive and complex view of what poetry is and how it satisfies. Eliot wants to remind us of 'that simple truth that literature is primarily literature, a means of refined and intellectual pleasure'.[2] However, he also realizes that this

---

[1] See I.A. Richards, *Science and Poetry* (London: Kegan Paul, 1926), 86. The remark is cited by Eliot (*TUP*, 124) in the course of an extended discussion of Arnold's and Richards' views. It is noteworthy that after Eliot's criticism of this assertion, Richards omitted it from subsequent editions of the book.

[2] See T.S. Eliot, 'Experiment in Criticism', *The Bookman*, 70 (1929), 227. See also *OPP*, 18.

truth is really not all that simple to understand or elucidate properly; for it does not mean (though it might seem to suggest) that literature is a mere means to obtain some external end of pleasure. Nor does it mean that in aiming essentially at pleasure, literature is confined to satisfying our sensual or emotional faculties, and is therefore not significantly connected with improving thought or communicating wisdom. For the pleasure is described as *intellectual* pleasure. Because of the likely misunderstandings that it is apt to provoke, Eliot's claim that literature is a refined game, that 'poetry is a superior amusement', is not confidently offered as an adequately 'true definition, but because if you call it something else, you are likely to call it something still more false' (*SW*, viii-ix). But what substance or value is there in Eliot's preferred view?

The idea of poetry as a superior game or amusement is developed in many ways throughout Eliot's critical corpus. We cannot consider them all, but the first we should consider concerns the character of pleasure or enjoyment derived from poetry. If poetry is a refined game, and since games are activities, the pleasure (enjoyment) of poetry would be that of an activity rather than that of a pleasant sensation. Eliot's idea of poetic pleasure is thus fundamentally Aristotelian.[3] Such pleasure is not a separate sensation or pleasant feeling external to and identifiable apart from the game played, but rather represents the attendant zest or satisfaction with which the game is played or the activity pursued.

For Aristotle, 'pleasure completes the activity' by the dual and reciprocal action of making it more rewarding and thus promoting it. Our pleasure intensifies our interest in the activity which makes us better pursue it, while displeasure conversely impedes it, as does submitting to alien pleasures from other activities. If the pleasures of different activities can conflict and impede their respective activities, then these pleasures must be distinguishable and are so in terms of the activities to which they attend. Our enjoyment of an activity thus logically depends on the constitutive structure of that activity and is inseparable from it. We therefore distinguish the pleasures of different games by the different game-activities to which they are bound. One may enjoy tennis, basketball, and football and perhaps feel similar pleasurable sensations from each. But the enjoyment of each game is clearly distinguishable and understood not in terms of these sensations but in terms of the different activities which constitute the formal object or ground of that pleasure. Different games or, more generally, different activities are differently enjoyable, and each has what Aristotle calls its own 'proper pleasure'. One could not get the pleasure of playing tennis from playing football, nor could one get the pleasure of playing poker from playing chess (*NE*, 1174b31-1175b15).

---

[3] The following sketch and citations from Aristotle's account of pleasure are taken from *Nicomachean Ethics*, bk. X, ch. 4-5, 1174a13-1176a29, in W.D. Ross's translation. A very helpful paper on this subject is J.O. Urmson's, 'Aristotle on Pleasure', in J.M.E. Moravcsik (ed.), *Aristotle* (New York: Doubleday, 1967), 323-333.

For Aristotle, as activities and the objects to which they are directed differ in nature and worth, so do their corresponding pleasures. As seeing is held superior to touching, and thinking superior to all sense perception, so are their corresponding pleasures; and the pleasure of contemplating a fine object is superior to that of contemplating a defective one (*NE*, 1174b15-30; 1175b35-1176a).

Similarly, for Eliot, since appreciating poetry essentially involves thought (albeit chiefly imaginative thought) rather than mere sensation; and since it is directed at a well-formed superior object, it provides a superior pleasure and constitutes a superior amusement. It may seem philistine to think of poetry or any art as an amusement pursued for pleasure, since we typically think of amusements as mere *means* to pass the time or to get pleasurable sensations; and we like to think that we pursue art for its own sake. But once we recognize with Eliot that the pleasure of literature is 'a peculiar kind of pleasure'[4] which only literature can provide and which is logically inseparable from literature itself, the idea that literature is a game or amusement pursued for pleasure no longer treats literature as merely an instrument or means for some external purpose. To pursue the pleasure of literature is thus to pursue it for its own sake, i.e. to appreciate it as literature. Moreover, the value of the literature that amuses us does not solely depend on or derive from its appreciators' enjoyment, but essentially derives from those features of the work whose appreciative understanding is the source of enjoyment; enjoyment being the by-product that attends and completes the appreciative activity. Eliot thus holds that 'every good poet ... has something to give us besides pleasure: for if it were only pleasure, the pleasure itself could not be of the highest kind.' Hence in good poetry the appreciation and pleasure always depends on 'the communication of some new experience, or some fresh understanding of the familiar, or the expression of something we have experienced but have no words for, which enlarges our consciousness or refines our sensibility' (*OPP*, 18).

Thus the pleasure of literature can be supplied only by literature because it is bound up with the activity of appreciating literature. However, since this activity requires that we understand literature, we cannot properly enjoy literature without understanding it. But our enjoyment in turn not only enhances our understanding by adding zest, it also prompts us to achieve a better understanding. We thus cannot sharply isolate the enjoyment of a poem from its understanding, though undoubtedly there are cases where we can say that we understand but do not enjoy, or that we enjoy but do not adequately understand. When Eliot claims that 'the essential function of literary criticism' is 'to promote the understanding and enjoyment of literature', he therefore urges that we 'not think of

---

[4] 'Experiment in Criticism', 232. Roger Scruton seems to make much the same point and argument with respect to aesthetic experience in general. See R. Scruton, *Art and Imagination* (London: Methuen, 1974), 80-83, 246.

enjoyment and *understanding* as distinct activities – one emotional and the other intellectual' *(OPP*, 115). This view is elaborated by Eliot in a passage which further shows the complexity and Aristotelianism of Eliot's view of poetic pleasure.

> To understand a poem comes to the same thing as to enjoy it for the right reasons. One might say that it means getting from the poem such enjoyment as it is capable of giving: to enjoy a poem under a misunderstanding as to what it is, is to enjoy what is merely a projection of our own mind. So difficult a tool to handle, is language, that 'to enjoy' and 'to get enjoyment from' do not seem to mean quite the same thing: that to say that one 'gets enjoyment from' poetry does not sound quite the same as to say that one 'enjoys poetry'. And indeed, the very meaning of 'joy' varies with the object inspiring joy; different poems, even, yield different satisfactions. It is certain that we do not fully enjoy a poem unless we understand it; and on the other hand, it is equally true that we do not fully understand a poem unless we enjoy it. And that means, enjoying it to the right degree and in the right way, relative to other poems ... It should hardly be necessary to add that this implies one *shouldn't* enjoy bad poems – unless their badness is of a sort that appeals to our sense of humour. (*OPP*, 115)

This view, which intimately binds the understanding and pleasure of literature, was meant to help criticism steer a course between two dangerous extremes which are apt to plague it: overemphasis on facts and knowledge about literature with the aim of erecting a science of criticism, and the contrary danger of repudiating the exacting efforts of understanding to exult with irresponsible freedom in the private pursuit of the pleasures of the text. As Eliot's early attack on impressionistic criticism was directed at exposing and correcting the latter danger, his later theorizing warns against the former, in the one-sidedly narrow search for 'scientific' interpretative knowledge pursued by both historico-biographical criticism and 'the lemon-squeezer school' of New Criticism (*OPP*, 107-118).

Today, in the surge of post-structuralist, deconstructive criticism, we are witnessing a violent reaction to New Critical and structuralist preoccupations with criticism as impersonal knowledge or science. We must be grateful to deconstruction for successfully undermining their scientistic and formalistic presumptions which unprofitably repressed our engagement with literature. Unfortunately, however, in the fervor of its reaction, deconstruction sometimes courts an extreme, unbalanced position where the idea and aim of interpretative understanding is totally rejected to pursue the self-satisfying pleasures of textual misreading. Indeed some deconstructionists have recognized this threat and therefore urge a radical return from pleasure to severe logical rigor.[5] Though Eliot

---

[5] The extremely hedonistic strain of deconstruction (e.g. in Barthes and Hartman) has been attacked by younger deconstructors like Culler and Norris who seek to depict the deconstructionist ideal as one of pure, uncompromising logical rigor, where the aims of

never witnessed the rise of deconstruction, he foresaw the see-saw dangers
of the polar extremes of knowledge and pleasure which continue to plague
critical theory. He therefore urged an account of poetic appreciation where
understanding and pleasure are essentially linked, and where criticism
pursues the golden mean between scientism and hedonism. Criticism
today might well benefit from Eliot's theory and practical wisdom.[6]

II

The intimate interrelation of understanding and enjoying poetry may
justify describing poetry as an amusement; but why liken it to a game?
Bird-watching, stamp-collecting and other hobbies are amusements which
link understanding with enjoyment and are pursued for their own proper
pleasures just as poetry. Yet they are not games, so why should poetry or
literature be considered particularly game-like?

The answer, I think, is that the notion of game, with its correlate notion of
play, displays an array of aspects which are also central to the appreciation
of literature and of art in general. Certainly many philosophers (Kant,
Schiller, and Gadamer, to name but a few) have characterized aesthetic
activity and understanding in terms of play. Perhaps the most crucial and
distinctive aspect of play which makes literary art especially game-like is
that of pretending or temporarily accepting an imagined 'world' that
somehow relates to and bears on what we generally call – in distinction
from games and art – the real world. This feature of pretending or
accepting, which is neither entirely believing nor disbelieving, is fundamental to the very perception of imaginative literature and is at the
heart of 'the issue of poetry and belief' (i.e. whether we can fully appreciate
a poem whose informing beliefs we reject) which so long and hauntingly
preoccupied Eliot. We shall come to this issue soon enough, but first let us
note two crucial functions of pretense in games and art: the taking on of real
seriousness, and the adoption of and self-identification with roles.

Though games are played primarily for amusement and are characteristically distinguished as play from the serious business of life, they
themselves must be taken seriously in order to be rewarding. If we play
tennis or chess with no serious effort to hit the ball or make the best move,
we will not enjoy the game. If we play only 'playfully' rather than seriously,

---

pleasure and appreciation of aesthetic richness are foresworn as temptations to logical
lassitude. [See, for example, J. Culler, *On Deconstruction* (London: Routledge, 1982), 220-225,
240-243; *Barthes* (New York: Oxford University Press, 1983), 91-100; and C. Norris,
Deconstruction: Theory and Practice (London: Methuen, 1982), 92-99.] Thus, for all its helpful
suspicion of misleading, complicity-concealing oppositions, deconstruction seems to have
been misled and divided by the dubious opposition of cognition and pleasure in reading. For
more on this point, see Chapter Eight, pp.219-221, below.

[6] Eliot's changing strategies to avoid the extremes of subjective hedonism and impersonal
scientism are discussed in more detail in Chapter Eight which treats his theory and exercise of
practical wisdom.

we will only be *'playing at'* the game rather than properly playing it. As Gadamer observes, 'only seriousness in playing makes the play wholly play. One who doesn't take the game seriously is a spoilsport' (*TM*, 92).[7] The same obviously goes for appreciating poetry, which can give but minimal enjoyment when not attended to seriously. Though 'seriously' does not mean 'solemnly' here, any more than it does in games.

In playing games seriously we do not typically mistake them for the serious matters of real life, but we temporarily pretend, as it were, that they are, often sparing no effort or risk to win. In the imaginary context or 'world' of the game, one *makes believe* (which is not really to believe) that one's fellow player is an adversary to be soundly beaten, even though he is still recognized as a devoted friend.[8] We temporarily take on new identities as players and as adversaries in play, and in doing so we may learn new things about each other and about our own selves: our playing abilities, our qualities of tenacity and concentration, our latent jealousies, our degree of sportsmanship, etc. Likewise, when we seriously read imaginative literature, even light literature for mere amusement, we take on the role of reader and the consequent identity of an interested, engaged onlooker or inhabitant of the imaginary world depicted by the work we read, a world we accept for the moment without questioning its reality. Such imaginative projections and pretended metamorphoses of the self (which, like games, can afford self-knowledge through self-forgetting make-believe) are what perhaps most clearly distinguishes games and literature from pastimes like stamp-collecting and bird-watching.

However, there is undoubtedly more to the game-literature analogy than pretense. Other important features are structure and the interaction of player or reader with the structure of the game or text. A game is not typically 'free play' but is instead defined in terms of rules, goals and tasks which give structure to the game, individuate it from other games, and distinguish it from the stream of ordinary life. One might argue, as Gadamer does, that no play is really free in an absolute sense, for that would mean it had no constraining structure; and as structureless, aimless activity, it could not be distinguished as play at all. This, however, does not entail that the term 'free play' is without meaning or application, but simply highlights again the pragmatic point that our distinctions (e.g. exact/inexact, complete/ incomplete, free/constrained) only have validity and workable meaning in terms of some context or purpose. 'Free play' takes the meanings it has from its contrast, in different contexts, to play (or work) that is more strictly or explicitly constrained or structured.

[7] H.-G. Gadamer, *Truth and Method* (New York: Crossroads, 1982). References to this book will appear in the text with the abbreviation *TM*.

[8] Of course, since games can be said to be a part of 'real' life or included in it (they are not dreams or illusions), the distinction between them is only a pragmatic one. One of the problems with professional sports is that this distinction between game and real-life business is made extremely tenuous and problematic; and this often sharply affects the spirit of the game.

Certainly our most rewarding games are governed by a network of rules and normative conventions, not all of which need be explicitly formulated. The rules constitute the structure or world of the game, e.g. its division into periods or sets, its touchdowns, runs, penalties, etc. As Gadamer notes, 'The particular nature of a game lies in the rules and structures which prescribe the way that the area of the game is filled' (*TM*, 96). But beyond the explicit rules, there are the unformulated 'rules', conventions, and playing traditions which constitute the particular character and spirit of the game. There is more to the proper play of cricket or tennis than can be learned from a rule book. We need to experience or at least witness the activity of playing in order to understand the nature of the game. As Wittgenstein apparently realized in abandoning the formal calculus model for the game model of language, the rules of a game must be interpreted and applied by the actual practice of players in order for these rules to mean anything.[9] Indeed without changing its explicitly formulated rules, a game may be drastically transformed by the players' changing the manner or spirit in which the rules are interpreted and applied.

A game thus constitutes a somewhat autonomous and make-believe world, replete with its own structure and spirit and distinguished from the actual world and its aims. The game's playing field, says Gadamer, 'sets the sphere of play as a closed world … over against the world of aims' (*TM*, 96). This world is at once limited (hence learnable) yet also complete and consistent in itself. The fact that it does not determine, for instance, whether its players are men or women, or whether or not they shake hands or shower when the game is finished does not make the game incomplete or somehow deficient. Of course, much the same is often said about the literary work and its world. We do not complain that *Hamlet* is deficiently incomplete because it does not specify Hamlet's courses and grades at Wittenberg or the color of his eyes.

Now in playing a game we enter its world, and by becoming players in it we take on new identities, imposing on ourselves the tasks, aims, and rules of the game. The more we get involved in a game, the more deeply we identify or 'lose ourselves' in our role as players in it, the more we submit ourselves to its challenges and constraints. This means that our skill, endurance, and intelligence are tested and exercised, allowing us to gain a better knowledge of our abilities and a greater breadth and aptitude in them. Gadamer thus seems right in maintaining that 'the attraction of a game, the fascination it exerts', allows it to 'master the players' so that whoever plays or 'tries' the game 'is in fact the one who is tried' (*TM*, 95).

But though the structures or rules of a game govern the player who submits to them, the game could not properly exist without its players and only achieves its 'full being' when it is played. Players and their play

---

[9] For more on this point see G.P. Baker and P.M.S. Hacker, *Wittgenstein: Meaning and Understanding* (Oxford: Blackwell, 1984), 48-51.

constitute an essential part of a game. A game whose rules have had no interpretative application, no practice of play, is not in fact a game but a set of rules for a game; and changing the interpretative practice of applying the rules in playing an existent game can radically alter the game's identity. Thus, a game requires an interaction of impersonal structures and rules with their interpretative realization or application by particular players. This vividly mirrors the interaction of the interpreting reader with the structures of the literary text. It is a commonplace that the structures of a literary text are lifeless abstractions until they are given imaginative recreation (interpretative application) by the reader, who (in Ingarden's term) concretizes the work in his reading.[10]

A game thus may be seen as a rule-structured make-believe world, limited but complete and coherent in itself, into which we project ourselves for our amusement; one in which we surrender and transform ourselves as we interpretatively respond to it and interactively actualize or play it out, and which, in testing and exercising us, can provide cognitive enlargement and self-knowledge. Conceived in this way, a game is a strikingly appealing model for literature and its appreciation. Eliot certainly seemed to think so, and his view of literature as a game or amusement is, not surprisingly, complemented by an emphasis on the literary work as an imaginary structured world which we imaginatively enter, interpretatively recreate, and respond to. The nature of this response is (or at least should be) typically more complex than the response of players in a game, since it also involves detaching oneself from the world one entered, and consciously criticizing it (and oneself as accepting, identifying reader) from an external standpoint. Through this complex response, literature can be a particularly rich source of knowledge, and perhaps even wisdom.

Eliot frequently urged that the literary work be appreciated in two different ways or stages, from 'two attitudes both of which are necessary and right to adopt in considering the work of any poet' (*OPP*, 145).[11] First, as an autotelic structured game, it must be sympathetically responded to and assessed on its own terms, i.e. in terms of the internal coherence of its rules and world, and the beauty and satisfaction they afford. This is when we imaginatively accept and enter the poet's world, 'when we isolate him, when we try to understand the rules of his own game, adopt his own point of view' (*ibid.*). For unless we at least provisionally accept and give ourselves

---

[10] See R. Ingarden, *The Literary Work of Art* (Evanston, Ill.: University of Illinois Press, 1973).

[11] Eliot sometimes speaks of the reader's appreciative response to the literary work as three-staged: 'you have to give yourself up, and then recover yourself, and the third moment is having something to say, before you have wholly forgotten both surrender and recovery.' [See T. S. Eliot's letter to Stephen Spender quoted in Spender's 'Remembering Eliot,' in A. Tate (ed.), *T.S. Eliot: The Man and His Work* (New York: Delacorte Press, 1966), 55-56.] This clearly suggests that in insistently pointing to two dimensions or stages of reading appreciation, Eliot is primarily interested in maintaining the complexity of the reading and critical process, not necessarily a rigid duality.

to the world, rules, and point of view of the work, we will be unable to get involved or caught up in the work and thus be unable to understand and enjoy it properly.

But, secondly, we must detach ourselves from the work we have entered and accepted, in order to examine it with respect to external standards involving the wider contexts of the literary tradition and even ultimately of the extra-literary world as well. This second stage is when a poet's work is assessed in terms of how it promotes the literary tradition, 'when we measure him by outside standards, most pertinently by the standards of language and of something called Poetry, in our own language and in the whole history of European literature' (*ibid.*). The first perspective should indicate, as it were, whether we are dealing with literature or sub-literature. The second perspective will help us decide whether it is literature that should be greatly admired or emulated; and here not only is consideration of the standards of the past and the literary needs of the present and future required, but philosophical, social, and ethico-religious considerations may also be appropriate.

Eliot demands and employs both perspectives. In his 1936 essay on Milton (from which we have most recently been quoting), Eliot concedes Milton's greatness from the first perspective but criticizes him from the second. In essays on Ben Jonson and Swinburne he takes the internal perspective to defend both poets against the charge of superficiality and lack of realism, by maintaining that the limited worlds they create to amuse us are satisfactory, consistent, and complete by their own rules, even if these worlds are much more meager than, say, Shakespeare's.[12] But, in Eliot's opinion, Jonson and Swinburne differ with respect to the second perspective. While Jonson's imaginary world presents a model and point of view which should be both appealing and instructive for contemporary literature, Swinburne offers a world which the modernist no longer finds very interesting or helpful in promoting literary progress.

Of Jonson and the alleged flatness of his world and characters, Eliot argues:

> We cannot call a man's work superficial when it is the creation of a world; a man cannot be accused of dealing superficially with the world which he himself has created; the superficies *is* the world. Jonson's characters conform to the logic of the emotions of their world ... and this logic illuminates the actual world, because it gives us a new point of view from which to inspect it. (*SE*, 156)

In its small-scale completeness, in its highlighting by flat simplification which makes it 'an art of great caricature', 'the "world" of Jonson is sufficiently large' so that we can derive not only enjoyment; but also, with regard to the second perspective, we can gain beneficial 'creative stimulus'

---

[12] See 'Ben Jonson' in *Selected Essays*, and 'Swinburne as a Poet' in *The Sacred Wood*.

as well as 'instruction in two-dimensional life' and the art of caricature (*SE*, 159, 147).

Neither is Swinburne's work to be condemned as a superficial 'sham, just as bad verse is a sham'. For it too does not pretend to be something it is not, i.e. a full representation of actual life. 'The world of Swinburne does not depend upon some other world which it simulates; it has the necessary completeness and self-sufficiency for justification and permanence ... The deductions are true to the postulates' (SW, 149), i.e. it is consistent as well as complete. However, though Swinburne passes muster from the internal perspective, he is disparaged from the external standpoint. For though his language 'is very much alive, with this singular life of its own', 'the language which is more important to us [i.e. modernists] is that which is struggling to digest and express new objects, new groups of objects, new feelings, new aspects, as, for instance, the prose of Mr. James Joyce or the earlier Conrad' (*SW*, 150).

III

More needs to be said about the complex interaction of reader and text in the appreciation of literature, particularly the interaction of his ordinary beliefs with those which inform the world of the text. This interaction may yield rich cognitive rewards for the reader but equally holds great epistemological and ethical dangers. The question of the cognitive value or disvalue of literary art, its status as purveyor of knowledge or corrupting falsehood, is among the oldest and most central questions of aesthetics. Dating back to Plato, it seems ultimately based on the distinction between art and reality but has since ramified into a host of more particular issues. Though Eliot was much concerned with the general question of literature's cognitive and educational value, he was especially preoccupied with a narrower issue pointedly raised by Richards' work on 'poetry and beliefs'.[13]

Can we, Eliot repeatedly pondered, properly appreciate a poem without sharing the beliefs expressed in or underlying the poem? If not, we could not properly appreciate the works of Shakespeare, Homer, and Dante which present scientific, theological, and moral beliefs which may sharply differ from our own. But since our appreciation of such works clearly seems undiminished by such differences of beliefs, it instead seems to follow that a work's beliefs are unimportant or irrelevant to its literary appreciation. However, if we try to subtract the beliefs from the poetry in order to appreciate it as pure poetry, our appreciation is drastically impoverished. For we are left at most with 'but a mere unrelated heap of charming

---

[13] See the chapters with that title in I.A. Richards, *Principles of Literary Criticism* (1924, repr. London: Routledge and Kegan Paul, 1970) and *Science and Poetry* (New York: Norton, 1926). See also his *Practical Criticism* (1929, repr. New York: Harcourt, Brace, 1956), 255-262. Among Eliot's more important discussions of this problem see *SE*, 229-231; *TUP*, 89-98; *OPP*, 258-63; and 'A Note on Poetry and Belief', *Enemy* 1 (1927), 15-17.

stanzas, the debris of poetry rather than the poetry itself' (*TUP*, 98). Moreover, if the beliefs expressed in literature are irrelevant, why has literature been so often praised and prized by its apologists as a source of knowledge and edification? Returning to the literature-game analogy may illuminate the problematic relations between literature, belief, and knowledge, and more particularly Eliot's proposed resolution of them.

Though pragmatically distinguished from ordinary life, games are not totally unrelated and alien to life (for in a way they too make up part of life). Indeed, games share and illuminate certain important aspects of ordinary, serious life (e.g. competition, teamwork, submission to rules, etc.) and are consequently considered of educational value. Now the invented world of a literary work typically differs from that of a game not in being more internally complete, but in being more analogous or representative of real life as a whole. It is peopled not by quarterbacks and goalies trying to score or prevent points on a narrow field, but typically concerns 'whole' (albeit largely invented) people, places, and actions which significantly resemble and reflect those of the world of real life. Moreover, a literary world (like a game) is very compact and coherently ordered compared to the ordinary world it reflects; thus in its compact surveyability and order, the literary work seems an excellent model to promote a better grasp of the world, 'to give us some perception of an order in life, by imposing an order upon it' (*OPP*, 86). It can do this not only by its similarity to the real world but by its differences, which can highlight aspects and orders of ordinary life which are apt to go unnoticed. It can help to teach us about various types of character and social relations; but more particularly it can, through our imaginative identification with its characters, give us a sense of what it is like to experience things we have never experienced and perhaps never could.

However, not withstanding all this apparent cognitive allure (and perhaps even to some extent because of it), literature is as likely to generate error and delusion as it is to produce knowledge. The dangerous tendency of literature to mislead is not only relentlessly attacked by Plato and his philosophical ilk, but is even attested to by literature itself. A host of novels paradoxically inculcate the theme that literature falsifies and misinforms, that it propagates, particularly in the young and naive, false ideas as to the nature of love, marriage, and life. Does literature, then, have any real cognitive value? Can it be said to provide the reader with new and significant knowledge of life, of the world, or of himself?

Eliot's answer to this troublesome old question is admirably clear, concise, and sensible. The cognitive value of a literary work depends not only on the work itself but also very much on how it is digested by the reader. Eliot again employs his two-stage model of response in reading literature. Though we must provisionally accept the work's world and the beliefs which inform it so that we can imaginatively realize and respond to it adequately, this alone does not give direct knowledge of life. Such knowledge only comes by means of the second 'stage of self-consciousness' and critical comparison which should be found in any intelligent, discerning reading. This stage is when we detach ourselves from the work's view of life and measure it against our own views and experiences, when we try to see, account for, and adjust the perceived differences of view in developing a new, more seasoned and superior perception of life.

> It is simply not true that works of fiction, prose or verse, ... *directly* extend our knowledge of life. Direct knowledge of life is knowledge directly in relation to ourselves ... in so far as that part of life in which we have participated gives us material for generalization. Knowledge of life obtained through fiction is only possible by another stage of self-consciousness ... So far as we are taken up with the happenings in any novel in the same way in which we are taken up with what happens under our eyes, we are acquiring at least as much falsehood as truth. But when we are developed enough to say: 'This is the view of life of a person who was a good observer within his limits, Dickens, or Thackeray, or George Eliot, or Balzac; but he looked at it in a different way from me, because he was a different man; he even selected rather different things to look at, or the same things in a different order of importance, because he was a different man; so what I am looking at is the world as seen by a particular mind' – then we are in a position to gain something from reading fiction ...; but these authors are only really helping us when we can see, and allow for, their differences from ourselves. (*EAM*, 103-104)

This two-stage account of reading and belief further helps Eliot explain two important phenomena: the extraordinarily powerful cognitive and behavioral effect of trivial literature read for mere pleasure, and the value of wide and critical reading in developing a full and sturdy personality and view of life. Our light 'pleasure reading' has such a powerful effect on our beliefs and attitudes because with such reading we typically do not trouble ourselves with the second, critical stage, since we know we are reading only for pleasure and not for cognitive enrichment or enlightenment. However, since any enjoyment of literature requires a first stage of imaginatively accepting and assimilating the work's world and outlook, omission of subsequent critical reflection on these features of the work will leave the attitudes or beliefs expressed in the work dangerously active, unconsciously and uncritically, in the mind of the reader. Hence it is 'the literature that we read for "amusement" or "purely for pleasure" that may have the greatest and least suspected influence upon us ... [since it is] read in this attitude of "purely for pleasure", of pure passivity.' And since popular contemporary literature is the literature most often and easily read in that attitude, it 'can have the easiest and most insidious influence upon us' and thus 'requires to be scrutinized most closely' (*EAM*, 105).

Eliot here provides the literary critic with a crucial role of culture criticism, exposing and critically examining the ideologies which inform contemporary popular literature and culture. If Eliot's own patently Christian execution of this task seems to us awkwardly heavy-handed and outdated, if not sometimes almost bigoted, this does nothing to invalidate his general theoretical doctrine that literature needs ideological criticism and that adequate, substantive literary criticism cannot ultimately afford to ignore it. Marxist and deconstructionist theorists who condemn Eliot's critical theory as insularly aestheticist, technical, and blind to the importance of the critique of ideas and ideologies in the criticism of literature are thus wildly off target.[14] Their difference with Eliot is not on the philosophical issue of the relevance of ideology but rather on the particular ideology to be used as a critical touchstone and pursued as a cultural end. Moreover, we are by now in a position to see that any attempt to charge Eliot with New Criticism's blindness to the crucial and complex role of reader-response can likewise be shown ludicrous by Eliot's repeated explicit attention to the reader's role and its complexity of stages.

Eliot's two-stage theory of reading also explains the great value of reading in the development of personality and view of life and in the achievement of self-knowledge. In reading a literary work, in imaginatively involving ourselves in and accepting its world, 'we are affected by it, as human beings, whether we intend to be or not ... during the process of assimilation and digestion' (*EAM*, 102). If we are very powerfully affected or 'captured' by a literary work, even the second stage of critical detachment and reflection will not altogether neutralize its effect and leave our beliefs and attitudes precisely as they previously were. For the work may have brought us, even after critical reflection, to see things rather differently. As Eliot remarked, when in order to understand and criticize a powerful author 'you have to give yourself up, and then recover yourself ... the self recovered is never the same as the self before it was given'.[15] The self thus undergoes expansion and development through its imaginative projection and transfiguration in reading.

Here again, literature's effect is a function not only of the power of the work or author but greatly depends on the reader, on the breadth, depth, and experience-proven firmness of his previous structure of belief, not to mention his capacity for imaginative understanding. When we are immature and not well-read, Eliot explains, '[what] happens is a kind of inundation, of invasion of the undeveloped personality ... by the stronger personality of the poet' (*EAM*, 102), an inundation which largely overcomes and submerges the critical reflections of the second stage. But the more experience and wider reading we assimilate, the more well-rounded, tempered, and sturdy our belief-structures (including the structure of our

---

[14] Eagleton and Norris are the prime perpetrators of this gross and tendentious misprision of Eliot's theory. See my discussion in Chapter One and their works cited in its notes 4, 5, and 9.

[15] Quoted in 'Remembering Eliot', 56. The problem of the reader's relation to a powerful author, is, of course, much more complex when the reader himself is an author, like Eliot. For an intriguing but highly speculative account of Eliot's anxiety about poetic influence, see Gregory Jay, *T.S. Eliot and the Poetics of Literary History* (Baton Rouge: Louisiana University Press, 1983), 68-91.

judgments of art) are apt to be; and consequently the less likely we are to be one-sidedly possessed and indoctrinated by the beliefs (or style, or critical taste) of any one author.

Moreover, since the views of different authors are often incompatible, digesting a variety of authors makes us critically compare and weigh their opposing views. This not only develops and sharpens our critical consciousness and power but elicits the formation and expression of our own selfhood in our comparative assessment and ordering of the different views. Wide reading is valuable, therefore, 'not ... as a kind of hoarding' or accumulation of information, but 'because in the process of being affected by one powerful personality after another, we cease to be dominated by any one, or by any small number. The very different views of life, cohabiting in our minds, affect each other, and our own personality asserts itself and gives each a place in some arrangement peculiar to ourself' (*EAM*, 103).

Thus, by projecting ourselves in reading into 'various worlds of poetic creation', we can not only enlarge and exercise our minds with the experience and opinions of others, but also thereby come to a better understanding of ourselves, a primary aim of hermeneutical inquiry. For entering and knowing these literary worlds and world-views provides us with a rich and articulate background of comparison and contrast which enables us more clearly, precisely, and assuredly to form, define, and assert our own identity and view of life in terms of the various views which we have come to know. Eliot therefore rightly insists that 'we make the effort to enter those worlds of poetry in which we are alien' so that we can better understand and appreciate the world, the beliefs, and the poetry we take most as our own.[16]

IV

The question, then, is how and to what extent is such adoption of alien beliefs possible? Eliot can here again avail himself of the game analogy and the two-stage model of critical response. In the first stage, when we imaginatively enter the fictional world and adopt its beliefs, we do not really believe them. We know, for example, that we are not in ancient Troy, and would not think of trying to contact Zeus to intervene in the action, for we do not believe he really exists. But nor do we simply suspend disbelief in the neutral contemplation of a possibility, for then we would not really be moved or affected as fiction does affect us. Instead, as in a game, we provisionally accept, *pretend*, or *make believe* the world and beliefs the work presents us.[17] These pretended beliefs are not fully or 'really'

[16] T.S. Eliot, 'Poetry and Propaganda', *Bookman*, 70 (1930), 602.

[17] For an excellent detailed analysis of the notions of 'fictional worlds' and the 'games of make-believe' which afford us 'entry' into them, see K. Walton, 'Fearing Fictions', *Journal of Philosophy*, 75 (1978), 5-27; and 'How Remote are Fictional Worlds from the Real World', *Journal of Aesthetics and Art Criticism*, 37 (1978), 11-23. Walton's account, which very much

believed, need not extend beyond the first stage or perspective of the game of reading, and may always be exposed to critical awareness of their pretended status through the second level of critical reflection. However, if we are unable in the first stage to make believe or pretendingly accept the contents of the work, we will fail to get adequately involved with it and thus be unable to appreciate it.

This failure may be as much the work's fault as the reader's. Its world and beliefs may seem so internally incoherent, so clumsily contrived or uninteresting, or so puerile and inadequate to our experience of life that we feel justifiably unable to surrender ourselves to them as we read. We feel justifiably unable to maintain sufficiently the imaginative acceptance or pretended belief (or even minimally the suspension of disbelief) necessary to enjoy the work in question. This is precisely Eliot's complaint against Shelley, whose insistent but 'shabby', 'muddled', 'puerile', and 'repellent' ideas obstruct enjoyment (*TUP*, 89-99). The world of a poem should therefore be 'reasonable' and appealing enough to induce the reader's imaginative '*acceptance*', which, as Eliot notes, is aesthetically 'more important than anything that can be called belief' (*SE*, 276-77).

Eliot thus is careful to maintain a pragmatic and recognizable distinction between poetic, pretended acceptance and real belief, while at the same time recognizing that the two are none the less recognizably related. 'For there is a difference ... between philosophical *belief* and poetic *assent*' (*SE*, 257). However, to command this assent 'the doctrine, theory, belief, or "view of life" presented in a poem [must be] ... one which the mind of the reader can accept as coherent, mature, and founded on the facts of experience, [so that] it interposes no obstacle to the reader's enjoyment'. It must strike the reader as a reasonably believable belief, 'whether it be one that he accept or deny, approve or deprecate. When it is one which the reader rejects as childish or feeble, it may, for a reader of well-developed mind, set up almost a complete check' (*TUP*, 96). This explains Eliot's insistence on 'the advantage of a coherent traditional system' of thought, an established 'framework of accepted and traditional ideas' as the most serviceable framework for creating intelligently satisfying and enjoyable poetic worlds, for it will make them easier to accept and abide in even if not fully believed (*SE*, 258; *SW*, 158).

Now when we find it hard to accept and appreciate the world of a poet who is held in the highest esteem, we should be more inclined to attribute this problem to our own limitations than to the author's. Our effort to understand and possibly overcome our difficulty in appreciation thus provides a further and especially rich opportunity for self-knowledge and

---

parallels Eliot's, distinguishes make-believe or pretense from real belief and suspension of disbelief, and construes the former (as Eliot does) in terms of acceptance. He also insists, like Eliot, that the reader must adopt a 'duality of standpoint', 'both from inside ... and from outside' the fictional world of the work and that failure to recognize and maintain these 'two perspectives' results in considerable theoretical confusion ('How Remote ...', 21-22).

development, since it demands that we examine our own limitations; and in exposing them to critical consciousness we may liberate our minds from their unconscious tyranny. 'In trying to understand why one has failed to appreciate rightly [the work of] a particular author, one is seeking for light, not only about the author, but about oneself ...: it is an effort to understand that work and to understand oneself in relation to it.' And in overcoming former antipathy to appreciate the work better, one achieves 'an important liberation from a limitation of one's own mind' (*OPP*, 209-210). Eliot performed this exercise of self-examination and overcoming most notably with respect to Goethe and Milton.

Although Gadamer may argue that any understanding 'affords unique opportunities [for] ... the broadening of our human experiences, our self-knowledge, and our horizon, for everything understanding mediates is mediated along with ourselves',[18] Eliot is surely right in emphasizing here that certain objects or projects of understanding are significantly more broadening and self-revelatory. He is also right to claim that the understanding of poetry is among the most edifying. For we have seen it involves not only understanding and sympathetically entertaining a variety of beliefs, world-views, and emotions but also understanding their similarities and differences to what we take as our own views and feelings.

Poetry, then, is a game which can provide knowledge and edification while amusing us on intellectual, emotional, and even sensual levels. Eliot goes so far as to suggest that it 'is the language most capable of communicating wisdom' (*OPP*, 226). This claim is hard to assess without a reasonably clear and adequate grasp of what wisdom is, and I cannot presume to supply one here. Eliot, however, though circumspectly confessing himself unequal to the task of defining wisdom ('There is no word ... more impossible to define, and no word more difficult to understand', *OPP*, 220) does in fact offer some account of this notion. Pending more detailed study in Chapter Eight, let us conclude this chapter by briefly considering Eliot's idea of wisdom to see how the understanding of poetry might contribute most significantly to its attainment.

In his essay on Goethe where Eliot makes this high claim for poetry and where Dante, Shakespeare, and Goethe are cited as great poets and wise men, Eliot characterizes wisdom as 'a native gift of intuition, ripened and given application by experience, for understanding the nature of things, certainly of living things, most certainly of the human heart' (*OPP*, 221). The wise man must have 'a very wide range of interest, sympathy, and understanding' held together in penetrating focus by some 'fundamental Unity', which is expressed in the particular coherent view that each great poet presents of 'life itself, the world seen from a particular point of view' based on intelligence and experience (*OPP*, 214). However, wisdom

---

[18] H.-G. Gadamer, 'Hermeneutics as Practical Philosophy', in *Reason in the Age of Science* (Cambridge, Mass.: MIT Press, 1983), 110.

requires not only having one's own ordered vision of the world but also recognizing it as only one possible point of view and consequently requires an openness and flexibility for accommodating new experience and a recognition and understanding of other world-views. In short, it requires 'the charity that comes from understanding human beings in all their variety ... and ... diverse beliefs' and thus cannot be identified with a set of 'logical propositions' or 'sum of wise sayings' (*OPP*, 221, 226). Since this charity involves the recognition that one's own view of life is not the only one that a wise man could adopt and that it is at best a fragile, partial, corrigible pattern imposed on a bafflingly unmanageable sea of experience, humility would also seem an essential part of wisdom.

If wisdom is indeed composed of these things, the appreciation of great literature should surely help us towards its attainment, though obviously cannot alone secure it. For the appreciation of such literature involves a deep understanding of a wide variety of coherent alien worlds of experience and belief which illuminatingly reflect an ordered perception of life and thereby test and develop our own beliefs and vision of the world. Literature also inculcates the charitable acceptance and appreciation of different points of view, both for the edification and the amusement they afford us in their aesthetically appealing forms of expression. Moreover, it is a commonplace that great literature communicates not only some perception of order in life but with it also a powerful sense of life's unfathomable mystery. It is no less obvious that in our effort to understand an author of genius and the nature of his genius we are powerfully made aware of our comparative inadequacy and limitation. Here, surely, great literature should at least provide humility, if no further wisdom. Indeed, one should not neglect Eliot's own suggestion, in a late poetic masterpiece, that humility may be the best wisdom we can hope to acquire, since whatever pattern human wisdom seems to perceive in life is apt to be challenged, if not falsified, by future experience.

> ... There is, it seems to us,
> At best, only a limited value
> In the knowledge derived from experience.
> The knowledge imposes a pattern, and falsifies,
> For the pattern is new in every moment
> And every moment is a new and shocking
> Valuation of all we have been ...
> The only wisdom we can hope to acquire
> Is the wisdom of humility: humility is endless.
>   'East Coker', II

V

I am reluctant to conclude with this seductive poetic flourish and on what may seem a cloyingly sanctimonious note. For surely most of us (though perhaps not the wise) would think humility an insufficient reward for the effort to understand literature. We may therefore be tempted to return to the first subject of this chapter and close by remembering with Eliot that, whatever else it may bring, the understanding of great literature gives great enjoyment. But here again caution overcomes temptation. For such 'humble' conclusions in the climate of today's intellectual ideology not only court the charge of self-satisfied and self-serving elitist piety, but invite the further charge of collusion with bourgeois conservatism's underlying inimical devaluation of literature as essentially a privately pleasurable but socially marginal pursuit. Given Eliot's association with the conservative establishment, such charges must be fully presented and faced, even if they cannot be fully answered.

One line of indictment would be this. By recommending humility as the only or highest wisdom while also advocating a humble respect for past literary masterpieces, the conservative elitist participant in high culture can at once assert and conceal his proud claim to superior knowledge through his privileged association with these literary sources of wisdom. For these sources are unfamiliar and insufficiently accessible to the culturally unprivileged who are and remain such largely through socio-economic and political domination. The seemingly self-deprecating humility before past literary glories is exposed as but a subterfuge for more powerful self-assertion through their privileging appropriation, just as Horkheimer and Adorno argued that our pious scientific respect for the facts of nature is but a ruse by which we aim to assert ourselves by dominating and exploiting her.[19] Moreover, the assertion that such humility is the height of wisdom is both an effective deterrent to new thinking and a pre-emptive criticism of any new ideas claiming to be wiser than the past. In short, the mask of humility belies a repressive assertion of superior authority through tradition, i.e. through special access to a privileged literary past which itself is the product of oppressive social and ideological forces. The idea that the objects of our cultural heritage, including our most cherished works of art, are wholly independent and innocent of unjust material and social conditions and untainted by the ideologies promoting those conditions (which largely constitute the conditions of these works' own production) is an illusion which contemporary cultural criticism has done well to expose. Is the call to humble appreciation of our literary past not a surreptitious and unavoidable invitation to adopt all its unworthy ideological prejudices?

Another major but related line of critique is that Eliot's assertion of the central role of pleasure in literary understanding plays right into the hands of the conservative, bourgeois agenda, which wants to trivialize and marginalize literature by rendering it a mere pleasurable pastime, detached from the struggles of history and devoid of any social and political

---

[19] See M. Horkheimer and T. Adorno, *Dialectic of Enlightenment* (New York: Continuum, 1986), 4-9, 54-57.

import. Moreover, it could be argued that Eliot's complementary emphasis on literature as an instrument of self-enlargement and self-enlightenment does not adequately counter this threat. For these are still projects of refinement of individual sensibility and understanding, circumscribed within the individual consciousness; and therefore they too allow a dehistoricization of literature which robs texts of their potential for raising class consciousness and promoting social change.

How could Eliot best reply to such a radical indictment of the wisdom of humility, the edifying pleasures of reading, and the value of culture? A satisfactory response, if one can be given, would involve nothing less than a full-scale defense of high culture, an updated 'Apologie for Poetry'; so I can here only sketchily project the directions an Eliotic reply might take.

It might well start by noting that the wisdom of humility is not necessarily wedded to conservative, conformist quietism but may equally promote that healthy sense of uncertainty which allows one to question the accepted wisdom of the day, including one's own dogmas, and to entertain alternative points of view which could initiate change. We should remember that it was Socrates who first made such wisdom famous in challenging the dogmas of Athenian thought as well as the sceptical certitude of the sophists. His humble wisdom of knowing that he did not know while still believing in the possibility of real knowledge was likewise condemned as a wily mask of proud superiority and self-satisfied assurance in his own beliefs. But surely we are not to accept the view of Socrates as a repressive enemy of free inquiry. Even if Eliot was a proud conservative, humility need not always be disguised pride and lust for power; and the facile global cynicism which is committed to interpreting it and similar virtues in this suspicious manner needs itself to be challenged for dogmatic and repressive blindness, for a brutal unwillingness to tolerate or entertain any act or motive not clearly reducible to its central category of self-asserting self-interest. This unhappy blindness would be seen by critical theorists like Adorno and Horkheimer as a heritage of Enlightenment scepticism and its total commitment to self-preservation through instrumental reason.[20]

Even linking humility with Eliot's admiration of the literary tradition does not entail a rigidly repressive conservatism which steadfastly holds to all and only what the past masters have written and believed. First, this would simply be impossible, since the various world-views embodied in our literature are, taken together, just far too inconsistent to be coherently maintained. Indeed, we saw that Eliot specifically advocated breadth of reading because the variety of different and incompatible authors' views encountered would keep our minds open and active in assessing their relative merits. Moreover, by Eliot's theory of reading, even the most revered masterpiece is never simply ingested and taken as true; it must be

[20] *Ibid.*, 28-35, 83-87.

exposed to that second stage of external criticism, where the experience of the present is used to test the putative wisdom of the past. Thirdly, the whole idea that commitment to tradition implies intransigence and blinkered devotion to the status quo rests on the false assumption, strongly challenged by Eliot, that tradition is fixed and determinate rather than something which always needs to be reinterpreted and gets continuously reshaped as it is constantly debated. Our tradition is contested and pluralistic, not oppressively monochrome. Eliot's dynamic historicist account of tradition will be analyzed at length in the next chapter.

Does Eliot's emphasis on the pleasurable edification of reading bespeak an attempt to trivialize and dehistoricize literature, to deprive it of ideological import and void its potency as an instrument for social change? It is hard to see how emphasis on the former implies exclusion of the latter. Eliot insists that edifying reading involves the exploration of different moral, social, and political worlds and affords self-understanding; he also insists that the effects of reading (even of what is read 'purely for pleasure') cannot be compartmentalized but instead strongly 'affects us as entire human beings', modifying our attitudes and 'our behaviour towards our fellow men' (*EAM*, 105, 100). Given this and the undeniable fact that social and political change require the raising of consciousness and the changing of attitudes, Eliot's account of reading is surely not inimical to literature's ideological and social appropriation. Moreover, the presumption that art must have direct political or social utility can itself be challenged as a dogmatic bias of instrumentalist ideology, reducing everything to a means. Adorno (though probably not Eliot) would go so far as to argue that part of art's value is in its comparative non-utility which serves as a tacit critique of our obsession with utilitarian instrumental thinking.

Finally, the most radical and troubling of these critical suspicions is that which condemns all culture as a massive and oppressive illusion. Enchantment with culture's glorious artistic products gives the lie to the miserable and cruelly unjust material conditions on which they were based. We are seductively lulled by art's satisfying beauty and perfection into thinking that its creators – mankind and society – have similarly approached perfection and satisfaction. Such escapist illusions help perpetuate social conditions which are no less deplorable when deplorably ignored, concealed by an enthralling aesthetic surface. The art of high culture seems even more oppressively deceitful when we recognize that despite traditional aesthetic theories (like Kant's) asserting an underlying natural foundation of taste common to all, the understanding and tasteful appreciation of art has largely been the protected domain of the culturally privileged and socially dominant. Aesthetic appreciation (through its inevitable distinction of superior from inferior taste) can be effectively wielded to underline and reinforce such domination.

Pious protestation that art is benignly innocent, essentially pure of social constraints and motives, is a foolishly empty reply that Eliot would scorn, since he instead insisted that art is significantly shaped by social forces and conversely shapes social attitudes. Culture's best defense lies in realizing art's social aspect and potency, while recognizing the complexity of its societal relations as well as the complexities of contemporary social relations of privilege and domination.

Historically, much art has served as an instrument of liberation and transformation. But even apart from works specifically concerned with social criticism and revolutionary causes, art's inviting vision of alien social worlds, ways of life, and discursive structures can help us realize that our own socially entrenched practices are neither necessary nor ideal, thereby opening the way for change. The eager rejection of all art as a lie unfaithful to the materialist evils of social reality betrays a dangerous tendency to assume that such reality is the ultimate criterion of truth and not itself the product of ideological illusion; it is to keep complicitous faith with that reality in refusing to consider art's alternative visions as worthy or serious. This, as Adorno remarks, is throwing out the baby with the bath-water; 'in face of the lie of the commodity world, even the lie that denounces it becomes a corrective truth.'[21]

Works of art need to be interpreted and most admit of different interpretations. Art's social import is therefore not fixed but depends on how art is interpretatively appropriated and deployed. Given the critical reading of literature that Eliot advocates, and certainly given the ingenuity of today's sophisticated readers in reading against the text, even a literary work expressly slanted in one direction may be eristically or deconstructively appropriated to advance opposing positions. Artistic masterpieces in our tradition are continuously being reinterpreted and redeployed as weapons in the continuing contest over socio-cultural legitimacy and dominance, a contest which reciprocally influences the relative valuation of these and other works.

In this contest for social privilege, it would be wrong to see high art as an unequivocal weapon of the most ruthlessly dominating class. This class or class fraction is comprised not of elite artists and their intellectual audience, but rather of big business, banking, industry, and advertising. Nor is elitist art its major instrument of domination. Instead it exploits, under the guise of democratic populism, the arts of popular culture (not to be confused with traditional folk art) and the manipulative art of advertising to produce a lucrative mass-culture industry. Apart from its own profit-taking, this industry promotes that docile conformism and worship of the superficially new which keeps the dominated consumer in a

[21] See T. Adorno, *Minima Moralia* (London: Verso, 1978), 43-44. Despite their huge differences in socio-political ideology, Eliot and Adorno share a number of important themes: the union of theory and practice, the rejection of positivism and instrumental method for practical wisdom or substantive reason, the value of discipline and suffering, the insistence on the redemptive potentiality of high art together with a taste for the austere art of high modernism, and the conviction that contemporary liberalism's cult of individuality too often merely represents and conceals a shameless conformism.

confused frenzy of changing fashion and thereby sets him up for ever more punishing rounds of profit-making.

In contrast, high art (along with education) represents perhaps the only serious rival to material capital as a source of social status and legitimation. The art of high culture, the appreciation of things that are not 'box-office', represents an alternative value still deeply entrenched and emotively potent in our tradition, perhaps partly as a repository for displaced religious feeling set free by the so-called death of God. This cultural capital, as Bourdieu[22] calls it, which is powerful enough to command at least the lip-service respect of both the common man and industrialist, constitutes the artist's and intellectual's prime weapon against the total hegemony of the dollar. And it is the dollar, not the poem or painting, which sustains and motivates the repressive conservative establishment deplored by so many of us.

Contemporary secular intellectuals, disenchanted with the socio-economic establishment and implicitly doubtful of their power to rebel against it, seem to have let out their frustration on the cultural objects which can best sustain them in their struggle, thus unintentionally colluding with the valuational motives of the power structures they wish to dislodge. Poetry, as Eliot realized (for more than theological reasons), cannot save us, but it can offer the social critic a great deal more than complicitous, escapist comfort.

---

[22] See P. Bourdieu, *Distinction: A Social Critique of the Judgement of Taste* (Cambridge, Mass.: Harvard University Press, 1984). Bourdieu is also very instructive in showing the simplistic error of lumping together as a single, coherent dominant class what is actually two warring class fractions which contest a whole range of fundamental values. The artists and intellectuals constitute the dominated of these (dominant) class fractions, dominated by the more dominant class of big business and material capital.

Chapter 7

The Concept of Tradition:
its Progress and Potential

Tradition cannot mean standing still.

After Strange Gods

I

That tradition is a hallmark of Eliot's thought is obvious and recognized. What is much less obvious and more maligned than properly understood is his conception of tradition. Most often it is perceived as a smug and pompous intransigence to change, a stodgy and wholly backward-looking traditionalism, self-satisfied with the way things have been and opposed to any idea of criticizing or changing them in any significant way. But closer study will reveal that Eliot saw tradition as requiring constant criticism and alteration with the aim of developing it and orientating it toward the future.

There are several reasons why Eliot's view of tradition is so widely misunderstood and so easily misrepresented as mere conservatism. First, his clear connection with the Church of England and the Conservative Party make it easy to pin him with the label 'conservative' and thus to forget his innovative achievements in poetry and criticism, and his advocacy of the need for change and continuous development in these fields. Certainly for those of us whose religion is secularism and whose politics are well left of center, there is a strong temptation to relegate Eliot's thinking *in toto* to the realm of the obsolescent past, especially when doing so makes our own critical and theoretical enterprises seem all the more novel and impressive. Secondly, understanding is hindered by the fact that Eliot's more famous discussions of tradition are rather fragmentary and unsystematic, while his more definitive and substantial treatments have received very little attention. Third, there is the problem that Eliot's view of tradition changed significantly (though not very dramatically) with his development as a critic. His very early but still most famous treatment of tradition in 'Tradition and the Individual Talent', which unfortunately reflects his juvenile objectivism and literary purism, evolved into a more balanced and general account which no longer sought to erect tradition into an immutably absolute ideal and purely artistic standard of objectivity for judging the meaning and value of authors and their work. Eliot's more mature and systematic view emphasizes tradition's need for perpetual criticism and change, warns of its dangers of rigidity and obsolescence, and insists on embedding literary tradition in a larger extraliterary social and cultural tradition, which is not transcendentally ideal but closely linked to our most concretely real and mundane ways of life. But this considered and definitive account remains sadly eclipsed by the familiar early view inscribed in Eliot's most famous and anthologized essay.

In this chapter I attempt to provide a better understanding of Eliot's conception of tradition by tracing its development. I hope also to afford a better grasp of the concept of tradition and its cognitive value by elucidating and supplementing Eliot's views with ideas from Gadamer (in whose thought tradition is similarly central though inadequately analyzed) as well as from other twentieth-century philosophers, both Anglo-American and continental.

II

Though it too readily lends itself to construing tradition in a transcendentally ideal and narrowly aesthetic fashion as 'an ideal order' of artistic 'monuments', even 'Tradition and the Individual Talent' shows Eliot's recognition that tradition involves criticism and change. For Eliot remarks that 'if the only form of tradition, of handing down, consisted in following the ways of the immediate generation before us in a blind or timid adherence to its successes, "tradition" should positively be discouraged' (*SE*, 14). This critical outlook needs to be directed not only at the immediate past but generally characterizes the writer's proper relationship to all past achievement: 'he can neither take the past as a lump, an indiscriminate bolus', nor simply embrace 'one preferred period' but 'must be very conscious of the main current, which does not at all flow invariably through the most distinguished reputations' (*SE*, 16).

Since tradition requires a critical understanding of the past which can cut through the mass of fossilized reputations to uncover 'the main current', Eliot maintains that 'tradition ... cannot be inherited' but only obtained 'by great labour'. To obtain it one needs 'the historical sense', which demands not only a critically structured grasp of the essential history of 'the whole of the literature of Europe from Homer and within it the whole of the literature of [one's] own country' but also requires that this literary structure be felt as a simultaneous ordered presence in our conscious present. 'This historical sense, which is a sense of the timeless as well as of the temporal and of the timeless and of the temporal together, is what makes a writer traditional' (*SE*, 14).

Despite this suggestion of tradition as a transcendental, timeless standard, Eliot must admit that tradition involves change, for otherwise the main current would not be a current but a stagnant pool. However, he is careful to assert that though 'the mind of Europe' through which tradition flows 'is a mind which changes ... this change is a development which abandons nothing *en route*, which does not superannuate either Shakespeare, or Homer, or the rock drawing of the Magdalenian draughtsmen' (*SE*, 16). The tension here, between recognizing change as inevitable and essential for continuing tradition and yet fearing it as a threat to the stability of standard sought from tradition, is particularly acute for a creative artist like Eliot. To give up the claims for change would make his own innovational creative efforts gratuitous; but entirely to give way to change could not only make Shakespeare but ultimately Eliot himself obsolete and irrelevant. Eliot's image of tradition as 'the main current' nicely captures not only his idea of tradition's selectivity but the desired balance between its change and identity: fluid movement in an essentially fixed course, a course whose direction or bearings are perhaps even timelessly fixed, even if its movement is limitless.

The essay's other, far more famous image of tradition – that of an ideal order of monuments – is similarly applied to the problem of fixity and flux. How can tradition maintain its claim to stable identity and unassailable validity in the face of real change in the arts, without altogether denying the importance and value of such change? If tradition represents a firm and unchallengeable standard against which new art must be judged, what room is there for any really new work of merit? It will either fail to conform to tradition's standard and thus fail as a work of art; or if it does conform it cannot be significantly new. Moreover, if it is not new, then by the traditional criterion of originality which Eliot seems to accept as necessary for art, it will not even reach the status of a work of art, failing to conform to the artistic tradition by simply conforming to it. 'To conform merely would be for the new work not really to conform at all; it would not be new, and would therefore not be a work of art' (*SE*, 15).

Caught in this aporia of tradition versus innovation, identity and change, Eliot tried to redefine tradition's relation to new work as a process of mutual conformity and readjustment, where the present can also alter the significance of the past and thus can modify the form of tradition rather than merely sustaining it. Tradition thus flexibly conceived hardly provides an unbending standard of objectivity; and Eliot, obviously uneasy about such concessions to the mutability of tradition, tries to recover what firmness he can by portraying tradition in the most solid and reverential imagery of monuments. This, however, stridently clashes with the idea of flexibility and movement he is compelled to recognize.

The existing monuments form an ideal order among themselves, which is modified by the introduction of the new (the really new) work of art among them. The existing order is complete before the new work arrives; for order to persist after the supervention of novelty, the *whole* existing order must be, if ever so slightly, altered; and so the relations, proportions, values of each work of art toward the whole are readjusted; and this is conformity between the old and the new. (*SE*, 15)

Visually realized the imagery is ludicrous. The great and sturdy existing monuments, firmly established in their assigned places as cornerstones of our literary tradition, suddenly start shuffling and nudging each other about so as to accommodate the new work to form a new 'complete' order, only to be upset again by the intrusion of another new work requiring more reshuffling and readjustment. Such adjustable monuments hardly provide tradition with permanent standards of objective value.

As the inherent flexibility of Eliot's concept of tradition is considerably contradicted and concealed by its metaphorical portrayal in terms of monuments and timeless orders, so the role of criticism in tradition is overshadowed by the suggestion (never explicitly stated) that within the literary past which includes both bad and good, there is embedded an 'ideal order', 'main current', or essence of tradition which is wholly good and calls for no criticism. Such a purified ideal literary tradition, once grasped through diligent study and efforts of critical and imaginative conscious-ness, could serve as a firm and compelling standard of objectivity; something that Eliot as a young, aspiring poet-critic deeply desired.

However, by the time he launched his next sustained discussion of tradition in *After Strange Gods* (1934), he had no use for such a purified ideal literary tradition to ensure objectivity.[1] First, his objectivist zeal had waned, and he had also come to regard the whole idea of judging literature in terms of a purely literary standard as a naive and narrow prejudice. In 1928 he already claimed to be more interested in 'the relation of poetry to the spiritual and social life', and by 1932 he was insisting that poetry's development and appreciation are largely the product of social forces which change over history and therefore that the idea of a purely literary or artistic appreciation is an unachievable and gainless figment (*SW*, viii; *TUP*, 21, 97, 109). Moreover, this historicist and sociological outlook could hardly harbor the idea of a transcendental, timeless order as an immutable standard of value.

Eliot's discussion of tradition in *After Strange Gods* reflects this new

---

[1] The metamorphosis of tradition from something culturally elite and obtained only by 'great labour' of consciousness ('the poet must develop or procure the consciousness of the past and ... should continue to develop this consciousness throughout his career', *SE*, 17) to something much wider, largely unconscious, and socially inherited (as in *After Strange Gods*) exhibits perhaps an intermediary stage in 'The Function of Criticism' (1923), where Eliot writes: 'A common inheritance and common cause unite artists consciously or unconsciously: it must be admitted that the union is mostly unconscious' (*SE*, 24).

perspective. Tradition is no longer conceived in narrow artistic terms; instead it embraces 'not solely, or even primarily, the maintenance of certain dogmatic beliefs' but rather the whole matrix of communal life and experience in which they function. 'What I mean by tradition involves all those habitual actions, habits, and customs, from the most significant religious rite to our conventional way of greeting a stranger, which represent the blood kinship of "the same people living in the same place" ' (*ASG*, 18). A real temporal community has replaced the ideal order of timeless monuments. Tradition is no longer a transcendental entity to be attained only through great conscious effort by the very gifted; it is rather an immanent part of our way of life, so that we can largely enjoy its possession without even being conscious of it. The following passage clearly brings out the historico-communal and largely unconscious character of tradition, while introducing two other crucial aspects, tradition's temporal vulnerablity and fallibility, and the need for its constant criticism and emendation through what Eliot calls orthodoxy.

> I hold – in summing up – that a *tradition* is rather a way of feeling and acting which characterizes a group throughout generations; and that it must largely be, or that many of the elements in it must be, unconscious; whereas the maintenance of *orthodoxy* is a matter which calls for the exercise of all our conscious intelligence. The two will therefore considerably complement each other. Not only is it possible to conceive of a tradition being definitely bad; a good tradition might, in changing circumstances, become out of date. Tradition has not the means to criticize itself; it may perpetuate much that is trivial or of transient significance as well as what is vital and permanent. And while tradition, being a matter of good habits, is necessarily real only in a social group, orthodoxy exists whether realized in anyone's thought or not. Orthodoxy also, of course represents a consensus between the living and the dead: but a whole generation might conceivably pass without any orthodox thought ... (*ASG*, 31-32)

Eliot never precisely formulates what he means by orthodoxy, but it is clear from his use of the term (as well as suggested by its etymology) that he takes it as a principle of right-thinking or belief, of critical intelligence to guide and correct tradition, which is largely unreflective.[2] The desired

[2] Orthodoxy is presented not as eternally fixed and articulated dogma but something which can change so that authors we find unorthodox can be 'orthodox enough according to the light of their day' (*ASG*, 58). Though its function is the rational criticism of our unreflective beliefs and feelings, orthodoxy is not like the Enlightenment's free and autonomous critical reason, but is instead a more substantive critical intelligence, like Aristotle's practical wisdom, emerging from and directed towards action and the achievement of right living, and alive to particular and changing circumstances. Its Aristotelian aspect seems further reinforced (in a lecture given the same year he delivered *After Strange Gods*) when Eliot expresses 'the wish that the classical conception of wisdom might be restored' and when he describes 'the way of orthodoxy' as 'a middle way', 'a way of mediation' between undesirable extremes (*EAM*, 117, 134-135). It is worth noting that Eliot's view of tradition as needing orthodoxy which itself can only exist in a tradition parallels Aristotle's view on the interdependence of virtue and practical wisdom; and Eliot's

amalgam of 'tradition and orthodoxy' is that of communal beliefs, practices, and feelings being articulated, refined, and updated to contemporary circumstances by rational reflective thought, 'the habits of the community formulated, corrected, and elevated by ... continuous thought' (*ASG*, 58). Recognizing that tradition requires criticism and correction to maintain its vigor and value ('Tradition cannot mean standing still', *ASG*, 25), Eliot simply assumes that the source of such criticism could only be from outside the tradition. Otherwise tradition seems not so much corrected as merely pursuing its own developing and changing course. Dominated here by a rigid inner/outer dichotomy and always very wary of immanent authority (e.g. his attack on Murry's 'Inner Voice' and Babbitt's inner check), Eliot feels compelled to posit orthodoxy as an external check on tradition. In this he is mistaken on at least two counts.

First, tradition admits of immanent critique. Even the most unified tradition will contain inner tensions or gaps which in the face of new circumstances would yield conflicting responses or troubling indecision as to how to behave. Such situations compel tradition to reflect critically on itself and to adjust or redefine itself to resolve them, where competing reconstructive interpretations of tradition stimulate further critical reflection. To suppose that tradition contains no possibility for internal conflict or different future projections is to conceive of it as a fully programmed and uniformly closed system, rather than the roughly fashioned, open-structured scheme of divergent elements which we know it to be.

Secondly, the idea of orthodoxy as a separate principle outside or independent of tradition is problematic. Such a purely external standpoint is not only unnecessary for criticism but seems non-existent or impossible. Orthodoxy cannot be the product or expression of pure, free, unmotivated reason, but is necessarily partly a product and dimension of tradition, building on and reflecting tradition's central interests and aspects, even while criticizing and reshaping others. Tradition not only prestructures orthodoxy's reflective thought, giving it its tools and tasks, but also serves as a measure of its adequacy – the value of reflection tested against a background of continuing shared ways of thinking, feeling, and acting, i.e. against tradition. Criticism of tradition is part of tradition, and 'the Enlightenment tradition' of the West is aptly characterized as a tradition of criticizing tradition.

Eliot's apparent error is in sliding from the reasonable view that tradition is largely unconscious and involves more than belief to the view that it involves no conscious concern with belief and is essentially

characterization of tradition 'as a by-product of right living' (*ASG*, 32) is, of course, one of Aristotle's ways to characterize virtue. The deeply Aristotelian character of Eliot's notion of wisdom and right-minded critical intelligence will be set out in detail in the following chapter.

uncritical and unthinking. His emphasis on tradition's unconsciousness may well be a reaction to his earlier view which took the other extreme of seeing tradition as something obtained only by superior critical consciousness. But jolting tradition from excessive intellectualism to near mindlessness leaves it without the means for its criticism and development. Hence, for Eliot, 'Tradition by itself is not enough; it must be perpetually criticized and brought up to date under the supervision of what I call orthodoxy' (*ASG*, 67). However, what he calls orthodoxy and never clearly defines is not specific dogma but essentially critical intelligence and its directives. Thus it is not in the least surprising that the essay initially speaks simply of intelligence rather than orthodoxy as providing guidance for tradition, where intelligence is not seen as something external to tradition but as belonging necessarily to any tradition of value:

> Tradition is not a matter of feeling alone. Nor can we safely, without very critical examination, dig ourselves in stubbornly to a few dogmatic notions, for what is a healthy belief at one time may ... be a pernicious prejudice at another ... What we can do is to use our minds, remembering that a tradition without intelligence is not worth having. (*ASG*, 19-20)

Eliot finally succeeds in maintaining a fully balanced grasp of tradition's conscious/unconscious, consensually preserving/critically reforming character in his later study of tradition, pursued under the different term (but for him the virtually identical notion) of 'culture'. This term was not only free from the unwanted associations (e.g. of timelessness and narrowly artistic scope) arising from Eliot's early use of the term 'tradition', but also seems much less controversially backward-looking and more general and suitable for scientific social theory. In any case, Eliot's subsequent theory of tradition is formulated as a theory of culture, which proves to be only an improved version of that of *After Strange Gods*, the central improvement being a greater recognition of conscious reflection and of diversity and division in the culture or tradition of a people. Both these factors help provide tradition with the means for self-criticism, thus obviating the need for a transcendental critical power.

In *Notes Towards the Definition of Culture* (1948), culture, like tradition before it, is described very broadly as the general matrix embracing the entire life of a community. It is not limited to high culture, which Eliot describes as simply more specialized and 'more conscious culture', but includes the whole spectrum of the societal community's activities and thus can only be adequately defined or understood 'in the pattern of the society as a whole' (*NDC*, 23, 48). Again like tradition, culture requires an historically extended consensual community united by 'an overlapping and sharing of interests', and involves transmission and development of itself from the past through the present and into the future. The prime medium for this is the culture's literature and language, which are also a crucial source of its unity (*NDC*, 24, 57). Moreover, like a tradition, 'culture is not merely the sum of [its] several activities' but represents the whole 'way of life' in which these activities are organized and the spirit in which they are pursued. Since it constitutes 'a peculiar way of thinking, feeling and behaving', culture (or tradition) is closely linked to religion in a wide sense. It follows from all this that a proper understanding of a culture or tradition requires 'an imaginative understanding' or some measure of empathetic identification with it (*NDC*, 41, 57, 31; cf. *ASG*, 31, 20, 43). Furthermore, since the matrix of our experience or way of life is not something that can be wholly grasped or perceived as a distinct object, tradition or culture can never be completely conscious, known, or controlled. 'Culture can never be wholly conscious – there is always more to it than we are conscious of; and it cannot be planned because it is also the unconscious background of all our planning', including 'the unconscious assumptions upon which we conduct the whole of our lives' (*NDC*, 94; *TC*, 76).

Eliot, however, is careful not to forget here that culture also includes an important conscious and critical dimension. In the cultural elite and their activities he finds the more conscious culture which includes the arts, sciences, philosophy, and theology. The elite functions both as a repository and preserver of high culture but also as the source of its criticism and modification. 'It is their function ... to transmit the culture which they have inherited; just as it is their function ... to keep it from ossification' by developing and altering it (*NDC*, 22-25, 42). The presence of more conscious and specialized cultural activities and groups greatly stimulates cultural criticism and change. For recognition of a plurality of cultural pursuits leads to creative friction and competition between them for cultural dominance, which leads in turn to mutual criticism and respective efforts by each field to outshine the others by improving itself. Thus, for example, though originally forming an 'inextricably interwoven' whole in primitive societies, 'religion, science, politics, and art become abstractly conceived apart from each other'; and with greater consciousness of their separate identities, they 'reach a point at which there is conscious struggle between them for autonomy and dominance. This friction is ... highly creative: [though] how far it is the result, and how far the cause, of increased consciousness need not here be considered' (*NDC*, 24-25).

More generally and throughout the book, Eliot emphasizes 'the vital importance for a society of *friction* between its parts'. A variety of competing classes, professions, regions, and religious ideas within a culture should 'lead to a conflict favourable to creativeness and progress', provided of course it does not lead to dissolving the underlying sense of unity which holds the cultural variety together. This desired 'pattern of unity and diversity' is a beneficial shift from *After Strange Gods'* one-sided emphasis on homogeneity which made it harder to account for the self-criticism and improvement of culture or tradition (*NDC*, 58-59, 81-82, 26; cf. *ASG*, 20).

A culture or tradition, then, requires a balance of unconsciousness with consciousness, consensual unity with pluralistic tension in order to maintain the desired balance of continuity with change which is necessary for its vigor. That tradition is not an ideal order of the immutably good but rather needs perpetual criticism and endless change was already most strongly urged in *After Strange Gods*. We must beware 'of confusing the vital and the inessential' in a tradition and therefore need criticism to determine 'what in the past is worth preserving and what should be rejected'. It is a 'danger ... to associate tradition with the immovable'; 'for the word itself implies a movement. Tradition cannot mean standing still'; 'it must be perpetually criticized and brought up to date'. 'For ... in even the very best living tradition there is always a mixture of good and bad, and much that deserves criticism' (*ASG*, 19-20, 25, 67).

Though no longer an ideal, timeless, unshakeable standard, tradition still plays a crucial role for literary creation and criticism. It indicates what has been done and thus what remains for the contemporary writer or critic to do; it helps to guide our assessment of literary and critical achievement not as an immutable yardstick but more as a flexible schema of coordinates. It provides writer and critic with access to a past which can inspire and enrich their work; and helps us all 'to renew our association with traditional wisdom; to re-establish a vital connexion between the individual and the race'; to establish, in other words, a larger, richer, more varied but still coherently united consensual community embracing both past and present (*ASG*, 53).

The task of sustaining tradition is delegated not only to great men of letters, but to 'men of the second or third or lower ranks as well ... The continuity of a literature is essential to its greatness; it is very largely the function of secondary writers [and critics] to preserve this continuity ... in forming the link between those writers who continue to be read' (*TC*, 147). For Eliot it had always been 'part of the business of the critic to preserve tradition'; yet no longer did this mean 'to see it beyond time' (*SW*, xv-xvi), but to see it instead as endlessly changing with time. Thus 'one function of criticism is to act as a kind of cog regulating the rate of change of literary taste', so that tradition steers a healthy course between the extremes of stagnating in past taste and admiring mere 'novelty as a sufficient criterion of excellence' (*TC*, 152). Besides this steady task of regulation, there is the occasional need for a rather large-scale readjustment or reshaping of tradition, at the hands of a 'master of criticism' or 'exhaustive critic' who reconstructs our literary past 'to set the poets and the poems in a new order' (*TUP*, 108-109).

III

Having traced the significant metamorphosis of Eliot's view of tradition, we can profitably compare his mature view to Gadamer's.[3] Like Eliot's, Gadamer's concept of tradition is globally comprehensive rather than elitely, aesthetically restricted. It is, moreover, immanently socially real and changing rather than transcendentally ideal and timeless. Largely unconscious, tradition is mainly transmitted through social breeding and imbibed through basic linguistic training, though some of its most conscious achievements demand a specially conscious effort to understand them. Tradition contains both good and bad, and requires constant criticism and change to keep it vital and worthy.

Though tradition is one of the most central concepts of Gadamer's philosophy, he offers no systematic analysis of it; probably because he rejects the very idea of representing tradition as a distinct object for analysis, seeing it instead as something which also underlies and prestructures our notions of object and analysis. For Gadamer, as for Eliot, tradition – being inextricably linked with language – constitutes the preconditioned and preconditioning matrix and medium of our thought. It is not a separate object we survey from an external standpoint. 'Rather, we stand always within tradition, and this is no objectifying process, i.e. we do not conceive of … tradition … as something other, something alien. It is always part of us' (*TM*, 250). And we are part of it: 'We belong to elements in tradition that reach us' from the past as a still living structuring force in the present, a force which is at the same time modified and 'motivated in a special way by the present and its interests' (*TM*, 420, 253). Therefore, Gadamer maintains, 'Tradition is not simply a precondition into which we come, but we produce it ourselves, inasmuch as we understand, participate in the evolution of tradition and hence further determine it ourselves', 'weaving the great tapestry of tradition which supports us' (*TM*, 261, 302).

As founded on community and hence communication, as the product of a dialogue between past and present, tradition is conceived by Gadamer as essentially 'linguistic in nature' and inextricably identified with language: 'tradition is not simply a process that we learn to know and be in command of through experience; it is language'. And language, perhaps more obviously than tradition, is 'the medium in and through which we exist and perceive our world' (*TM*, 321; *PH*, 29). If language embodies, transmits, and 'is the reservoir of tradition', so conversely tradition, broadly conceived by Gadamer as 'that which is societally transmitted', must in turn include and transmit language (*PH*, 29). 'Linguistic tradition is tradition in the literal sense of the word, i.e. something handed down' (*TM*, 351). This puzzling mutual subsumption of language and tradition would not be, for Gadamer,

---

[3] The abbreviations I employ in referring to Gadamer's works are explained in Chapter Five, n. 5.

a cause for dismay but a sign of their intimate identification and of the folly of objectifying them as distinct delimited entities.

Another reason not to treat tradition as a distinct determinate object is that it is continually modified, developed, and reshaped through its appropriation and criticism by its participants. Tradition can exist only through its use or practice, but this means its application to particular situations by its participants who appropriate and implement tradition in relation to their particular situational interests and needs. Then, since these perpetually change with time and context, tradition must be perpetually reinterpreted and modified accordingly to maintain its applicational value and relevance. Since 'it is the nature of tradition to exist only through being appropriated', and since there is no limit to appropriations and their change, it follows that there is no possible consciousness which can grasp tradition as a complete totalized object (*TM*, xxv, 430). Moreover, since the 'historical life of a tradition depends on constantly new assimilation [i.e. appropriation] and interpretation', which must be adapted to the changing situations encountered, it follows that 'tradition exists only in constant alteration' (*TM*, 358; *R*, 307).

It is therefore wrong to think of tradition as intransigently predetermined, fixed, and opposed to all criticism or change through the agency of critical intelligence or reason, which itself is an aspect or outgrowth of tradition and not a purely external transcendental faculty. Here too, Gadamer concurs with Eliot, as he does in maintaining that a tradition or parts thereof may be 'resisted with revolutionary fervour when ... found to be lifeless and inflexible' (*KS*, I, 160). Gadamer also shrewdly points out that reason functions not only in critical reform but in decisions to preserve elements of the tradition. 'Even the most genuine and solid tradition does not persist because of the inertia of what once existed. It needs to be affirmed, embraced, cultivated. It is, essentially, preservation, such as is active in all historical change. But preservation is an act of reason, though an inconspicuous one' (*TM*, 250).

There is, however, a misleading ambiguity in Gadamer's assertion. Though it is obviously true that preservation *can* be an act of reason (e.g. when it involves a deliberate conscious decision to preserve), given the largely unconscious nature of tradition surely much of its preservation is simply the unreflective or unconscious continuing of social habits. And here there is hardly room to speak of preservation as an act of reason. Criticism and reform, on the other hand, require at least consciousness of what is being criticized, if not also deliberation as to the desirability of alternatives. Reason, then, is not alien or inherently opposed to tradition, but it does not pervade or operate in all areas of tradition, though perhaps no part of tradition can in principle be immune or impenetrable to reason's scrutiny.

The strikingly deep affinities between Eliot's and Gadamer's theories of tradition will be further demonstrated in the project which occupies the remainder of this chapter: a ramified account of why the concept of tradition is theoretically valuable to Eliot and how it helps to provide a more promising middle course between the poles of an unconvincing, self-repressing absolute objectivism and an unwanted, self-imprisoning subjectivism. My account will focus on five crucial features of the concept of tradition which give it great explanatory power and enable it to combat the vitiating oppression of the objective/subjective dichotomy. These features are prejudice, community, authority, language, and compound explanatory unity. We may begin where Gadamer and Eliot agree that all understanding must begin – with prejudice.

IV

(1) The term 'prejudice' has so long been linked with such abominations as racism and sexism that it has absorbed (like the term 'discrimination') a distinctively pejorative connotation. So prejudiced are we against the idea of prejudice that any imputation of prejudice is taken as censure and invariably answered by protestations of denial. Yet Eliot and Gadamer agree that we are fortunately never lacking in prejudice, which is a necessary condition for our understanding or knowledge of the world. We cannot confront the world free from all preconceptions, prestructuring categories, formative interests and desires. Instead we always confront it from within a tradition which embodies such orientating prejudices, many of which we subscribe to unconsciously. We might imagine trying to rid ourselves of all preconceptions, interests, and desires (though with unconscious ones this hardly seems possible[4]) with the aim of attaining a wholly unprejudiced objective view of the world. But such a supremely purified vision is itself highly motivated or tainted with interest, and arguably an interest of a narrow and perverse sort. For there would hardly seem much use for a view of the world significantly devoid of relation to our interests in dealing with the world.

A wholly unprejudiced view of the world would, moreover, be incomprehensible to us.[5] It could not be properly expressed or translated into our

---

[4] The pragmatist Peirce effectively puts this anti-Cartesian point: 'We cannot begin with complete doubt. We must begin with all the prejudices which we actually have when we enter upon the study of philosophy. These prejudices are not to be dispelled by a maxim, for they are things which it does not occur to us *can* be questioned'. [*Collected Papers of Charles Sanders Peirce* (Cambridge, Mass.: Harvard University Press, 1931-35), 5.265, p. 156]. Prejudices however can be tested in experience and corrected, though this is done holistically together with the structures of belief which depend on them.

[5] It is arguable, therefore, that even the very idea of distinguishing *the* world itself, independent of any linguistic or conceptual tools through which human intelligence conceives and deals with it, is ultimately empty and unintelligible. The point is cogently made by N. Goodman, 'The Way the World Is', *Problems and Projects* (Indianapolis: Bobbs-Merrill, 1972), 24-32, and *Ways of Worldmaking* (Indianapolis: Hackett, 1978), 1-22, 91-140. On the problems this raises for the traditional scheme/content distinction, see D. Davidson, 'On the Very Idea of a Conceptual Scheme', in *Inquiries into Truth and Interpretation* (Oxford: Oxford University Press, 1984), 183-198. Though I feel the

language, whose semantic concepts and categories reflect our culture's preconceptions and interests – carving out the semantic field, individuating entities, actions, and qualities in terms of what is already taken as worth individuating and referring to. For to express or translate it in our terms must introduce contaminating prejudice. But since any language involves predetermined categories which involve prejudices, and since all understanding is mediated by language, it would follow that all understanding involves prejudice.[6]

However, understanding is not always wrong because it never achieves a purely unprejudiced God's-eye view which is alleged the only true understanding. For such an idea of objective understanding, as Eliot realized, is a chimera; since any point of view is prestructured or limited, 'there is no *absolute* point of view' (*KE*, 22). A completely unprejudiced and unstructured vision would not see anything at all. Our aim is therefore not pure, unprejudiced objectivity but a satisfactory or workable understanding based on fruitful prejudices, which may be corrected, rejected, or supplemented when they and the understanding they afford are found wanting. Gadamer, too, insists 'that all understanding inevitably involves some prejudice' (*TM*, 239), but does more than Eliot to elaborate the positive, knowledge-producing dimension of prejudice.

> Prejudices are not necessarily unjustified and erroneous, so that they inevitably distort the truth. In fact, the historicity of our existence entails that prejudices, in the literal sense of the word, constitute the initial directedness of our whole ability to experience. Prejudices are biases of our openness to the world. They are simply conditions whereby we experience something – whereby what we encounter says something to us. (*PH*, 9)

Tradition, with its medium of language, embodies and maintains these prejudices or forms of orientation through which we are able to cope with the world, forms which have been slowly fashioned and hammered out through long centuries of trial and error. We would not like to start from scratch, uncorrupted by cultural prejudice like some feral child, even if we could. But besides transmitting and sustaining the prejudices which inform our thought, tradition also provides the means for revealing and removing those which rather hinder than promote fruitful understanding. Eliot, we recall, remarked that a tradition has 'always a mixture of good and bad', of helpful and harmful predispositions of thought and feeling; and Gadamer explicitly distinguishes between illegitimate 'false prejudices' which need to be rejected and 'legitimate prejudices', 'justified prejudices productive of knowledge' (*TM*, 246-247). But how do we distinguish

---

pragmatist power of this line, I shall not try to purge my language here of such notions of structuring the world or experience, for to do so would invite misinterpretation as naive objectivism.

   [6] As Gadamer writes, 'We are always already biased in our thinking and knowing by our linguistic interpretation of the world' (*PH*, 64).

between them, and how can tradition help us here?

We cannot sort out the productive from the pernicious prejudices by the exercise of a pure, unprejudiced transcendental faculty of reason, since its existence is denied. We instead determine the validity of prejudices by repeatedly testing them against new experience and new situations. Since they are neither proved by one success nor falsified by one failure, their necessary repeated testing requires that prejudices be maintained through time; and tradition achieves this, enabling past prejudices to be tested by the present and future and 'their limitations [to] become manifest in the perspective of history'. Tradition 'performs the filtering process ... of distinguishing the true prejudices, by which we understand, from the false ones by which we misunderstand', and letting the latter die off so that 'those that bring about genuine understanding ... emerge clearly as such' (*TUP*, 142; *TM*, 266).

Apart from this test of time, tradition provides another means of testing and improving prejudices – playing them off against each other. We can test those prejudices which currently dominate our thinking by confronting them with past prejudices which are no longer very dominant or influential in our thought but which still belong to our tradition and can still reach us as embodied in and transmitted through its language, most particularly and powerfully through its works of literary art. When we read the epics of Homer and the tragedies of Sophocles, or even the works of Dante and Jane Austen, we encounter worlds shaped by prejudices and attitudes which we no longer share. In opening ourselves to these old prejudices and in setting them against our present ones, we may find that ours are far less satisfactory, rewarding, and indubitable than we had previously assumed them to be.

'For Gadamer,' as Richard Bernstein remarks, 'it is in and through the encounter with works of art, texts, and more generally what is handed down to us through tradition that we discover which of our prejudices are blind and which are enabling ... It is only through the dialogical encounter with what is at once alien to us, makes a claim upon us, and has affinity with what we are that we can open ourselves to risking and testing our prejudices.'[7] Bernstein's account, though correct as far as it goes, requires important supplementation. We not only need such an encounter with tradition to distinguish the good and bad in our prejudices, we also often need it to discover what our prejudices actually are. For some of our most potent prejudices are hidden from us; and it may take confrontation with significantly different prejudices embodied in a text to highlight through contrast the prejudices which unconsciously direct us, thereby bringing them up into consciousness so that they may be assessed, criticized, and perhaps amended. 'It is impossible to make ourselves aware of [our prejudice] while it is constantly operating unnoticed, but only when it is, so

---

[7] R.J. Bernstein, *Beyond Objectivism and Relativism* (Oxford: Blackwell, 1983), 128-129.

to speak, stimulated. The encounter with a text from the past can provide this stimulus' and 'make conscious the prejudices governing our own understanding' (*TM*, 266).

Eliot had similarly urged encounter with tradition's texts as a means to escape our temporal parochialism where we are so immersed in present attitudes that we are unaware of them and implicitly take them for granted as inevitable. Not only did he claim that we must 'enter those worlds of poetry in which we are alien' in order to approach 'full consciousness' of the poetic vision of life we endorse as our own,[8] he also advocated the same sort of value in reading past criticism, 'a value which all study of the past should have for us: that it should make us more conscious of what we are, and of our own limitations, and give us more understanding of the world in which we now live' (*OPP*, 192).[9]

Yet another way in which tradition helps to distinguish legitimate prejudices and even seems to supply legitimation is in terms of the consensual, shared character of tradition's prejudices. Accepting the inevitability of prejudice and discarding the ideal of absolute, mirroring objectivism, we are left to interpret objectivity or validity in terms of consensus. Prejudices embodied in and shared by the tradition can appeal to considerable consensus, and the longer and deeper an existing prejudice is embedded in a living tradition, the greater its consensus and its *prima facie* claim to legitimation. Such deeply shared prejudices of tradition may be sharply distinguished from merely personal prejudice or individual bias, which cannot be justified by appeal to consensus but rather stand out as eccentrically deviant from and threatening to consensus. However, even the shared prejudices of a tradition are shared by individuals and help constitute their individual thought and personality. Such prejudices therefore defy the objective/subjective dichotomy. On the one hand, they belong to subjects and are inconceivable without them; on the other, they are clearly more than subjective. They represent a standard of objectivity or legitimacy external to the particular individual – the standard of consensus with a tradition, agreement with a wide community of competent and fruitful thought extended and tested over an impressive length of time.

(2) This leads us to the second feature of tradition to be discussed – its consensual community over time. We may begin by noting the obvious fact that any tradition requires a significant degree of consensus among individuals with respect to actions, beliefs, habits, and attitudes. It almost seems a conceptual truth that tradition requires some consensus, for one

---

[8] T.S. Eliot, 'Poetry and Propoganda', *Bookman*, 70 (1930), 601-602.

[9] Eliot may have learned this lesson from Hulme who advocated the study of history as 'necessary in order to emancipate the individual of certain *pseudo-categories* ... of which we are as a matter of fact unconscious. We do not see them, but see other things *through* them ... Once they have been brought to the surface of the mind, they lose their inevitable character' (*Speculations*, 37-38).

could hardly speak of the unique tradition of an individual, though we can already speak of a family or club tradition. Tradition, then, is inseparable from a consensual community, and in participating in a tradition the individual cannot help but act and think in ways that are not merely subjective or private.

Twentieth-century pragmatists who reject the realist idea of an unmediated, unprejudiced, timeless objectivity have sought to avoid the subjectivist alternative by adopting consensuality as either the proper model of objectivity or as an alternative standard of validity. Nor is their idea of consensual objectivity an ethereal idealist intersubjectivity of similar mental content and judgment, but rather a consensus that is materially embodied and hammered out in the real world of practice and history. Thus Rorty holds that 'our only usable notion of objectivity is agreement rather than mirroring' and Margolis defines objectivity as 'the consensually accepted' which ' "belongs" within the life of a given society'.[10] In anchoring objectivity or validity in community, they are only returning to ideas emphasized by some early twentieth-century philosophers who were influential at Eliot's Harvard. Peirce, the original pragmatist, stressed the dependence of knowledge on a community of inquirers, maintaining even that the 'very origin of the conception of reality shows that this conception essentially involves the notion of a COMMUNITY, without definite limits, and capable of a definite increase of knowledge'.[11] Josiah Royce, Eliot's graduate teacher whose later philosophy was avowedly influenced by Peirce's pragmatism and had emerged right at the time Eliot came under his tutelage, similarly insists on the primacy of consensual community. 'The existence of this community', argued Royce, not only 'is presupposed as a basis of every scientific inquiry into natural facts', but is also the necessary basis for any knowledge of the self.[12] This is because self-knowledge cannot be acquired immediately through intuition or perception as a particular datum or universal character, but instead is the goal of a continuing process of interpretation which requires comparison with other selves and thus requires community. Self-knowledge, self-development, and self-identity are thus largely a product of social construction and differentiation based on participation in 'a community of interpreters'. The inconceivability of one's individual self without a socially real community entails the untenability of radical subjectivism and any

---

[10] R. Rorty, *Philosophy and the Mirror of Nature* (Princeton: Princeton University Press, 1978), 337 and J. Margolis, 'Relativism, History, and Objectivity in the Human Studies', *Journal for the Theory of Social Behavior*, 14 (1984), 9.

[11] See *Collected Papers*, 5.265, 5.311, pp. 157, 186-187.

[12] J. Royce, *The Problem of Christianity*, 1913 repr. (Chicago: University of Chicago Press, 1968), 332. Eliot's solution to solipsism was essentially Roycean, arguing that we cannot say we know only the self and its thoughts because the self is not an entity or idea immediately given in experience (i.e. given as opposed to an external world which has to be inferred) but is itself only 'an intellectual construction'. Eliot recognizes that 'I only know myself in contrast to a world' and other selves (*KE*, 150, 152).

rigid dichotomy between the subjective and consensually objective.

Eliot's doctoral thesis displays his appreciation of the consensual model of objectivity advanced by his Harvard predecessors. Reality is described as a function of community consensus in pragmatically interpreting experience: 'the real world ... consists in the common meaning and "identical reference" of various finite centres.' It is 'a construction by the selection and combination of various presentations to various viewpoints'; and it is only 'one world because there is only one world intended ... [and] we are able to intend one world because our views are essentially akin' (*KE*, 140, 142, 144). Reality thus depends on the cooperative consensus of men and women to intend the same objects, and this consensual cooperation is ultimately motivated by their shared pragmatic aim of coping satisfactorily with their experience. The existence of any common object 'depends upon our recognition of [its] community of meaning' (i.e. its being intended by and its presenting similar qualities to a community of observers on different occasions); 'and this community' of meaning is ultimately practical' (*KE*, 161). Thus 'reality is a convention' created and modified by what 'practical purposes demand'; 'the world ... a construction essentially practical in its nature' (*KE*, 98, 136).

When Eliot first turned to literary criticism, and the pragmatic idealism of his doctoral philosophy gave way to a more robustly objectivist criticial stance, the idea of consensual objectivity was still operative in his themes of tradition and 'the common pursuit', though temporarily overshadowed by a realist correspondence model of objectivity. Eliot's subsequent literary theory displays an increasing and manifold dependence on the idea of consensus. Its community serves as a necessary precondition and, to some extent, also a measure or goal of good literature. Kermode's view to the contrary notwithstanding,[13] Eliot rejects the Romantic ideal of the isolated artist. He instead insists that any writer not only 'needs a small public of substantially the same education as himself, as well as the same tastes; [but] a larger public with some common background with him; and finally he should have something in common with everyone who has intelligence and sensibility and can read his language' (*TC*, 158). For Eliot, the very 'survival of English literature' requires this consensual background, continually nourished by some shared education and tradition, 'for upon this depends the possibility of a general audience, the possibility both of the author's being able to communicate with people in all walks of life, and of their being able to understand each other' (*TC*, 158, 155). This deep commitment to the idea of consensus helps explain why, despite his reputation as an elitist poet, Eliot's poetic ideal was to reach the largest audience and affect the greatest community. This is evident in his praise of Dante and Shakespeare, but even more so in his advocacy of the poetic

---

[13] See F. Kermode's *Romantic Image* (London: Fontana, 1971), 153-177, which treats Eliot as subscribing to the Romantic-Symbolist doctrine that the artist's essential isolation from society is crucial to his superior vision.

drama and in his own dogged and difficult struggle to achieve a wider audience by turning to the theatre. 'I believe that the poet naturally prefers to write for as large and miscellaneous an audience as possible ... I myself should like an audience which could neither read nor write ... The ideal medium for poetry, to my mind, [therefore] is the theatre' (*TUP*, 152-153).

Consensus is also the motivating ground for Eliot's 'ideal of a common style' and 'a community of taste' which are necessary for the creation of any work of classic stature (*OPP*, 57-63). It must also be present in a high degree for any progress to be made in those 'purer' forms of criticism that provide 'minute and scrupulous examination of felicity and blemish' (*TUP*, 25, *OPP*, 191). But more significant than any of his specifically literary or critical applications of the idea of consensus is Eliot's recognition that a certain degree of consensus, a certain background of shared beliefs and agreed ways of thinking, is necessary for any productive communication. Even debate or controversy 'can only usefully be practised when there is common understanding. It requires common assumptions; and perhaps the assumptions that are only felt are more important than those that can be formulated' (*ASG*, 11).[14]

Though we began by arguing that tradition requires a consensual community, we must similarly recognize that any durable and substantial consensual community needs a tradition. Without it, i.e. without a perceived form of continuity of agreement through the past into the present, whatever consensus the present seems to reveal may well be a momentary, fragile, arbitrary coincidence. Tradition provides consensus *over time*, an abiding or enduring consensus which gives the notion of consensus the sort of stability or durability we demand of a model of objectivity or validity. It also provides the sort of unifying, sustaining story which distinguishes a real historical community from a mere collection of co-existents. As Royce argues, the very notion and identity of such a community involves the perception of its members' sharing a tradition or common past.

> The psychological unity of many selves in one community is bound up, then, with the consciousness of some lengthy social process which has occurred, or is at least supposed to have occurred. And the wealthier the memory of a community is, and the vaster the historical processes which it regards as belonging to its life, the richer – other things being equal – is its consciousness

---

[14] Gadamer likewise argues that community consensus provides the necessary background for any valid understanding or rationality. 'Solidarity ... is the decisive condition and basis of all social reason' (*RAS*, 87). Instead of Cartesian 'foundationalist ... apodictic evidence of self-consciousness', he posits 'participation', the sharing of 'a common world of tradition and interpreted experience', as the basis and model of human understanding (*HS*, 64). For Gadamer, as for Eliot, the necessary 'communality of all understanding [is] grounded in its intrinsically linguistic quality ... Discussion bears fruit when a common language is found'. For in speaking a common language we 'are continually shaping a common perspective' through the shared assumptions that any common language requires (*RAS*, 110).

that it *is* a community, that its members are somehow made one in and through and with its own life.[15]

By providing a consensus of the present with a long and abundantly fruitful past, tradition makes our community's consensus much wider and richer, and hence more convincing and reassuring; or, as it were, by the consensual model of objectivity – more objective. Thus, for pragmatists like Rorty, committed to consensuality and ethnocentric rather than transcendental truth, 'the desire for objectivity is not the desire to escape the limitations of one's community, but simply the desire for as much intersubjective agreement as possible, the desire to extend the reference of "us" as far as we can'.[16] This desire, which Eliot shared (at times to the point of intolerance to non-conformity), brought him to celebrate and bolster tradition as a means to its satisfaction, to the achievement of a greater consensus. For tradition, of course, 'represents a consensus between the living and the dead', a vast though largely unconscious communality of belief, action, and sensibility, whose valuable presence Eliot labored to bring to our conscious appreciation, hoping thereby to engage our cooperative efforts to sustain and develop it.

The abiding, abundant, and coherent consensus that tradition provides the present also serves to promote consensus in the future. It does so not merely by inertia but by supplying a precedent of agreement which future attempts to achieve consensus can effectively employ or emulate. The underlying idea here (meticulously elaborated in Lewis's study of convention) is that when we share a desire for consensus or conformity of behavior, we can achieve it without explicit agreement but simply on the basis of rationally held 'concordant mutual expectations'.[17] These, when acted on and fulfilled by consensual behavior, become reinforced or more strongly expected which in turn leads to their being (in a recursive fashion)

---

[15] Royce, 243-244. The most central and basic Roycean conception of community, one without which the notions of self, other, and object would be meaningless, is what he calls 'the Community of Interpretation'. The idea of such community extended over history comes close to Eliot's idea of tradition, and perhaps, as Piers Gray suggests, influenced it [P. Gray, *T.S. Eliot's Intellectual and Poetic Development, 1909-1922* (Sussex: Harvester Press,1982), 96-104]. The Roycean-Eliotic idea of an historically extended community of interpreters through which both the objects and subjects of experience are constituted clearly prefigures Stanley Fish's recently influential theory of 'interpretive communities' as the fundamental factor determining textual meaning. See S. Fish, *Is There a Text in This Class?* (Cambridge, Mass.: Harvard University Press, 1980), 11-17. The Roycean-Eliotic concept of community is arguably superior because it is portrayed in more comprehensive terms, reflecting enduring social and historical realities, and thus not as arbitrary and relativistic as Fish's seems to be.

[16] R. Rorty, 'Solidarity or Objectivity?' in J. Rajchman and C. West, *Post-Analytic Philosophy* (New York: Columbia University Press, 1985), 5.

[17] D.K. Lewis, *Convention: A Philosophical Study* (Cambridge, Mass.: Harvard University Press, 1969), 34. For a more concise account of this idea, and a critical analysis of Lewis's theory, see my 'Convention: Variations on a Theme', *Philosophical Investigations*, 9 (1986), 36-55.

reciprocally fulfilled and further reinforced, making the means and achievement of future consensus more obvious and easy. Tradition, with the precedents it provides, is probably the most potent source of such consensus-generating expectations. Yet, conversely, these expectations themselves, as tradition itself, already reflect and require the existence of some consensus.

Since Eliot shares the pragmatist aim of enlarging consensus, and since tradition provides the best (if not only) precedent or available model for consensus, it is not surprising that he should advocate tradition as the means for constructing the future's consensual community: 'Our problem being to form the future, we can only form it on the materials of the past; we must *use* our heredity instead of denying it' (*FLA*, 102).[18] This, of course, does not mean that tradition's materials cannot be supplemented or changed, just as our desire for cultural consensus is not a desire for complete cultural uniformity which would deny the productive variety of tradition necessary for its self-criticism and progressive evolution.

(3) Its provision of an authoritative precedent for promoting consensus points to a third feature of tradition – authority. Like prejudice, authority is a notion much disparaged by our Enlightenment heritage and liberal conscience. But again like prejudice, it seems necessary for the achievement of any adequate, workable understanding of the world. One of Gadamer's points in what he calls 'the rehabilitation of authority and tradition' is that we simply cannot do without traditional authority. As finite, historical beings we are precluded from achieving the Cartesian project of 'the total reconstruction of all truth by reason' and its authority alone. For our very conception of reason, not to mention the (often unconscious) presuppositions on which it works, depends largely on tradition as the historical context and structuring matrix into which we are born and through which we learn to act and think effectively.

> That which has been sanctioned by tradition and custom has an authority that is nameless, and our finite historical being is marked by the fact that always the authority of what has been transmitted – and not only what is clearly grounded – has power over our attitudes and behaviour. All education depends on this, and even though ... the educator loses his function when his charge comes of age and sets his own insight and decisions in the place of the authority of the educator, this ... does not mean that a person becomes his own master in the sense that he becomes free of all tradition. (*TM*, 249)

---

[18] This emphasis on the resources of the past – for materials and for wider consensus – is what makes Eliot's pragmatism seem so different from Rorty's, which aims at 'overcoming the tradition' and making a better future not so much by using the past as by 'inventing new vocabularies'. Since we can plausibly talk of a consensual community embracing past and present, if we share Rorty's aim of maximizing community, this aim would seem much better served by relying more on shared past vocabularies than on the invention of new ones. Rorty's anti-traditionalism and panacea of new vocabularies are criticized in the next chapter but more fully in my 'Deconstruction and Analysis: Confrontation and Convergence', *British Journal of Aesthetics*, 26 (1986), 311-327.

The ineliminable and productive role of traditional authority in our knowledge and action may be demonstrated by the following argument. Since thought and social interaction are essentially linguistic, and since language can only be acquired through a training which involves submission to linguistic authority, i.e. the authority of traditionally established rules or conventions of language as embodied in the practice and instruction of competent speakers of language, it follows that thought, knowledge, and social interaction ultimately rely on the authority of tradition.

Reliance or dependence on tradition's authority does not, however, entail mere slavish, passive submission to it. There is in fact a dialectic between obeisance to and mastery of it, a dialectic which Eliot always intuitively grasped and profitably employed in speaking authoritatively for tradition, but which eludes and confounds his early theorizing on the issue of inner judgment versus external authority (*SE*, 23-24). This dialectic of submission and mastery can be clarified by supplementing MacIntyre's views on the notion of a practice with some of Wittgenstein's remarks on rules.

For MacIntyre, to engage in any practice or discipline (i.e. 'any coherent and complex form of socially established cooperative activity' aimed at achieving the goods and standards of excellence partially definitive of that activity) requires the recognition of traditional authority in the form of the standards and models of achievement already operative in the practice.[19] Since a 'practice involves standards of excellence and obedience to rules ... [to] enter into a practice is to accept the authority of those standards and ... to subject my own attitudes, choices, preferences and tastes to the standards which currently and partially define the practice'. Though the already existing rules or standards are not 'immune from criticism' and though we can eventually come to criticize them, 'none the less we cannot be initiated into a practice without accepting the authority of the best standards realised so far'. One cannot properly learn to compose or appreciate a sonnet without first submitting one's judgment to and guiding one's efforts by what has already been established as proper and worthy in this genre. 'It is thus the achievement, and *a fortiori* the authority, of a tradition ... from which I have to learn.'

Though MacIntyre rightly asserts the need for subordinating ourselves to tradition's authority, this image of self-subordination to an external authoritative standard is apt to cause confusion. For in an important sense, the tradition's authoritative rules and standards do not simply exist autonomously as a distinct external master; they rather belong to, are mastered by, and even extended and reshaped by the individuals participating in the tradition or practice. Initial subordination is necessary for, but typically issues in, a competence or mastery of rules and standards

---

[19] A. MacIntyre, *After Virtue* (London: Duckworth, 1981), 175-181. My quotations in this paragraph are from pages 175, 177, 181.

which internalizes or transforms them into dispositions of the individual participants, who thereby, in pursuing the practice, intuitively perform or recognize what is right without appealing to the mediation or confirmation of an external, articulated rule. For true competence or mastery of the rules of a practice requires, as Wittgenstein noted, knowing 'how to go on', how to go beyond mechanical applications to familiar instances, how to interpret the rules and to see that in some cases they need to be extended or modified to sustain and develop the practice. Though I must first learn the rules and be 'drilled' in them from an outside source, I come to absorb and master them as expressions of my own disposition. Thus, as Wittgenstein remarks on aesthetics, 'I develop a feeling for the rules. I interpret the rules' beyond their present or explicit determinations. Successful and influential innovative practitioners may also modify the rules. For the rules or standards of an aesthetic practice are not autonomously given entities, governing from the outside its circle of competent practitioners, but rather an expression of their shared dispositions, 'an expression of what certain people want'.[20]

Thus there is no essential, ineluctable antinomy between traditional authority and individual judgment. Individuals not only imbibe tradition but are essentially formed, bred, and motivated by its rules and bearings. We would not be the individuals we are without tradition's formative training, and we can therefore generally conform to tradition in the free pursuit of our own (tradition-fashioned) dispositions rather than through reluctant, constrained obedience to an outside authority, imposing its external objectivity on an utterly internal, lawless subjectivity. Here again, tradition helps free us from a blind and blighting rigid dichotomy of objective and subjective, typically reinforced here by the captivating picture of a clearly separated outer versus inner.

In the pragmatism of his doctoral thesis, Eliot realized that 'the distinction between inner and outer, which makes the epistemologist's capital, cannot stand' in any foundational principled sense (*KE*, 138). But later, in the sway of his early objectivism and in the heat of an important polemic with Middleton Murry, who advocated a romantic faith in 'the inner voice' over the classical 'principle of spiritual authority outside the individual', Eliot foolishly rushed into a dichotomous terminology of debate where he should have feared to tread.[21] Though circumspectly noting that 'outside' and 'inside' are terms of too 'base coinage' for serious psychological discourse, Eliot presumes that for his literary 'purpose these counters are adequate' and offers the following feeble definition of the outside he champions: 'If you find that you have to imagine it as outside, then it is

---

[20] L. Wittgenstein, *Lectures and Conversations on Aesthetics, Psychology, and Religious Belief* (Oxford: Blackwell, 1970), 5.

[21] One reason Eliot could not forego the debate with Murry and wanted to attack him head-on concerns a matter of literary-journalistic politics. Murry's advocacy of Romanticism and the inner voice was a manifesto for his newly founded journal, *Adelphi*, an obvious rival to Eliot's classically orientated *Criterion*, founded only the year before. As a dedicated new editor and able polemicist, Eliot could not allow Murry's challenge to go unanswered.

outside' (*SE*, 26-27). That this definition of the outside aporetically relies on the *inner* voice of one's imagination, and is moreover sharply inconsistent with the essay's insistence on hard facts and the dangers of imagination helps betray the untenable confusion of Eliot's binary thinking here.

Contrasting the outer to the inner, traditional authority to individual judgment, as if they were unproblematic dichotomous terms, Eliot is here unable to see that tradition is not at all a clearly separable, external object but exists only as embodied in the practices and achievements of the individuals who reciprocally belong to it and sustain and develop it. Blinkered by the polemical hypostatizing opposition of 'Inner Voice' to 'Outside Authority' (*SE*, 29), Eliot temporarily fails to realize that one's inner voice may well express the rules and standards of traditional outside authority from which it learns to speak. For the inner voice, to speak at all, must speak in forms that it did not create but received from a tradition which extends beyond the particular individual and in that sense exists outside him, yet which can also exist in him and can only exist in some group of individuals. The inner voice can and has to speak in external public tones, as Wittgenstein's private language argument effectively shows. Eliot's entire internal/external polemic is a red-herring, while the true issue of objectivity here is one of consensus. The location of the voice is irrelevant. What is dangerous is not its internality but its disruptive, dissonant deviance from the norm; what is desired is not its externality but its consensual harmony.

That a judgment can issue from an individual's inner sense of what is right and can yet be based on and appeal to the authority of tradition is crucial to Eliot's critical enterprise. In failing to emphasize this possibility while maintaining a privileging opposition of traditional authority over individual judgment, Eliot makes himself vulnerable to charges of inconsistency, hypocrisy, and hubris. For having demanded that the individual ignore his inner voice or sacrifice his individual judgment in obeisance to the 'external' authority of tradition, Eliot reveals himself as an individual who offers his own views. He thus appears to allow himself what he denies to others or, still worse, to presume the unique identity of *his* inner voice with tradition. But raising one's own voice in the name of and defense of tradition only seems a problem when we assume an essential opposition of inner voice and outside authority. Yet the example of language shows that the former can express the latter. We have no trouble accepting that a competent English speaker can rely on his inner judgment to determine whether certain sentences are or are not grammatical; and we would not regard it as overweening pride for him to say that his inner voice expresses here the authoritative verdict of the English language. The critic's voice and the inner voice of one's moral conscience can similarly speak with the authority of a literary or ethical tradition. The perceived differences in the voice's authority in these cases only seems to be a question of difference in degree of consensus in the field. We enjoy more agreement in syntax than in morals or aesthetics; but perhaps we have to, since language provides the basis for both and for all tradition.

(4) Language and tradition may be distinguishable but are inseparable; 'flip-sides', as it were, of our most common currency. Language, as Wittgenstein contended, is more than an abstract calculus but depends upon a shared form of life, communal practices and customs which extend with continuity and regularity over time – in short, upon tradition. Like any activity involving rules, language requires a traditional factor both for the repeated regularity and for the public or communal accessibility (and hence possibility for confirmation or correction) that are essential to the very notion of following a rule. 'It is not possible that there should have been only one occasion on which someone obeyed a rule ... To obey a rule, to make a report, to give an order, to play a game of chess, are *customs* (uses, institutions)' (PI, 199). Rule-following similarly requires a consensual community to provide the normative aspect of a rule, its being more than a mere regularity but something which can be correctly or incorrectly followed. The idea of purely private rules thus makes no sense, for it would void the distinction between obeying the rule and merely thinking one was obeying it. Hence Wittgenstein's view of the impossibility of a private language, and the necessary grounding of language in community 'agreement in ... form of life'. 'If language is to be a means of communication there must be agreement not only in definitions but also (queer as this may sound) in judgments'; e.g. 'what we call "measuring" is partly determined by a certain constancy in results of measurements' (*PI*, 241-242). Thus, for Wittgenstein, 'to imagine a language means to imagine a form of life' (PI, 19) shared by a temporally extended consensual community; which means to imagine a tradition.

If language depends on the shared practices of tradition, so conversely does tradition depend on language which helps to structure and transmit the shared practices and ways of feeling and thinking that constitute a tradition or form of life. Almost all the ordinary activities of civilized people involve language and require it for their smooth functioning; many (e.g. bargaining, arguing, reporting, reading, writing, etc.) would be inconceivable without it. And if all thought requires language, then the notion of a language-less tradition is as empty as that of a private language.

Like Wittgenstein, Gadamer recognizes 'the unity between language and tradition', explicitly declaring that 'tradition ... is language' (*TM*, 400, 321). Most obviously 'tradition is linguistic in character' because it exists 'in the medium of language' through which it is transmitted and sustained, whether through oral repetition or more powerfully and enduringly in a written, literary form. But tradition needs language not only for language's communicative power of transmission but also for its communicative power of unification, which helps to connect and bind individuals in a common structuring orientation to the world and thus helps to constitute tradition's consensual community. 'We are continually shaping a common perspective when we speak a common language and so are active participants in the communality of our experience of the world' (*RAS*, 110). For language 'is the middle ground in which understanding and agreement concerning the object takes place between two people' (*TM*, 345-346). Since conversation and hence community require a shared language, if none exists they must immediately create one or cease to be. Thus tradition's consensual community both requires and is required by language. 'All forms of human community of life are forms of linguistic community: even more, they constitute language' (*TM*, 404).

Eliot's account of tradition highlights the same two functions of language: preservational transmission and unification. He maintains 'that for the transmission of a culture – a peculiar way of thinking, feeling, and behaving – and for its maintenance, there is no safeguard more reliable than a language. And to survive for this purpose it must continue to be a literary language', because literature expresses and preserves ways of feeling and thinking likely to be ignored in scientific writing (*NDC*, 57). Eliot likewise insists on language as a force which gives distinctive unity to a particular tradition or culture, 'because speaking the same language means thinking, and feeling, and having emotions [in much the same way but] rather differently from people who use a different language' (*NDC*, 120).

Eliot here points to a dominant theme of twentieth-century philosophy (common to thinkers as different as Goodman and Gadamer, Davidson and Derrida, Croce and Wittgenstein) – the fundamentally linguistic character of our experience and understanding of the world, a world which itself is largely and unavoidably constituted by the structures of language. Like these philosophers, Eliot realized that we 'live in' a language (*OPP*, 65) and that the language we live in greatly determines the direction, limits, and quality of our thought and feeling. 'Every language has its own resources and its own limitations' (*OPP*, 54); but the particular constraints that this places on our understanding are not irremediable or final. First, a language may be developed by the creative and critical efforts of its users, whose intellectual achievements extend the language's capacities for thought and feeling. This is one of the functions of philosophers, scientists and poets. Secondly, our capacities for understanding can be extended by acquiring foreign languages and their literatures which provide new worlds and ways of thought and experience.

With respect to the first point, we may recall Eliot's praise of Russell's mathematical logic for extending the capacities of English language. 'The *Principia Mathematica* are perhaps a greater contribution to our language than they are to mathematics', because they make it closer to 'a language in which it is possible to think clearly and exactly on any subject'.[22] And many years later Eliot was still maintaining that 'certain languages ... have

[22] T.S. Eliot, 'Commentary', *The Criterion*, 6 (1927), 291.

become, because of the work done by scientists and philosophers who have thought in those languages, and because of the traditions thus created, better vehicles than others for scientific and abstract thought' (*NDC*, 56). What the scientist and philosopher do for a language's abstract thought, the poet must do for its capacity to communicate feelings, which Eliot recognized as even more closely linked to the particular language of a culture: 'the impalpable differences of feeling between one people and another, differences which are affirmed in, and developed by their different languages' are what makes 'no art more stubbornly national than poetry' and nothing more difficult to translate (*OPP*, 19-20).[23]

Eliot therefore recommends the enlargement of the individual's range of feeling and understanding through the acquisition of foreign languages and literatures, though he is more careful than Gadamer in noting the dangers of such cultural excursions.[24] 'One of the reasons for learning at least one foreign language well is that we acquire a kind of supplementary personality; one of the reasons for not acquiring a new language *instead* of our own is that most of us do not want to become a different person' (*OPP*, 19). Eliot himself admits that he gave up his absorbed pursuit of Oriental philosophy because his increased immersion in it risked his 'forgetting how to think and feel as an American or a European: which, for practical as well as sentimental reasons, [he] did not want to do' (*ASG*, 44).

The intrinsic linguistic nature of thought and feeling thus implies a necessary linguistico-cultural dimension of personal identity, which obviates the threat of a vitiating solipsistic subjectivism. For even if we try to strip away the social dimension of our identity to reach a private personal

[23] As Eliot notes, 'It is easier to think in a foreign language than to feel in it'; so even if a local language is superseded by a greater one for scientific or business communication, there is still a need for its poetic use to express its characteristic feelings. Though poetry is primarily concerned with the expression of emotion and feeling, Eliot recognizes that it also needs 'intellectual content or meaning', for without it there could be no sense to the poem and hence no expression of feeling (*OPP*, 19-20). Indeed, the sharp separation of thought and feeling was one of the dangerous dichotomies that Eliot opposed and tried to overcome, as we can see in his theory of the dissociation of sensibility.

[24] Gadamer, who echoes Eliot in affirming that 'to learn a language is to increase the extent of what one can learn' (*TM*, 400), confidently asserts: 'If, by entering into foreign linguistic worlds, we overcome the prejudices and limitations of our previous experience of the world, this does not mean that we leave and negate our own world. As travellers we return home with new experiences. Even if we are emigrants and never return we can still never wholly forget' (*TM*, 406). Gadamer sanguinely neglects the serious problems of alienation and identity that extensive linguistic-cultural travelling may generate along with its positive enriching and enlarging effects. It may make a previously comfortable inhabited world seem in some ways uncomfortably and arbitrarily constraining, though for practical or personal reasons it may remain a world we cannot escape. The problem is not at all of 'wholly forgetting' what we were but rather of reconciling the conflicting directions of thought and feeling in which the different linguistic cultures pull us, so that we do not suffer from a deeply divided personality or the sense of alienation of not belonging fully to any community. Eliot's own personal experiences of linguistic-cultural migration and adjustment made him more alive to its dangers. Not surprisingly, the rootless cosmopolitan in his or her unhappy isolation is a dominant figure and theme in Eliot's poetry.

core, it must to some extent re-emerge in the language of even our most private thoughts, which to be thought at all presuppose a common language and hence enough community of belief to ensure the identity of reference and shared meaning necessary for viable communication. That our own language cannot be *only* our own shows that the self and personality are not immaculately private and autonomous, but are largely constituted by and only known through participation in a tradition and interaction with and within a community.

Our insistence that language is necessarily consensual and shared should not be construed as denying that different individuals may have their distinctive particularities of style, idiom, or associative imagery. But such divergent individual styles or idiolects can only emerge and be understood on the background of a common dialect, an underlying agreement in usage, which is typically a general conformity and need not be an exceptionless uniformity. Nor should the recognition that language ineluctably depends on communal tradition be taken as legislating against the linguistic originality of creative individuals. Eliot, therefore, addressed considerable thought to the issue of linguistic change and originality and to the poet's particular role as both a preserver and innovator of language.

The first important point to be noted is that language must involve change and creativity, because of its functions as the structuring medium of our experience and as a tool which both reflects and serves our needs and interests in coping with the world. As our experience, needs, and interests change, so must language. Though demanding some (though not necessarily the same) stable background of regular usage, and though embodying and sustaining the values and experience of the past whose historical continuity has helped fashion it, a language must handle and therefore (in Gadamer's words) necessarily 'reflects not only what is persistent but also the changing nature of things' (*TM*, 407).[25] For Eliot, as for Gadamer, the healthy state of language, tradition, and historical consciousness requires a proper proportion between the old and the new, so that we suffer neither stagnation nor a dizzyingly disruptive and unmanageable flood of hurried change. Since in modernist and postmodernist times the latter danger seems more proximate and acute, there is pragmatic justification for greater emphasis on tradition and our historical and linguistic continuity with the past. Having seen how Eliot's championing of tradition carries the proviso that tradition must be flexible and open to criticism and change, we should expect his similar insistence that change and creativity are

[25] There is, says Gadamer, 'a constant process of concept formation by means of which the life of a language develops', a process which reflects the changing 'system of man's needs and interests. What a linguistic community regards as important about a thing can be given a common name with other things that are perhaps of a quite different nature in other respects, so long as they all have the same quality that is important to the community' (*TM*, 388, 394).

necessary to the vitality of a language and thus ultimately to its preservation and survival. For Eliot, therefore, the consequent

> wobbliness of words is not something to be deplored. We should not try to pin a word down to one meaning, which it should have at all times, in all places, and for everybody. Of course there must be many words in a language which are relatively at least fixed always to one meaning ... and must have meant essentially the same thing throughout the history of the language ..., [e.g.] *table* and *chair*. But there are also many words which *must* change their meaning, because it is their changes in meaning that keep a language *alive*, or rather, that indicate the language *is* alive. If they did not change, it would mean either that we were living exactly the same life as our ancestors (the rate of change in the meanings of words in the language of a primitive tribe I should expect, other things being equal, to be very slow) or else that our language was no longer adequate to our needs – in which case, the more progressive language of some neighbour might supplant it. (*TC*, 65-66)

Not suprisingly, Eliot connects the need for continual linguistic development with the continuous need for literature. If life and language are fixed, creative literature is perforce confined to repetition and imitation, and is thus in a sense both unnecessary and not really creative literature at all. Therefore, Eliot holds as 'a necessary condition for the continuance of a literature, that the language should be in constant change'; and he consequently reserves highest praise for 'those rare writers who have brought their language up to date, and in so doing, "purified the dialectic of the tribe" ' (*TC*, 49, 54). Yet change must not be too quick or violent so as to breach linguistic continuity. For that would deprive the literary artist and his audience of smooth access to the language of the past and the traditional feelings and values therein enshrined, and thus would immeasurably impoverish the language's resources. Eliot therefore contends that 'poetry should help not only to refine the language of the time but to prevent it from changing too rapidly: a development of language at too great a speed would be a development in the sense of a progressive deterioration' (*OPP*, 160). Moreover, on the grounds of the combined dangers of linguistic stagnation and discontinuity, Eliot propounds a most original argument why literature must be continously written, 'why we cannot afford to *stop* writing poetry' (*OPP*, 20): otherwise a gap will necessarily emerge and increasingly widen between the literature of the past and the language of the present devoid of literary embodiment. This gap between a literary past and a non-literary linguistic present may become too great to bridge satisfactorily, so that we can no longer understand, express, or even experience the range of sensibility enshrined in our literary heritage.

> if we have no living literature we shall become more and more alienated from the literature of the past; unless we keep up continuity, our literature of the past will become more and more remote from us until it is as strange to us as the literature of a foreign people. For our language goes on changing; our way of life changes, under the pressure of material changes in our environment in

all sorts of ways [so that without a living literature linked to a literary past] ... our own ability, not merely to express, but even to feel any but the crudest emotions, will degenerate. (*OPP*, 21)

Just as the health, enrichment, and refinement of language depend on a living literature, so does the quality of literature depend on that of its language: 'for a poet must take as his material his own language as it is actually spoken around him. If it is improving, he will profit; if it is deteriorating he must make the best of it' (*OPP*, 22). It thus behooves the poet for both egoistic and altruistic reasons to work to improve his language, which again is both his own and more than his alone. In this work of linguistic maintenance and refinement Eliot saw the prime social function of the poet, a function of both preserving the past and serving the present and future.

> We may say that the duty of the poet, as poet, is only indirectly to his people: his direct duty is to his *language*, first to preserve, and second to extend and improve ... Poetry can to some extent preserve, and even restore, the beauty of a language; it can and should also help it to develop, to be just as subtle and precise in the more complicated conditions and for the changing purposes of modern life, as it was in and for a simpler age ... [The poet has the duty-bearing] privilege of contributing to the development and maintaining the quality, the capacity of the language to express a wide range, and subtle gradation, of feeling and emotion; his task is both to respond to change and make it conscious, and to battle against degradation below the standards which he has learnt from the past. (*OPP*, 20, 22, 37-38)

Eliot suggests at least three ways in which the poet can extend and improve his language. The first, already noted, is to bring poetic language more up to date by making it encompass the realities and speech of modern life and give them more subtle, precise, and satisfying linguistic expression. The second is to give linguistic expression to what people vaguely feel, which allows them to feel it more consciously and thus differently, thereby enlarging the range both of feeling and of language (*OPP*, 20). The third and loftiest way that the poet can extend the range of language is in his 'attempt to extend the confines of the human consciousness and to report of things unknown, to express the inexpressible' (*OPP*, 169).

For Eliot, 'the great poet should not only perceive and distinguish more clearly than other men' the sights, sounds, and feelings of ordinary experience; he should also 'perceive ... beyond the range of ordinary men and be able to make men see and hear more ... than they could ever see without his help' (*TC*, 134). Moreover, it is not simply that great poets as a group see and feel somewhat differently from ordinary men; each great poet 'is also individually different from other people, and from other poets too, and can make his readers share consciously in new feelings which they had not experienced before' (*OPP*, 20). The poet, entrusted with the task of extending his own consciousness and language so as to extend that of his linguistic community, can only succeed if his individual explorations do not altogether lose touch with the common tradition which gives him a dialect and grammar of thought and feeling to create in and refine. The great poet, then, must stand out from the common fold, but not outside it; he must be exceptional but not eccentric. Invested with 'the obligation to explore, to find words for the inarticulate, to capture those feelings which people can hardly feel, because they have no words for them', the poet is also obliged to remember 'that the explorer beyond the frontiers of ordinary consciousness will only be able to return and report to his fellow-citizens, if he has all the time a firm grasp upon the realities with which they are already acquainted' (*TC*, 134).

This is why Eliot so often insists 'that poetry must not stray too far from the ordinary everyday language which we use and hear' (*OPP*, 29), and it is how he distinguishes 'the eccentric or mad' writer from 'the genuine poet'. 'The former may have feelings which are unique but which cannot be shared, and are therefore useless; the latter discovers new variations of sensibility which can be appropriated by others. And in expressing them he is developing and enriching the language which he speaks' (*OPP*, 20). For Eliot, then, the extension of perception and sensibility and that of language 'are not to be thought of as separate or separable. The task of the poet, in making people comprehend the incomprehensible, demands immense resources of language; and in developing the language, enriching the meanings of words and showing how much words can do, he is making possible a much greater range of emotion and perception for other men, because he gives them the speech in which more can be expressed' (*TC*, 134).

Since the poet's primary social function is to maintain and extend his language and the consciousness it informs, Eliot holds that any great poet or 'master of a language should be the great servant of it' (*TC*, 133). Such service 'makes a difference to the speech, to the sensibility, to the lives of all the members of a society, to all the members of the community ... whether they read and enjoy poetry or not'. For language is the communal property of the tradition and a writer's linguistic refinements and extensions 'will work themselves into the language gradually ... and ... become well established' (*OPP*, 22, 21). Thus, without the meliatory service of past poets 'the current speech of a people with a great language would not be what it is', and the successful performance of this sustaining and transforming service is the mark of poetic greatness, shared by Dante, Shakespeare, and Dryden: 'To pass on to posterity one's own language, more highly developed, more refined, and more precise than it was before one wrote it, that is the highest possible achievement of the poet as poet' (*TC*, 133).[26]

---

[26] Here Eliot rewardingly exploits the ambiguity of the phrase 'one's own language' to convey with rich economy both the poet's achievement of passing on to posterity his or her own personal linguistic accomplishments embodied in works of art, and also the achievement of simply having made the language shared with the community and passed on

As a practicing poet, Eliot felt an acute responsibility to keep alive the rich experience and language of the past as enshrined in its poetry, and to use the lessons, resources, and sense of responsibility that its appreciation provides to inspire further refinements and extensions in the future. He therefore tried to evoke through his own poetry a heightened awareness of the past and its continuing value in the present; and through this heightened appreciation of our tradition's past he sought to inspire our efforts to sustain its future unity, richness, and growth. The depth of Eliot's dedication to a continuing literary-linguistic tradition, one that looks both backward and forward, not only resounds in the innumerable literary allusions, borrowings, and echoes which richly season his verse. It is also explicitly confessed in the last of his *Four Quartets*, his culminating poetic achievement, in the mouth of the 'familiar compound ghost' who is both 'myself' and 'someone other'

> ...our concern was speech, and speech impelled us
> To purify the dialect of the tribe
> And urge the mind to aftersight and foresight.
>   'Little Gidding'

(5) One reason why tradition is such an attractive explanatory concept, abundantly able to make sense of things, to give them meaning and value, is that it amalgamates the two most basic modes of explanation – the structural and the genetic. The first explains something in terms of its formal or functional relations with other elements in a larger structure or system. This is the mode of explanation favored by varieties of critical formalism, including structuralism. The genetic mode instead explains something in terms of its origins or sources, and is employed by historical, biographical, and intentionalist criticism, which formalists have attacked for perpetrating 'the genetic fallacy' (the intentional being one of its species).[27] These two basic explanatory modes are not confined to criticism but can be found in the sciences and even in everyday life. For instance, we can structurally explain the presence of a standing lamp in the corner of our room as serving to complement the similarly styled table lamp in the opposite corner and to combine with the proximate easy chair to make a cosy reading corner. On the other hand, we could genetically explain it as a gift from a dear friend which needs to be displayed. The explanations are clearly different, yet both are plausible and can be right.

The compatibility is important to note because it is generally assumed, as Derrida argues, that the validity of the distinction between the

---

to its future members an improved and developed one. This point and others relating to Eliot's view of the poet's duty to language are illuminated in A.V.C. Schmidt, 'Eliot and the Dialect of the Tribe', *Essays in Criticism*, 33 (1983), 36-48.

[27] For an attack on the genetic approach in criticism, see M. Beardsley, *Aesthetics* (New York: Harcourt Brace, 1958), 456-60, and more specifically on intention in interpretation, 17-21.

structural and the genetic somehow entails their essential conflicting opposition and inconsistency.[28] But there is no reason to assume this, unless we confuse difference with antagonistic incompatibility by taking our distinctions as rigid metaphysical divisions rather than flexible pragmatic tools, which Derrida would surely not wish us to do. There are countless cases where both structural and genetic explanations are combined and even fused in a common idiom (e.g. explaining a microwave cookbook or set of training wheels as 'coming with' the oven or bike). As Eliot once remarked in response to the charge of 'confusing the genetic with the structural standpoint', 'I can only urge that I have found the two organically related' rather than intrinsically conflicting (*KE*, 133). I think that one place where the genetic and structural modes of explanatory ordering are most fruitfully united is in the concept of tradition (another is in the hermeneutic circle's dual dimensions); and I believe that by incorporating the genetic and hence temporal dimension, the structure of tradition avoids being a closed or static system fixedly inscribed by the past, but is instead a fundamentally open structure which demands the idea and ideal of future development.

Tradition is most frequently taken, as Derrida takes it, as simply a genetic mode of explanation; and tradition's genetic aspect – its emergence and development from the past and its account of present features by relating them to the past – is obvious enough not to belabor here. What needs to be emphasized is that tradition also affords a structural standpoint, since many of tradition's past elements are still actively present alongside what they have helped generate and are thus available as terms of relation for structural accounts of the meaning of later elements. In other words, a tradition is not a mere sequence of clusters of random items, but a sequence of structures structured by the past and structuring the present and future.[29] The main point in Eliot's early rehabilitation of tradition was this living presence of past tradition and the consequent conception of tradition as a structural and not merely genetic order, and hence 'as a principle of aesthetic, not merely historical, criticism' (*SE*, 15).

[28] See J. Derrida, ' "Genesis and Structure" and Phenomenology', in *Writing and Difference* (Chicago: University of Chicago Press, 1978), 154-168.

[29] I borrow the terminology of 'structured and structuring structure' from Pierre Bourdieu's theory of the *habitus*, as presented in his *Outline of a Theory of Practice* (Cambridge: Cambridge University Press, 1977) and *Distinction* (Cambridge, Mass.: Harvard University Press, 1984). Traditions are structured in that they are the ordered consequences of past efforts of social and cultural organization, and are inherited or transmitted through such organization. Traditions are structuring because they provide formative categories of our thought and action and largely determine the direction of our interests and inquiry, and the vocabularies with which we may pursue them. Traditions are structures because they contain a variety of ordered and classifiable activities or features coherently organized into meaningful interrelations and profitable interaction. The remarkable affinity between Bourdieu's theory of *habitus* and Eliot's view of tradition and culture cannot, however, be pursued here.

The structural standpoint views things in terms of a relational system or organic whole. It sees the meaning of things within the system as not independently inherent in the things themselves but instead as a function of their relations with other things in the system. What constitutes a given phoneme is not a particular acoustic sound but a systematic set of relations of functional contrast with other phonemes in the system. The meaning or value of an American dollar is not in the nature of the paper or coin in which it is found but in the relations it has with other elements in the U.S. (and world) monetary system. Eliot recognized that any literary tradition comprises such an organic structure or system, and thus he thought of literature – 'of the literature of the world, of the literature of Europe, of the literature of a single country, not as a collection of the writings of individuals, but as "organic wholes", as systems in relation to which, and only in relation to which, individual works of literary art, and the works of individual artists have their significance'. 'No poet, no artist of any art, has his complete meaning alone. His significance, his appreciation is the appreciation of his relation to the dead poets and artists', a structural relation of 'contrast and comparison' and not of mere causal genetic sequence (*SE*, 23-24, 15).

The enduring nature of past elements preserved in a tradition make it capable of functioning as a synchronic structural system, so that we can treat 'the whole of the literature of Europe' (or any sub-tradition thereof) as having a 'simultaneous existence' and composing 'a simultaneous order' of synchronic structural relations. These, however, must be constantly revised by new systemic relations generated by the introduction of new elements to the order.

> The existing order is complete before the new work arrives; for order to persist after the supervention of novelty, the *whole* existing order must be, if ever so slightly, altered; and so the relations, proportions, values of each work of art toward the whole are readjusted; and this is conformity between the old and the new. (*SE*, 15)

We obviously see here how poorly the notion of completeness suits a temporally open structure like tradition, but we should also note how subtly Eliot links the structural and genetic by assimilating the genetic-temporal relation of old and new to the patently structural relation of different parts in an organic whole. Old and new elements derive their meaning from their reciprocal relations of contrast and coherence in a larger whole of tradition, which they themselves constitute as parts. Tradition thus presents an analogue of the hermeneutic circle, a holistic framework which can enlarge meaning and understanding by enlarging the contextual whole in which any individual element is understood. Tradition provides not only the widest of holistic contexts, but, so long as the future of language and literature is open, ever new and wider ones. This helps explain why Eliot and Gadamer see interpretation as inexhaustible.

Each generation confronts a given literary work within a new complex of structural relations linking that work to the whole of tradition as it currently, temporarily, stands. Understanding demands an account of this new relational meaning, hence a new interpretation. Moreover, tradition's complex of relations includes not only those between different works of art but also those between the different interpretations that each has received in the tradition. Hence any new interpretative response calls for a further interpretative response to link and assimilate it to the interpretative tradition that has helped form the work's meaning.

This fundamental openness of tradition's structure must be emphasized. For the charge usually directed against structuralist forms of explanation is that they are necessarily closed and totalizing systems, that they leave no room for historical change and amendment, for openness to innovation. Tradition hardly seems vulnerable to such a charge, since historicity and openness to change and development though time is deeply built into the concept in its genetic aspect. Tradition thus includes a structural opening to something outside its present structure, not simply to forgotten or abandoned features of the past but more importantly to an open future which will continue to shape tradition as it is also shaped by it.

Both Eliot and Gadamer realize that tradition's value is as much in its open prospect as in its retrospect; its function being to make a better present and future, not to serve futile attempts to restore the past.[30] Indeed, given Gadamer's claim that the meaning of human experience 'always contains an orientation towards new experience', that our history is thus 'only present to us in light of our futurity' (*TM*, 319; *PH*, 9), it follows that if our tradition were perceived as having no future, it would lose the meaning it would otherwise have for us. As Eliot remarks, 'If we cease to believe in the future, the past would cease to be fully *our* past: it would become the past of a dead civilisation' (*OPP*, 65). Thus, even to preserve the value of past tradition means projecting tradition into the future; not as a fixed or rigid articulated code to be slavishly obeyed, but as a time-fashioned, flexible, and complexly structured structuring structure (e.g. of rules, categories, customs, habits) which needs to be intelligently applied or interpreted to present situations, or criticized and modified in their light.

That the concept of tradition is intrinsically open to the future does not ensure the future of any given tradition. Indeed it is only because traditions can die that the injunction to preserve them is in any way compelling and intelligible. Traditions can die a variety of deaths; they may be destroyed by material extinction or simply killed off by other traditions, which either completely obliterate them or absorb and assimilate them into their own. Rather than try to catalogue these different forms of death, which may be as diversely numerous as the ways traditions are individuated, I shall close

[30] In this connection they both distinguish between (present-mediated, forward-looking) 'preservation' of tradition, and 'foolish' (since futile) attempts at 'restitution' or 'restoration of the past'. See, for example, *TM*, 149-150; *SW*, 62; *OPP*, 105-106.

my discussion of tradition's evolving genetic-structural unity by mentioning two dangers likely to destroy this unity.

The first is stagnation or lack of development, which will tend to result in the tradition's being abandoned for or crushed by a superior one. Such stagnation can result from insufficient resources for development or from lack of stimulation. Both deficiences derive from a tradition's being excessively uniform. For diversity in a tradition provides more possibilities for development simply by providing more features to develop and more combinations of their developmental interaction. It also provides rivalry over the relative importance and value of these different features, which stimulates competition as to how the tradition should be interpreted and best preserved and continued in the future. This 'conflict favourable to creativeness and progress' was, as we noted earlier, what made Eliot insist on a tradition's diversity or a culture's variety. For him, 'a *uniform* culture would be no culture at all'. 'We need variety in unity'; and '[t]he variety is as essential as the unity' (*NDC*, 59, 62, 120; *OPP*, 23) A living tradition, then, is what Gallie has called an essentially contested concept, one that invites (like 'democracy' and 'art') rival interpretations because it is both internally complex and positively appraised.[31] As MacIntyre put it more recently: 'A living tradition ... is an historically extended, socially embodied argument, and an argument precisely in part about the goods which constitute that tradition.'[32]

But if a developing tradition requires diversity and conflict, it also needs enough unity not to fall apart and die by disintegration. Given the open, mutable, and contested nature of a tradition, we can hardly appeal to a necessary, unchanging essence to anchor and ensure its unity. Indeed we have no accepted formula for determining whether sufficient unity obtains, no algorithm for measuring how unified a tradition is. We simply have to perceive or experience a tradition's unity or fragmentation; we have to see how well things hang together and how we could make them cohere better. One way to achieve a greater sense of coherence in a time of conflict and division, one way thus to strengthen tradition's unity, is to place the rifts of the present scene within the structural narrative context of the tradition which engendered them. This not only makes the conflicts more intelligible and thus more manageable by revealing their roots, but it also defuses the threat and sense of violent rupture by diffusing disagreement over an extended continuous history of coherent debate within a common tradition. Thus, a strong sense or awareness of tradition is a potent force for maintaining its unity and continuity, particularly when it is in danger of deterioration through fragmentation and rapid change. Conscious of this and painfully perceptive of the radical changes and conflicts in modern

[31] See W.B. Gallie, 'Essentially Contested Concepts', *Proceedings of the Aristotelian Society*, 56 (1956), 167-199; repr. and revised in his *Philosophy and the Historical Understanding* (New York: Schocken, 1968, 157-191.
[32] MacIntyre, 207.

thought and society which threatened to disintegrate and remove us from the European traditions which he so cherished, Eliot was right to emphasize the paramount importance of tradition. For those today whose experience of the world is more of alienated confusion than coherent community, for those who sense with sadness that the so-called glories of our literary and intellectual past no longer command much interest, let alone respect, there is reason to review if not repeat Eliot's message.

Of course, tradition is not a panacea whose mere presence or mention will resolve all our decisions or difficulties. Indeed, in order to bring tradition to bear on a problem demands that we decide how to interpret or apply it with respect to that problem. To preserve and continue a tradition demands, as Eliot insisted, that we learn how to extend, develop, and modify it in the light of changing circumstances. It demands that we employ our practical intelligence to steer a middle course between damaging extremes so as to achieve the proper proportion of fixity and change, unity and variety, old and new. Tradition, in Eliot's pragmatic mind, is not one of those ideas which James disparagingly calls 'magic words' or 'solving names', like 'God', or 'the Absolute', where 'you can rest when you have them [being] at the end of your metaphysical quest'. Instead tradition represents the object of an open, worldly quest; something whose 'practical cash-value', in James' terms, must be continuously elucidated, tested, and set at work within the stream of experience. 'It appears less as a solution, then, than as a program for more work.'[33] Eliot's pragmatism with its emphasis on practical wisdom is as evident in his theory of tradition as it is elsewhere in his criticism and theory. Having often but fleetingly touched on Eliot's pragmatism throughout our study, we ought to conclude with a closer and more sustained look at it.

[33] W. James, *Pragmatism and Other Essays* (New York: Simon and Schuster, 1963), 26.

Chapter 8

Pragmatism and Practical Wisdom

Where is the wisdom we have lost in knowledge?
Where is the knowledge we have lost in information?

'Chorus I' from *The Rock*

I

One of the features of Western tradition that Eliot most wanted to revive and restore to a position of cognitive centrality and cultural recognition is the classical idea of practical wisdom, a form of knowledge which treats of the contingent and changing, and which cannot be reduced to any articulated system, doctrine, or formula. This idea, elaborated by Aristotle in terms of the intellectual virtue *phronesis* and effectively sustained by the Aristotelian tradition through the Middle Ages and Renaissance, has largely been eclipsed and discredited in modern times by the alternative ideal of science, with its promise of immutable laws and systems based on infallible foundations and providing extraordinary predictive precision through adherence to standardized methods and universalizable formulae. The great success of the natural and technological sciences in improving our knowledge and control of the natural world have made the idea of science seem to modern eyes the only form of knowledge worthy of the name.

The result is the long familiar dilemma of the humanities: either be scientific or abandon all claims to supply real knowledge. Thus we find the seemingly endless and often ludicrous attempts of humanistic disciplines of learning (including literary criticism) to mimic 'scientific method' and presume scientific status so as to insure their cognitive respectability. When the project of assimilation to natural science seems especially dubious or distasteful, as in criticism, the reaction is typically not to argue that there are other important forms of knowledge, but to eschew cognitive claims entirely and to treat criticism as an art whose reward lies only in the 'pleasure of the text'. Important as pleasure is to us all, this trivializes the value of literary study. What we need to recognize (apart from the inalienable link between pleasure and understanding discussed in

192

Chapter Six) is that there is more to knowledge than science, that non-scientific ways of thinking can provide genuine and indispensable cognitive rewards, and even supply the necessary background of social interaction and thought without which scientific thinking could not exist.

Eliot's idea and ideal of practical wisdom may thus be very relevant for contemporary criticism. Yet, surprisingly, this notion has been ignored by Eliot's critics and commentators, even though it deeply informs both his literary and social theory. In this chapter, we shall examine Eliot's idea of practical wisdom, not only by relating it to its Aristotelian source but by showing how it incorporates central ideas of twentieth-century pragmatism.

Eliot was exposed to pragmatism at Harvard, where it was born and still sufficiently flourishing to make Royce, Eliot's teacher, recast his idealist philosophy in an avowedly pragmatist mold as 'absolute pragmatism'. Whatever the extent to which Eliot formally imbibed pragmatism, it was certainly a philosophy well-suited to his intellectual temperament – his characteristic blend of scepticism and belief, and his tough-minded, practical, yet deeply devoted attitude toward art, criticism, and even religion. As his biography makes abundantly clear, Eliot not only was a master of the practical-political art of creating a literary reputation; he was psychologically deeply driven by a need for practical tasks and for 'useful' (i.e. more than 'writerly') employment, perhaps as a ballast to his creative and critical literary activity. This is why he held fast for eight years to his banking job at Lloyd's, refusing to leave for a career as an academic or full-time literary journalist, until he found an equally business-like job at the publishing firm of Faber and Gwyer (later to become Faber and Faber and to have Eliot as one of its directors and most published authors).[1]

We have traced significant shifts and developments in Eliot's criticism and theory which some have seen as laming inconsistency. Even the apparent constant of tradition is differently interpreted as Eliot matures. One reason for many of these shifts and one of the most constant and formative factors through his changing critical and theoretical pronouncements is the pragmatic impulse. As the current state of poetry and criticism changes, so to some extent must the critic's and theorist's response. This should not be seen cynically as altogether abandoning the pursuit of valid theory for an unprincipled opportunism of trying to pander to changing fashion. It does, however, reflect a pragmatist's view of knowledge and theory as something at least ultimately aiming at real and fruitful consequences. Eliot's thinking was primarily motivated not by the wish for neutral, accurate reflection of what is or logically must be the case, but by the desire to effect a worthy change or improvement. His goal was not so much to get things descriptively right as to make things better. This pragmatic view of theory – where theory emerges from practice and is

---

[1] See P. Ackroyd, *T.S. Eliot* (London: Hamish Hamilton, 1984), 78, 91, 277, 152, 101.

judged pragmatically by its fruits in the practice which it also helps produce – is manifested throughout Eliot's intellectual career, whether he was theorizing about poetry, criticism, society, religion, or even theory itself. He came to realize and unashamedly affirm that as a theorist he had an essentially 'practical mind' with little interest in 'abstruse reasoning' for its own sake (*TUP*, 77).[2]

Eliot's pragmatic view of theory emerged as early as his doctoral thesis, which held that our world is a collaborative practical construction or interpretation of impinging experience which we must objectify or conceptualize in order to handle it, refer to it, and thus even experience it intelligibly. Apart from the plane of metaphysical speculation with its longing for the Absolute, when it comes to judging any theory or truth about the world 'all that we care about is how it works'; 'we must ... put our theories to the pragmatic test' (*KE*, 169, 161). For Eliot, 'the theoretical point of view is the inevitable outgrowth of the practical' (*KE*, 137). But if theory is dependent upon practice, it is not merely fruitlessly parasitic; for theory – critical reflection on practice – effectively influences practice, reinforcing or altering it. 'Theory and practice are', Eliot concludes, 'inextricable: for without theory we should not have our present practice, and without the practice in which it finds its application the theory would be meaningless' (*KE*, 155-156). One could hardly find a better key to understanding Eliot's future theorizing as a literary critic than the pragmatist declaration of his thesis: 'our theory will be found full of practical motives and practical consequences' (*KE*, 137-138).

We have seen how Eliot abandoned the metaphysical stance and abstract idiom of his thesis to embrace, in his early years as a critic, a more robust realism and faith in concrete empirical facts and analysis. Part of the reason for this shift, we have argued in Chapter Two, was to put criticism on a more profitable course, away from both the 'narcotic fancies' of impressionistic criticism and the turgid, empty 'abstract style' of Hegelian philosophical criticism, by modeling it on the most promising philosophical method of the day – the analytic empiricism of Russell and Moore. But when Eliot soon came to see such philosophy as inadequate, as being 'crude and raw and provincial' and plagued by 'irresponsibility and lack of wisdom' despite its enormous technical sophistication (*SE*, 449), he in turn abandoned it for an historicist, hermeneutic philosophy which we have tried to outline in Chapters Four to Seven, and whose salient pragmatist character is our focus here.

Eliot was often explicit about putting theories, philosophies, even religions to the pragmatic test. In reviewing (and rejecting) the theory of

---

[2] Eliot thought literary theory valuable to the extent that it could improve literary and critical practice, and enhance appreciation, 'refining our sensibility by increasing our understanding' (*TUP*, 143). Theory's practical consequences, however, need not be immediate, nor more (or less) confined than the notions of literature and criticism it works with, which for Eliot, of course, went beyond the narrowly aesthetic.

the Crocean literary critics, Eliot characteristically contends: 'The test, of course, of any critical programme or platform ... is the sort of criticism which it produces.'[3] Religions and philosophies were also to be judged by their results, central among them the art they produce. This is 'the esthetic sanction': 'the partial justification of these views of life by the art to which they give rise.' For Eliot, *ceteris paribus*, 'any way or view of life which gives rise to great art is for us more plausible than one which gives rise to inferior art or to none.'[4] It is thus not surprising that both before and after his religious conversion Eliot thought a Church should be assessed pragmatically: 'a Church is to be judged by its intellectual fruits, by its influence on the sensibility of the most sensitive and on the intellect of the most intelligent, and it must be made real to the eye by monuments of artistic merit' (*FLA*, 13). And speaking as an Anglican Catholic, Eliot declares 'that the Catholic Faith is also the only practical one' (*EAM*, 134) and that Anglican Catholicism is preferable to the Roman in being more practical in its flexibility 'to take account of changed conditions' (*SE*, 375).

II

The year Eliot spent at Oxford (1914-15), the last year of his formal instruction in philosophy, was devoted to the study of Aristotle under the tutelage of Harold Joachim, a close disciple and colleague of Bradley at Merton College. The primary text of study was the *Posterior Analytics*, but Eliot's subsequent writings display a wide-ranging knowledge of Aristotle's work, and more significantly a deep appreciation of it. For Eliot, Aristotle was (in the eponymous essay) 'The Perfect Critic' and the consummate philosopher, 'a man of not only remarkable but universal intelligence ... [who] could apply his intelligence to anything'. But the

---

[3] See T.S. Eliot, 'Creative Criticism', *Times Literary Supplement*, 1280 (12 August, 1926), 535. Eliot's special reasons for thinking that the Crocean program was not likely to bear much worthy fruit will emerge more clearly later in this chapter, when we consider deconstruction.

[4] T.S. Eliot, 'Poetry and Propaganda', *Bookman*, 70 (1930), 599. It is noteworthy that Eliot's only real criticism of pragmatism as a philosophy was itself distinctly pragmatist, that 'the great weakness of Pragmatism is that it ends up by being of no *use* to anybody' (*FLA*, 67; Eliot's emphatic italics). This criticism merely amounts to saying that pragmatism, unlike more traditional philosophies, does not offer very much in the way of positive philosophical theories. It does not supply any inspiring definition of the essence of reality, knowledge, goodness, or beauty which can be used as a handy criterion to save us the difficult toil of inquiring into the messy particular questions concerning these matters. But pragmatism deliberately refuses to supply such theories, because it believes, as Eliot at least came to believe with respect to poetry and criticism, that such philosophical theories are bound to be vacuous or misleading, since there are no essences anywhere for philosophical theories to be usefully about; and that there can be no wholesale philosophical solution or substitute for the complexities of actual inquiry and the continuous debate and deliberation of intelligence in deciding how inquiry should be pursued. In sharing these and other pragmatist views and in elevating practical wisdom over standard philosophy, Eliot shows that his commitment to pragmatism is deeper than any occasional criticism of it.

greatest value from Aristotle is not obtained by accepting all his specific doctrines 'in a canonical spirit' but by seeing through his example that in many areas of thought 'there is no method except to be very intelligent'. Aristotle's 'eternal example ... of intelligence itself' flexibly operating in a variety of subjects is a model for 'what is called the scientific mind ... [but] might better be called the intelligent mind', for it goes beyond the specific methods of 'the ordinary scientific specialist' and can be found also in the arts and letters (*SW*, 10, 11, 13).

What Eliot came near to expressing in this early essay's ideal of Aristotelian intelligence was the Aristotelian idea of practical wisdom, which he later more clearly endorsed, voicing 'the wish that the classical conception of wisdom might be restored' (*EAM*, 117).

Phronesis is Aristotle's term for practical wisdom, which many (including Eliot) prefer to translate simply as wisdom since it is productive of truth, e.g. of what is good for human beings or feasible in certain situations, even if such truth is attained for the purpose of action rather than mere contemplation.[5] A major and necessary part of *phronesis*, but not in itself sufficient for its full attainment, is natural intelligence or cleverness (*deinotes*), which needs to be developed by training and informed by moral virtue to achieve true wisdom. Aristotle distinguishes wisdom as the intellectual virtue concerned with truth about the contingent and variable and 'about what sorts of things conduce to the good life in general' (*NE* 1140a23-b6). In this it is contrasted to the intellectual virtues of science (*episteme*) and theoretical wisdom (*sophia*) which deal with things necessary and eternal, lofty objects superior to man's mutable, contingent state.

Moreover, unlike these theoretical virtues, *phronesis* is practical, directed at effecting some desired end and typically issuing in action to effect it (*NE* 1139a5-b13, 1140b31-41b23). It is essentially deliberative, since it deals with the variable and contingent things of human life that do not admit of scientific demonstration or self-evident intuition. 'Practical wisdom ... is concerned with things human and things about which it is possible to deliberate; ... but no one deliberates about things invariable, nor about things, which have not an end, and that a good that can be brought about by action' (*NE* 1141b8-13). Nor can one deliberate 'about things that are impossible for him to do' (*NE* 1140a33), so practical wisdom requires a sense not only of what is ideally or generally good, but of what good is possible to achieve in the particular given circumstances. It requires an acute perception of the particular needs of the situation, 'for it is practical, and practice is concerned with particulars' (*NE* 1141b16,

[5] See A. Kenny, *The Aristotelian Ethics* (Oxford: Clarendon, 1978), 164. My quotations from Aristotle's *Nicomachean Ethics* are from W.D. Ross's translation. Though Eliot most often talks simply of wisdom, he sometimes speaks of 'worldly wisdom' (*FLA*, 67). On several occasions, however, he is careful to remark that if worldly wisdom is 'merely worldly' or crassly expedient, i.e. unguided by virtue or 'spiritual wisdom', it is not 'true worldly wisdom' and can be 'as vain as folly itself' (*EAM*, 117-118, 120; *OPP*, 220). On another occasion, he suggests the same point in distinguishing 'cleverness' from 'wisdom' (*ICS*, 49).

1142a25-28). Since in our variable world the particular situations and particular feasible goods are continually changing, wisdom cannot be reduced to a fixed formula or law. That is why it is a matter of intelligent deliberation, not scientific demonstration or mechanical application of a method. Here, in Eliot's words, 'there is no method except to be very intelligent'.

Despite his early flirtations with science (outlined in Chapters Two and Three), Eliot came to a very similar contrast of wisdom and science, and to an increasing elevation of the former. Though post-Aristotelian science no longer claimed to treat only the necessary, eternal, and immutable, it still hoped to treat everything in its putatively universal purview in terms of necessary and invariable laws, independent of the orientation, tools, and practical interests of its investigators. The view that science stands pure, above and detached from the social conditions and human vicissitudes of inquiry is given little credence by today's philosophers of science. But it was more or less unquestioned dogma when Eliot challenged it in the heyday of positivism by asserting science's insufficiency and need to be guided by wisdom. As Eliot realized, none of us, not even the hard-nosed scientist, could 'get on for one moment without believing *anything* except the "hows" of science'.[6] Indeed, the very pursuit of science cannot exclusively rely on verified scientific knowledge and scientific method. For even if we have a law-like scientific theory, it needs to be interpreted into real-world or laboratory conditions in order for it to be tested and confirmed; and the determining of such conditions and assessment of confirmational testing require more than is given by the theory or by strict scientific method. Thus philosophers of science like Putnam and Polanyi contend that even exact science 'typically depends on unformalized practical knowledge', on tacit, socially acquired skills and sentiments, and that the scientist must '*rely on his human wisdom*'.[7]

Less concerned with science itself than with society as a whole, Eliot insisted on the importance of wisdom to counter the unhealthy 'exaggerated devotion to "science"' in modern society.[8] 'A really satisfactory working philosophy of social action ... requires not merely science but wisdom'; and 'wisdom, including political wisdom, can neither be abstracted to a science, nor reduced to a dodge' (*EAM*, 116, 118). He similarly warned against scientific purism in philosophy: 'Philosophy without wisdom is vain' and 'unbalanced' (*FLA*, 67). And in rejecting the idea 'of

[6] See T. S. Eliot, 'Literature, Science, and Dogma', *Dial*, 82 (1927), 242.

[7] See H. Putnam, *Meaning and the Moral Sciences* (London: Routledge and Kegan Paul, 1979), 72-73; and M. Polanyi, *Personal Knowledge* (London: Routledge and Kegan Paul, 1958). See also M. Grene, 'Perception, Interpretation, and the Sciences: Toward a New Philosophy of Science', in D. Depew and B. Weber (eds.), *Evolution at a Crossroads: The New Biology and the New Philosophy of Science* (Cambridge, Mass.: MIT Press, 1985), 1-20.

[8] See T.S. Eliot, 'Religion Without Humanism', in N. Foerster (ed.), *Humanism and America* (New York: Farrar and Rhinehard, 1930), 108.

pursuing criticism as if it was a science, which it can never be' (OPP, 117), Eliot was advancing the idea that criticism should instead be informed by practical wisdom, concerned with effecting real goods in particular situations and not with mere truth.

Like Aristotle, he realized that as it involves the particulars of changing human situations as well as general knowledge of human good, wisdom cannot be reduced to standardized rules formulable in 'logical propositions' nor can be 'arrived at by a strictly logical conclusion from agreed premises'; it requires 'excellence in deliberation' and astute perception of particulars (OPP, 226; EAM, 119; NE, 1140a30-35, 1142a28-b33, 1143b1-5). For Eliot, then, even the best of philosophies or religions cannot provide 'an infallible calculating machine for knowing what should be done in any contingency … [but always needs] perpetual new thinking to meet perpetually changing situations' (EAM, 134). There can be no substitute for wisdom, which he characterizes in strikingly Aristotelian style as 'a native gift of intuition, ripened and given application by experience, for understanding the nature of things … [and particularly] of the human heart', 'understanding human beings in all their variety of temperament, character, and circumstance' (OPP, 221). Thus 'wisdom is … well gained only through both … a study of human nature through history … and a study through observation and experience of the men and women about us as we live' (EAM, 116-117).

However, for Eliot as for Aristotle, intelligent understanding and intuition are not enough to produce true wisdom. Phronesis requires a moral component as well, which is what distinguishes it from mere intelligence or cleverness. For wisdom is not only a question of cleverly finding the best means to secure a given end but also a question of choosing the right ends; not only of knowing but wanting what constitutes a good life. The same intelligence directed at improper ends would not be wisdom but clever roguery or 'smartness' (NE, 1139a21-b1, 1144a25-35). But what helps us to choose or want the right ends is moral virtue, which is a disposition to right action and right feeling based on natural capacity for virtue but needing to be developed by proper training, 'made perfect by habit', and guided by phronesis. In short, wisdom and moral virtue are inseparable, each enabling the other and both resting on natural gifts of intelligence and human feeling, while requiring their proper ripening through inculcating training, education, and discipline (NE, 1103a24-b20; 1144a20-24, b30-32, 1178a16-18). It is noteworthy that Aristotelian wisdom and moral virtue are not concerned simply with knowing, willing, and performing the right actions, but also with feeling the right feelings. As naturally endowed human beings can be trained to think and act properly, so can their emotions be educated and refined by habituation and discipline (NE, 1103b15-25, 1104b9-16, 1106b16-23). As wise and virtuous action is action according to the mean determined by right reasoning (kata ton orthon logon), so the feelings of the wise and virtuous seek the right mean (*NE*, 1107a1-b9).[9]

Eliot similarly affirmed the moral dimension of wisdom without which it would be mere 'expediency' or the 'merely worldly wisdom' of 'a dodge' (*EAM*, 118). He further recognized that true wisdom cannot be achieved without a society whose strong and coherent training and reinforcement would inculcate the right habits of thought, action, and feeling (those three aspects of human experience through which he defined tradition and culture). Understandably drawn to social theory to promote such a society, Eliot was paradoxically forced to the pragmatic realization that the betterment of social life is ultimately not achieved by theoretical inquiry nor by simple social engineering, but requires 'a moral conversion' involving 'the discipline and training of emotions'. This discipline he thought so difficult for the modern mind as to be 'only obtainable through dogmatic religion'.[10] Here in a nutshell is Eliot's pragmatist justification for rejecting secularist liberalism for a religious perspective which offers a definite vision of the good life and a solid, reinforcing community and practice for its pursuit. The rejoinder of today's secular pragmatist is that dogmatic religion has been too dead to too many for too long to make it believable and in any way effective for ethical and social regeneration. We either need a more living and compelling myth or meta-narrative, or need to make do without any transcendental support whatever in convincing others to what we think would make a better society and way of life.

The idea that *phronesis*'s right reasoning directs action and feeling to a proper mean between two undesirable extremes (*NE*, 1106a25-1109b28) is surely the best known feature of Aristotle's theory of practical wisdom, and the one most emphasized and employed by Eliot. We shall not probe the specifics of the Aristotelian mean by inquiring whether he was right to suggest that the mean can always be seen as lying on a quantitative scale between the extremes of excess and deficiency. Nor shall we puzzle over whether the extremes are first identified and then define the mean or vice versa (which might seem preferable, as defining the extremes not in any fixed sense but as directions of deviation from what is right). What must be stressed, however, is that the doctrine of the mean is no mechanical algorithm which can take the place of the deliberative intelligence and intuitive perception of *phronesis*. The desirable mean is no fixed or recursively applicable 'arithmetical proportion' given in the nature of things, but needs to be determined anew in relation to us and the changing particulars of our situation (*NE*, 1106a29-b8, 1141b8-23). We should moreover note Aristotle's realization that although 'the intermediate state

---

[9] Central to Aristotle's idea of wisdom and virtue is *prohairesis* (often translated 'preferential choice'), since the wise and virtuous individual not only knows and chooses the good but desires it. Aristotle elsewhere defines *prohairesis* as 'reason desiring or desire reasoning' (*NE*, 1139b4), which is as close as one can get to Eliot's ideal of the unification of sensibility, of thought and feeling.

[10] The quotations are from *EAM*, 130; and 'Religion Without Humanism', 110.

is in all things to be praised', circumstances are often such 'that we must incline sometimes towards the excess, sometimes towards the deficiency ... [in order to] hit the mean and what is right' (*NE*, 1109b25-28).

The ideal and strategy of the mean is ubiquitous in Eliot's thought. Whether he is treating art or criticism, church or state, all roads lead to the *via media*. The Anglican Church and Elizabethan policy (Eliot follows Aristotle in substantially identifying practical and political wisdom) are praised for their practical wisdom and pursuit of the mean. 'The *via media* which is the spirit of Anglicanism was the spirit of Elizabeth in all things; ... her intuitive knowledge of the right policy for the hour and her ability to choose the right man to carry out that policy, determined the future of the English Church' (*FLA*, 12). In similar fashion Eliot praises John Bramhall's philosophy as sounder than the extremism of his contemporary Hobbes. While Hobbes 'thought in extremes' even in such political and social matters where 'the extreme is always wrong', Bramhall displayed an urbane, well-balanced practical wisdom 'with his sense of realities and his ability to grasp what was expedient ... His thinking is a perfect example of the pursuit of the *via media*, and the *via media* is of all ways the most difficult to follow' (*FLA*, 33-34). If these remarks powerfully recall Aristotle's regard for the practical and his view that 'to hit the mean is hard in the extreme' (*NE*, 1109a33), we should not be shocked at Eliot's appreciation of the pragmatism of Machiavelli, who is commended as 'a doctor of the mean' and 'a partial Aristotle of politics' (*FLA*, 50-51). For Eliot, the mean or middle way seems almost part of his idea of orthodoxy, the right-minded critical reflection needed to guide and develop a tradition. Orthodoxy is not an articulated dogma or formula but the right-thinking and deliberative critical intelligence of *phronesis*. 'There must always be a middle way, though sometimes a devious way when natural obstacles have to be circumvented; and this middle way will, I think, be found to be the way of orthodoxy; a way of mediation, but never ... a way of compromise' (*EAM*, 134-135).

The balanced mean between two undesirable extremes was not only a rational ideal but a recurrent practical strategy in Eliot's thinking, perhaps the closest thing he has to a method. His theoretical essays are most fréquently built on a contrast between two opposing principles or approaches, either of which in its extremity proves pernicious. Through his polemics on the dangers of the two extremes, the superiority of an alternative middle way is suggested (though at times only very vaguely and implicitly suggested rather than clearly fleshed out and affirmed). In 'The Perfect Critic' the contrast is drawn between the extreme subjectivism of 'impressionistic criticism' and the excessively 'philosophic' or 'abstract style in criticism', easily side-tracked 'into a metaphysical hare-and-hounds' and lost in vague generalities and 'verbalism' which do nothing to illuminate the works of art which occasion such discourse. Between these unappetizing extremes, we are offered the superior middle way of Aristotle (and de Gourmont) which combines acute concrete perceptions (rather than merely personal impressions) with intelligent analysis and generalization to enhance our understanding not only of the particular work 'as it really is' but of the more general artistic principles which underlie it; 'intelligence itself swiftly operating the analysis of sensation to the point of principle and definition' (*SW*, 1-16).

'Religion and Literature', as we saw in Chapter Six, navigates between the extreme that fictional literature is cognitively valueless falsehood and the equally unacceptable contrary that it provides the greatest truth, to emerge successfully with an eminently sane intermediate view. We have similarly seen how Eliot's discussion of belief rejects the extreme alternatives that belief is either essential for proper appreciation of poetry or that it is irrelevant, and instead proposes a middle way of make-believe, pretense, or poetic acceptance, which also helps to explain fiction's ability to help one achieve truth and wisdom. Indeed, as Eliot elsewhere remarks, between the improper extremes of taking poetry as mere entertainment or as joylessly somber spiritual edification, 'there is a serious *via media*' (*TUP*, 137).

'Tradition and the Individual Talent' attempts to mediate between blind obeisance to past tradition and the ignorant, tradition-blind pursuit of novelty by urging the poet to a critical adoption of tradition as open-ended and malleable so that he can at once conform to it and modify it. This middle way of balancing acceptance and criticism, preservation and change, old and new in pragmatically sustaining and reshaping a continuing tradition was, we saw, increasingly emphasized in Eliot's later treatment of tradition, which likewise emphasized a balance of conscious and unconscious elements, and yet another golden mean between unwanted extremes. I refer to his ideal of complex unity in variety, of rich coherence of competing diversities (of class, region, profession, sect, etc.), which eludes, on the one hand, a moribund monotonous uniformity and, on the other, an incomprehensibly chaotic tangle of fractious factions unable to share any common ground for fruitful communication. This desirable mean is also expressed as the right balance between the conflicting claims of order and freedom, neither of which must be taken to extremes. 'The danger of freedom is deliquescence; the danger of strict order is petrifaction'; either extreme will result in 'cultural deterioration' (*NDC*, 81).

The proper mean between rigid, stultifying order and an anarchic disintegrating freedom, the ideal pattern of unity and diversity, pertains not only to the macrocosms of tradition, culture, and society but to the microcosms of particular works of art. As early as 1917, Eliot was insisting (after Pound), that a 'work of art is a compound of freedom and order', an agreeably stimulating 'state of tension ... between free and strict' (*TC*, 171-172). And elsewhere that same year, he defined the refreshing sense of freedom on a background of order, a balancing 'contrast between fixity and flux', as 'the very life of verse' (*TC*, 185; cf. *OPP*, 160-161). Good poetic diction must likewise steer between the extremes of a monotonous, flat simplicity and an overwrought complexity, which by 'losing touch with the spoken language' loses the power to speak effectively to its audience (*OPP*, 59).

We could uncover many more instances where Eliot employs the principle of the mean of practical wisdom.[11] But rather than try to catalogue them all, let us examine two cases which are especially interesting. For in each we find the principle at work in different, changing pragmatic contexts and thus applied in different ways to effect different rebalancing adjustments of practice, yet steadily aimed at what is seen as the proper balance. This should go some way to answering the possible charge that such talk of 'the mean' or 'balance' is just evasive, empty hedging, devoid of any definite practical directive or payoff.[12]

The first case concerns Milton and the proper balance of sound and sense in poetry. Though all poems can be said to provide both oral and semantic properties, they obviously differ in their emphasis on these two aspects. 'Poetry, of different kinds, may be said to range from that in which the attention of the reader is directed primarily to the sound, to that in which it is directed primarily to the sense' (*TC*, 32). Both the poet and the evaluating critic thus must face 'the problem of the emphasis on sound or on sense. [For while the] greatest poetry ... passes the most severe examination in both subjects ... there is a great deal of good poetry, which establishes itself by a one-sided excellence. The modern inclination is to put up with some degree of incoherence of sense ... so long as the verse sounds well and presents striking and unusual imagery.' But if *we* are too 'easily seduced by the music of the exhiliratingly meaningless', by 'melodious raving', the age of Johnson could be too easily contented with good clear sense 'set forth in pedestrian measures'. And 'to exceed in one direction or the other is to risk mistaking' the true and more durable balance of sound and sense. 'Between the two extremes of *incantation* and *meaning*' we are to find the proper mean (*OPP*, 169).

The practical aim of achieving the desired balance in the face of changing poetic and critical contexts very neatly and convincingly explains Eliot's notorious changing evaluations of Milton in his essays of 1936 and 1947. The first essay, while conceding Milton's greatness, proceeds to devalue him with sharply derogatory criticism. Milton is 'blind', i.e. lacks 'visual imagination'. His style and diction are excessively 'dictated by a demand of verbal music, instead of by any demand of sense'; his lines are arranged exceedingly 'for the sake of musical value, not for significance' and 'can

[11] For example, Eliot also seems to recommend some mean between the extreme self-conscious attention to compositional technique, which reached the apparent limit of its value in Valéry, and the still worse extreme of a poetry wholly devoted to spontaneity and the all-importance of subject matter (*TC*, 40-42).

[12] The mere notion of the mean, like that of tradition, is not in itself a solution to anything. No mechanical algorithm, it needs to be interpreted and applied to real situations (which requires *phronesis*), but Eliot was well aware of this.

hardly be enjoyed while we are wrestling with the meaning'. Thus, 'although his work realizes superbly one important element in poetry, he may still be considered as having done damage to the English language from which it has not wholly recovered'. His influence in overemphasizing sound over sense was 'an influence for the worse', 'an influence against which we still have to struggle' (*OPP*, 138-145).

In the 1947 essay, Eliot modifies much of the original obloquy, but does not (as some mistakenly supposed) repudiate his earlier criticism.[13] Indeed, one aim of the essay is to defend or justify it for its time by presenting its *pragmatic* motivation, by trying 'to make clearer the causes, and the justification, for hostility to Milton on the part of poets at a particular juncture' (*OPP*, 159), who aimed at revolutionizing English poetry and restoring the lost balance by insisting on sense.

> It inevitably happens that the young poets engaged in such a revolution will exalt the merits of those poets of the past who offer them example and stimulation, and cry down the merits of those poets who do not stand for qualities which they are zealous to realize. This is not only inevitable, it is right ... Milton does, as I have said, represent poetry at the extreme limit from prose; and it was one of our tenets that verse should have the virtues of prose ... And the study of Milton could be of no help here: it was only a hindrance. (*OPP*, 159-160)

Eliot is not ashamed that his harsh evaluation of Milton was motivated by the pragmatic interest of improving poetry. (Why should he be? For what worthier aim should criticism have, especially if we adopt a pragmatist's scepticism regarding the value of truth in itself for its own sake?) Nor is he ashamed of greatly weakening his censure once the apparent success of his poetic (and critical) revolution made it pragmatically no longer so necessary. Thus Eliot ends his later essay by remarking that by now 'poets are sufficiently liberated from Milton's reputation to approach a study of his work without danger, and with profit to their poetry and to the English language' (*OPP*, 161).

The second case of pragmatic critical shifting in pursuit of the mean of *phronesis* through changing circumstances concerns the balance between pleasure and knowledge in appreciating, poetry. Just as all poetry combines sound and sense, so, Eliot realized (as we saw in Chapter Six, with Aristotle's help), in poetic appreciation, enjoyment and understanding are fundamentally, conceptually linked and should ideally be inseparable; so that to 'understand a poem comes to the same thing as to enjoy it for the right reasons ..., enjoying it to the right degree and in the right way, relative to other poems' (*OPP*, 115). But as there can be an impairing imbalance in the basically inseparable sound and sense, there can be a

---

[13] Eliot himself confirms that those who took the second essay as a recantation of his earlier one have misunderstood it and that it is rather 'a development' of the first essay's basic line (*TC*, 23-24).

damaging imbalance of emphasis on either pleasure or understanding, especially when the two are frequently regarded as clearly separable and conflicting alternatives.

Eliot began his critical career in an environment of literary appreciation generally imbalanced toward the hedonistic and personal, in the wake of the anti-scientistic, anti-moralistic wave of turn-of-the-century aestheticism. Against this perceived excess of self-centered, pleasure-seeking impressionistic criticism, the young Eliot vigorously and successfully rebelled; reversing the emphasis on subjective pleasure for a radical privileging of objective and impersonal knowledge, 'the sense of fact' and technical 'analysis'. Seeing a need to establish the real cognitive worth and seriousness of criticism, to transform its self-image from that of salon chatter and the adulating twaddle of 'the Browning Study Circle', Eliot emphasized (indeed one could say profitably overemphasized) criticism's cognitive dimension. Seeking cognitive respectability and believing then that science was the unquestioned paradigm of knowledge, he sometimes even went so far as to liken criticism to science and to praise 'the scientific mind' of (in his eyes) its ablest practitioners, such as Aristotle and de Gourmont (*SW*, 2-3, 5, 10; *SE*, 31-34). Yet alongside, though overshadowed by, his early polemics for facts and knowledge, Eliot still maintains the essential unity of enjoyment and understanding, rejecting 'the torpid superstition that appreciation is one thing, and "intellectual" criticism something else' and seeking not mere 'Blue-book knowledge but the enjoyment of poetry' (*SW*, 15, 53).

However, when he delivered 'The Frontiers of Criticism' in 1956 the critical situation had vastly changed. Literary criticism was by then a sizeable and still expanding industry of knowledge, firmly established and institutionalized in the universities and spewing out a flood of scholars and scholarly publications utterly dedicated to the tireless, often tedious, accumulation of literary historical knowledge and analyses of texts. Seeing the balance had become excessively reversed towards knowledge (ironically through critical movements which his early work had inspired), Eliot now takes the opposite line to redress it. He stresses the dangers of single-minded devotion to facts, 'of mistaking explanation for understanding'; and he warns that unrelenting commitment to technical analysis and the scrutinizing mode of reading of 'the lemon-squeezer school of criticism' could render poetry less enjoyable, making us so intent on taking the poetic 'machine to pieces' that we are unable or loath to see its parts as fully reunited and constituting a satisfyingly unified whole (*OPP*, 109, 113-114). (New Criticism is thus prophetically seen as issuing in deconstruction.) Rather than impersonal facts, Eliot now emphasizes the *enjoyment* of understanding and the valuable *personal* aspect of interpretation, that 'a valid interpretation [of a poem] ... must be at the same time an interpretation of my feelings when I read it' (OPP, 114). Asserting here the fundamental unity of enjoyment and understanding, Eliot obviously is after a mean which will be unfair to neither, but he recognizes with Aristotle that with changing circumstances we must incline sometimes toward one extreme or the other in order to approach the mean. He is eminently aware of this pragmatic shifting of weight to secure a better, more rewarding balance, and his retrospective conclusion needs no gloss:

> If in literary criticism, we place all the emphasis upon *understanding*, we are in danger of slipping from understanding to mere explanation. We are in danger even of pursuing criticism as if it was a science, which it never can be. If, on the other hand, we over-emphasize *enjoyment*, we will tend to fall into the subjective and impressionistic, and our enjoyment will profit us no more than mere amusement and pastime. Thirty-three years ago, it seems to have been the latter type of criticism, the impressionistic, that had caused the annoyance I felt when I wrote on 'the function of criticism'. Today it seems to me that we need to be more on guard against the purely explanatory. (*OPP*, 117-118).

III

The idea of *phronesis* has recently been enjoying a remarkable renaissance of interest, concomitant with our growing disenchantment with scientism. Besides being a central feature of Gadamer's hermeneutic philosophy,[14] it finds significant expression in contemporary American pragmatism through Putnam and Rorty. Eliot, I think, is best seen as a pragmatist in both criticism and theory. Viewing him thus will not only explain and justify many of his shifting and apparently inconsistent pronouncements, but will also place him in the context of an American tradition of thought which seems destined to be as dominant today as it was when Eliot encountered it at Harvard. The most plainspoken, outspoken, and uncompromising of contemporary pragmatists is Richard Rorty, whose account of pragmatism may be used to show Eliot's deep affinity to this way of thinking.

Rorty's 'first characterization of pragmatism is that it is simply anti-essentialism applied to notions like "truth", "knowledge", "language", "morality", and similar objects of philosophical theorizing'.[15] Eliot, as seen in Chapter Four, extended this anti-essentialist line to poetry and criticism. It might be wonderful to penetrate their variety of types and changing forms and reveal the true and eternal essences of poetry and criticism, which could ensure their identity and integrity against distortive corruption of practice and also serve as a firm and sure criterion for distinguishing the good from the bad. However, Eliot realized that (in Rorty's words) 'there are no essences anywhere in the

---

[14] See, for example, *TM*, 278-289.

[15] R. Rorty, 'Pragmatism, Relativism, and Irrationalism', in *Consequences of Pragmatism* (Minneapolis: University of Minnesota Press, 1982), 162. Future references to this collection will appear in the body of my text after the abbreviation *CP*.

area ... to direct, or criticize, or underwrite, the course of inquiry' (*CP*, 162). Poetry and criticism, as products of human practice and interests rather than fixed natural kinds, can only depend on such practice for their continued survival and flourishing. We cannot count on some science or philosophical theory to help us by discovering their necessary laws or essences since none such exist. Unable to rely on science or *theoria* to grasp the necessary and unchanging, we must rely on *phronesis*, practical wisdom applied to the contingent, mutable, and historically conditioned human good.

Rorty understandably makes substituting *phronesis* for *theoria* the second defining feature of pragmatism. This substitution expresses the pragmatist desire to dispense with the metaphysical idea of truth (as something having substantive and transcendental content beyond being what is good or justified in the way of belief) and placing in its stead an emphasis on 'utility, convenience, and the likelihood of getting what we want' in the practice we pursue, be it scientific, moral, or aesthetic (*CP*, 163). What is supposed to save this program from degenerating into crass means-end efficiency and opportunism is *phronesis*, the ability to deliberate well and to desire what we *should* want. Pragmatism rejects the scientistic ideal of reducing all rationality to a rule or method. 'For the pragmatist, the pattern of all inquiry – scientific as well as moral – is deliberation concerning the relative attractions of various concrete alternatives' (*CP*, 164). And we have just seen these very themes in Eliot's case against the claims of science and for the primacy of *phronesis* and practice.

Yet the primacy of practice in no way entails that theory is banefully gratuitous, as Fish and other new pragmatist critics have recently argued.[16] Though right to assert that theory is impossible without practice and ultimately inseparable from it, they are wrong to conclude that 'theory has no consequences' for practice, apart from political and institutional ones. Theory – as critical reflection on practice, involving imaginative reflection on possible modifications or alternatives to the given practice – surely *can* have and *has* had significant consequences for literary study. Fish's argument, that theory's conscious-heightening critical reflection does 'not necessarily' issue in change of practice and that such heightened consciousness and change can be produced by other means, does not in any way refute theory's power of intervention. It only denies the exclusivity of that power. Justifiably dissatisfied with one traditional idea of theory as standing outside of but founding and governing practice, Fish and his disciples neglect another traditional idea of theory, the Baconian, in which theory is seen as providing tools for

---

[16] See S. Fish, 'Consequences', and S. Knapp and W. B. Michaels, 'Against Theory', in W. J. T. Mitchell (ed.), *Against Theory* (Chicago: University of Chicago Press, 1985). The quotations from Fish are on pp. 115, 121.

transforming reality instead of merely reflecting its putative essential and invariable features.[17]

Rorty's third defining feature of pragmatism is its recognition of 'the contingent character' and inalienable social and historical aspects of the context of inquiry. Our 'starting-points' are not dictated simply by the nature of the objects we encounter and wish to understand; they are largely determined by our location in the particular human history of inquiry which we are continuing, by the vocabularies and directions that are available and most promising at our point of entry into the cognitive conversation of the cultural tradition to which we belong. In giving up the false dream of uncontaminated reflection of naked reality from a God's-eye view, in accepting the historical and social contingency of our understanding, Rorty offers pragmatism's alternative comfort and quest: 'we may gain a renewed sense of community. Our identification with our community – our society, our political tradition, our intellectual heritage – is heightened when we see this community as *ours* rather than *nature's*, *shaped* rather than *found*, one among many which men have made' (*CP*, 166). We may thereby come to see our apparent quest to converge on the truth more clearly as a quest for greater convergence of belief within our community and for making the convergent beliefs more rewarding. All this is powerfully expressed in Eliot's ideas of tradition, of the historicity of understanding, and of 'the common pursuit of true judgement' as interpreted on the consensual model outlined in Chapter Three.

Yet another key feature of Rortian pragmatism concerns the status and role of distinctions. For Rorty, pragmatism's anti-essentialism means a proclivity to holism. Once we deny that the world of discourse is ontologically carved up into distinct natural kinds, each having its definitive essence, then the distinctions we make between various kinds of objects and modes of inquiry lose their appearance of being necessary and inviolable. They lose their guise of being more than distinctions which people have made to help serve their interests and which can be superseded when no longer helpful. In particular, pragmatism aims to undermine what it sees as unwarranted and stymieing dichotomies, like the dualisms of objectivity versus subjectivity, the rationality of science versus the irrationality of the arts, understanding versus pleasure. Rorty's 'holistic strategy, characteristic of pragmatism (and in particular of Dewey), is to reinterpret every such dualism as a momentarily convenient blocking-out of regions along a spectrum, rather than as a recognition of an ontological, or methodological, or epistemological divide'.[18] But if distinctions and criteria are not foundational or

---

[17] This notion of theory is noted by P. Rieff, *The Triumph of the Therapeutic* (New York: Harper and Row, 1966), 55-56, and is affirmed by Rorty in his essay 'Freud and Moral Reflection' in J.Smith and W.Kerrigan (eds.), *Pragmatism's Freud: The Moral Disposition of Psychoanalysis* (Baltimore: Johns Hopkins University. Press, 1986), 14-15.

[18] R. Rorty, 'Texts and Lumps', *New Literary History*, 17 (1985), 8.

ontologically grounded, they can none the less be valid and justified in the best way things are justified, by serving 'specific utilitarian ends ..., in order to get something done' (*CP*, lxi).

Eliot was just as forthright in maintaining that the only justification of theoretical distinctions relating to poetry and criticism is in their pragmatic power of illumination. In surveying the attempts of critics like Dryden, Johnson, and Coleridge to distinguish the faculties of invention, imagination, and fancy, Eliot cautions that their distinctions should not 'be taken too seriously, as final psychological or philosophical truth, when they are merely analyses of pragmatic validity, to be tested by their usefulness in helping us to weigh the merits of particular poets' and to understand better their 'particular pieces of poetry'. This is why such distinctions, though very imprecise and problematic, can still be felt to 'have enduring usefulness' (*OPP*, 188-189; see also *TUP*, 77).

Much the same attitude characterizes Eliot's view of the distinctions between literature, literary criticism, and other related but distinct disciplines. We saw how he recognized that their distinctive identities could not be founded on their peculiar and permanent essences because they had none such, and that 'it is impossible to fence off *literary* criticism from criticism on other grounds' or purify poetry from all non-literary interests. A purely ' "literary appreciation" is an abstraction, and pure poetry a phantom' (*TC*, 25; *TUP*, 98; *OPP*, 116; *SE*, 271). Eliot thus seems to approach Rorty's pragmatist, holist position of blurring the distinctions between the traditional disciplines and subject matters (i.e. between the sciences, philosophy, criticism and the arts) and instead 'promoting the idea of a seamless, undifferentiated "general text" '.[19]

But Eliot, I think wisely, refuses to take this plunge. For recognition that our distinctions are neither ontologically underpinned nor wholly unproblematic should not lead the pragmatist toward a distinctionless abyss of holistic monism. That would be to deny the validity or reality of distinctions by mistaking what distinctions are or must be to be valid. It would be to assume falsely that they need ontological grounding to be real and justified, when all they need is to be meaningfully made and helpful. The distinctions and boundaries we have, through time, embroidered between our different disciplines are surely, Eliot would argue, more helpful than harmful so long as we recognize them as homespun human products and do not mistake them for ontologically given and eternally inscribed verities. To maintain a sharp enough focus and a reasonably definite agenda for pragmatic problem-solving, literary criticism should be constantly defining its aims and limits (in the light of the needs and circumstances of the present but with the experience and guidance of the past), even if these aims and limits are destined to be repeatedly revised and overrun. 'Literary criticism is an activity which must constantly

[19] R. Rorty, 'Deconstruction and Circumvention', *Critical Inquiry*, 11 (1984), 3.

define its own boundaries; also, it must constantly be going beyond them.'
Like any productive discourse it needs some structuring limits, for 'unless
you limit fields of discourse, you can have no discourse at all' (*OPP*, 215;
SE, 270).

Eliot would therefore fiercely oppose the proposal that literary criticism
should simply and irrevocably dissolve itself into a general 'theory of
discourse' or 'culture criticism' or 'rhetoric of signifying practices' as Rorty
and literary theorists like Culler and Eagleton would have it.[20] This does
not mean that literary criticism should not be informed by and deal with
such wider semiological, social, and philosophical concerns. Eliot would
hardly deny that the literary critic can be a social, moral, and political
critic as well, for he himself was certainly one. But the literary critic can
do all these things and probably do them better without repudiating the
continuing worth of literary criticism (and literature) as traditionally
practiced and distinguished from such other but related textual practices,
however vague and historically contingent such distinctions may be. So
much of the literary critic's cultural entitlement and prestige, so much of
his power to intervene in culture and society, depends on his traditional
role as specifically devoted to and entrusted with the interpretation of
great, canonical literary works of art. For in our secular society these are
the closest things we have to sacred texts. Thus the idea that the critic
could play a greater and more productive role in society by abandoning
the high palace of art for the general plane of discourse theory and the
nitty-gritty of sociology of culture is surely ill-conceived, no matter how
well intended.

Another central issue where Eliot's pragmatism differs significantly
from Rorty's is in its emphasis on preservation of the past alongside
concern for future development. Eliot would agree with Rorty's
pragmatist premise that since criticism's nature is *made* rather than
permanently given to be discovered, theorists should aim not at neutrally
revealing what criticism is but at making it into what we want it to be.
However, Rorty's general pragmatist strategy to 'get us what we want' is
by introducing 'new ways of speaking' or new vocabularies. This strategy,
Rorty believes, is particularly right for literary works and criticism, since
what we 'want [of] both these works and the criticism of them [are] *new*
terminologies' (*CP*, 150, 142). Not surprisingly, one of the most striking,
pervasive, and recurrent themes of Rortian pragmatism is the need and
goal of 'overcoming the tradition'.[21] Eliot would challenge this imbalance

[20] See J. Culler, *On Deconstruction: Theory and Criticism after Structuralism* (Ithaca:
Cornell University Press, 1982), 8-12; and T. Eagleton, *Literary Theory: An Introduction*
(Oxford: Blackwell, 1983), 204-217.

[21] Rorty's essay of that title (*CP*, 37-59) and his most pointed attacks on tradition are of
the philosophical tradition. But his anti-traditionalism is global and pertains to literary
studies as well, as can be seen in his defence of deconstructionist criticism in 'Nineteenth
Century Idealism and Twentieth Century Textualism' (*CP*, 139-159) and in his support of
an undifferentiated general text.

toward the new, asserting that the best if not the only way 'to form the future ... [is] on the materials of the past; we must *use* our heredity, instead of denying it' *(FLA*, 102). Nor is Eliot the only pragmatist to emphasize tradition's value. Dewey's aesthetic equally insists on art's and (criticism's) deep 'dependence upon tradition' even 'for original vision and creative expression'.[22] And beyond Dewey and aesthetics, this more conservative perspective is endorsed by contemporary pragmatists like Quine and Goodman,[23] who emphasize linguistic and scientific tradition (a shared and well-entrenched background language and web of scientific belief) as the necessary basis for any cognitive progress, effective prediction, or indeed any real meaning at all. Confining ourselves here to literature, we can reinforce Eliot's tradition-respecting perspective by adducing axiological and epistemological objections of distinctly pragmatic import against Rorty's program of inventing and proliferating new vocabularies.

The axiological objections concern the moral and cultural damage likely to be incurred by the invention and free-wheeling manipulation of vocabularies to make texts perform the tricks we momentarily want them to perform. Rorty, himself aware of the moral danger, describes it not only as violating the author's integrity by the willful misreading of his work, but also as isolating the misreading word-maker from his fellow members of society, who share a common language and a common set of beliefs that language both requires and informs. The search for new vocabularies as 'stimulus to the intellectual's private moral imagination ... is purchased at the price of his separation from his fellow-humans' *(CP*, 158). Rejecting the common language of the logocentric, willful misreaders become alienated and egocentric. What goes for the moral imagination also goes, I think, for the aesthetic. Private improvisations are pursued at the price of rejecting participation in a shared appreciative understanding of the works that constitute our cultural tradition. But besides this social and historical alienation, there is self-alienation as well. For our familiar, traditional ways of talking are a

---

[22] See J. Dewey, *Art as Experience* (New York: Putnam, 1980), 265. The following lines of Dewey could easily be taken for Eliot's: 'When the old has not been incorporated, the outcome is merely eccentricity. But great original artists take a tradition into themselves. They have not shunned but digested it' (p. 159).

[23] Quine has called his pragmatic principle of cognitive conservatism 'the maxim of minimal mutilation': 'warping ... scientific heritage to fit' new experience so as to maintain as best we can our inherited web of belief. See W.V. Quine, *From a Logical Point of View*, (New York: Harper & Row, 1961), 46; and *Philosophy of Logic* (Englewood Cliffs, N.J.: Prentice-Hall, 1970), 100. The necessity of a shared background language for the possibility of reference is argued in Quine's *Ontological Relativity and Other Essays* (New York: Columbia University Press, 1969), 26-28. Goodman's recognition of tradition is clear in his claim that all rightness of description and representation, as well as of categorial predicates for inductive inference, is largely 'a matter of fit with practice [or antecedent "habit"] ...', effected by evolving tradition'. N. Goodman, *Ways of Worldmaking* (Indianapolis: Hackett, 1978), 97, 128, 138.

major part of the intellectual's own life, and ardently striving to replace or confuse them with new vocabularies would seem to endanger very basic and still satisfying ways of self-experience.

Recognizing with Rorty that ways of talking are made, one need not conclude that radically novel ones made today are necessarily better (particularly for talking about texts from the past). Though it be naive to think that past tradition will save us, it is no less naive to think that inventing new vocabularies will solve our problems. This is just another form of metaphysical comfort, a faith in future language. Similarly, recognizing 'pragmatism's claim that all vocabularies, even that of our own liberal imagination, are temporary historical resting-places' (*CP*, 158), one need not accept Rorty's further demand that we programatically seek new terminologies, which will only make our admittedly temporary resting-places increasingly ephemeral and restless. That would be like arguing that since marriages aren't made in heaven for eternity, we should be contantly seeking new partners. The attitude is neither healthy for marriage nor for language. Moreover, in not questing for new vocabularies, we need not fear our ways of talking must become stagnant, unproductive, and incapable of coping with change. For, as Eliot recognized, even without any neologistic zeal, our ways of talking will change, as they always have changed, when compelled by changes in context and ways and perceptions of life, and without conscious 'attempts to change the common meaning by violence' (*TC*, 64-65, 72, 74). And if this is all that Rorty really means, one must challenge his misleadingly novel and overdramatic way of saying it.

A more epistemological objection to Rorty's proposal of using vocabularies to make texts do what we want is that this seems to undermine the hermeneutic project of 'edifying conversation' (Rorty's Gadamerian alternative to foundational epistemology) by turning all conversation into self-centered monologue. By making texts mean what one wants them to mean, one denies the alterity of the text and its ability to maintain a different point of view; but this is to deny what makes literature so edifying and mind-expanding. In discussing Eliot's dialogical account of reading in Chapter Six, we saw instead that to learn from and properly enjoy literature we must to some extent submit ourselves to the work, even if ultimately we must critically assess it against our own experience and view of life. Paradoxical as it sounds, we do not always want poems (or people) to say and do just what we want them to. One reason we cherish and learn from literature and people is that they resist being manipulated as mere text-objects or sex-objects.

A further epistemological objection against multiplying vocabularies without necessity and playing about with them to gain one's momentary satisfaction is that we may be left with no common vocabulary, no reasonably stable and shared linguistic practices to enable very effective thought and communication. However we interpret Wittgenstein's private-language argument, the role of consensual community (whether as actually constituting linguistic rules or merely as providing the necessary background for them)[24] seems clearly crucial for the possibility of effective language. And Rorty's own commitment to consensual solidarity over foundational objectivity requires a community of language and belief 'to make fruitful conversation possible'.[25] But this ambition of linguistic community would seem threatened by Rorty's willingness to deny any 'common vocabulary in which critics can argue' so that one can do with language what one wants (*CP*, 158). Perhaps one *can* do with language what one wants, but one must weigh the value of immediate momentary gains against the likely and perhaps irremediable losses. One must, Eliot might say, distinguish between the dazzling performance of critical cleverness and the more sober exercise of practical wisdom. He might wish to repeat with increased emphasis the view he voiced in 1956 that the 'criticism of our time ... [has] been ... a brilliant period in literary criticism ... It may even come to seem, in retrospect, too brilliant' (*OPP*, 118).

To conclude, then, our Eliotic pragmatist critique of Rorty's postmodern pragmatism: Although change is inevitable, and with it acceptance of change, this does not mean that change itself be simply equated with progress and that any change be consequently regarded as a desired improvement. This is too neat a way of ensuring that we shall always get what we want. Similarly, we can gladly accept that words wobble and multiply without advocating a perpetual shake-up and intensified spawning of new vocabularies. Though apparently wary of deadly dualisms, Rorty himself seems misled by the erroneous assumption that we can only choose between the uselessly superannuated language of the past and the radically new language of the future, evidently inspired by Derrida's apocalyptic vision of a new writing born through deconstruction's dismantling of logocentrism.[26] Yet why assume that we have no choice but between the hopelessly archaic and the still-to-be-created new? Our traditional language, one which Rorty employs with captivating power, is neither but rather embraces and links past, present, and future. There is no convincing argument for denying that such language could be maintained and developed to serve our current and coming cultural needs, one of which is to prevent our alienation from our community and from our past.

Finally, on this historicist note, the ineluctably provisional nature of

[24] Kripke suggests the former interpretation, which Baker and Hacker criticize in maintaining the latter. See S. Kripke, *Wittgenstein on Rules and Private Language* (Oxford: Blackwell, 1982), and G.P. Baker and P.M.S. Hacker, 'On Misunderstanding Wittgenstein: Kripke's Private Language Argument', *Synthese*, 58 (1984), 407-450.

[25] R. Rorty, 'Solidarity or Objectivity?' in J. Rajchman and C. West (eds.), *Post-Analytic Philosophy* (New York: Columbia University Press, 1985), 13.

[26] For Rorty's appropriation of Derrida, see especially his 'Philosophy as a Kind of Writing: An Essay on Derrida' (*CP*, 90-109) and 'Deconstruction and Circumvention'.

man's theories and vocabularies does not entail that the ideas and words we have inherited can no longer speak profitably to us and must be scrapped for new ones. Such a conclusion betrays a naively ahistorical confidence in the present and its independence from the past. As Eliot's theory of tradition shows, recognition of historicism need not mean the denial of history; tradition provides our present with a living presence of the past. One pressing task for contemporary criticism is to help preserve and develop our critical heritage by distinguishing and fruitfully employing traditional modes which still seem potentially potent and profitable. One important task for philosophers of criticism is to protect such old and still satisfying ways of reading from the threat of a rash and wholesale discrediting dismissal through the philosophical arguments of literary theorists. This threat has lately seemed all too real with criticism's recent preoccupation with one subversively exciting and aggressively overpowering novel critical mode – deconstruction, based on a radically sceptical philosophy bearing the same name.

Here is not the place to defend old ways of reading by challenging the totalizing and privileging claims of deconstruction. Such a task, which I have briefly undertaken elsewhere,[27] would require a book-length project of its own to do sufficient justice to deconstruction's complexities and valuable insights before pronouncing with any confidence on its limitations. But since our study of Eliot's philosophy of criticism has tried to emphasize its enduring relevance to contemporary literary theory, we should not conclude without speculating on its relation to deconstruction. Certainly, Eliot would not reject deconstruction merely for seeming revolutionary. For he recognized the need for 'revolutionary theories' to supply 'the violent stimulus of novelty' (*TC*, 184) when a tradition or practice became crustily complacent; and we saw his dissatisfaction with the entrenched academic criticism of the 1950s, whose hegemony deconstruction has successfully undermined. Moreover, Eliot surely would have endorsed deconstruction's attack on the idea that interpretation is ever a faithful reflection of a determinate meaning fully present in the work, since Eliot himself launched a similar critique. But how might he have reacted *against* deconstruction?

One way to speculate on this inevitably speculative issue is to examine Eliot's response to deconstruction's perhaps closest prefiguration – Croceanism, a philosophy which dominated aesthetics and literary criticism in the early part of this century as much as deconstruction does today. Though Croce and Derrida may seem at first blush a shockingly odd couple, they share a common heritage and problematic stemming

---

[27] See R. Shusterman, 'Deconstruction and Analysis: Confrontation and Convergence, *British Journal of Aesthetics*, 26 (1986), 311-327. My critique of deconstruction does not aim to gainsay its valuable contributions to theory and criticism but challenges its essentialism and its totalizing and exclusive claims to penetrate and capture the necessary essence of all texts and all interpretations.

from the anti-positivist backlash of the late nineteenth century, re-enacted in Derrida's anti-positivist, anti-structuralist revolt. More significantly, they share some very important philosophical themes and strategies. Of course, Croce's aesthetic formula that intuition is expression seems utterly remote from Derrida's *différance* and indeed painfully susceptible to Derridean deconstruction. (Croce's equation would be construed not only as a pathetically unconvincing begging of the question and a graphic admission of the alterity of intuition and expression, signified and signifier, presence and trace; it would also be seen as a poignant example of the distortive longing for closure and stasis through the complete commensurability and union of signifier [expression] and signified [intuition]).[28]

However, beyond this and other differences which distinguish Derrida from any philosopher in the onto-theological tradition, we find remarkable affinities with Croce's thought which justify associating them. Both are anti-realist, abjuring the idea of any reality wholly external to language with which language could be compared and judged for accuracy of representation. Both suggest that what we call reality is basically a temporary linguistic construct, 'a provisional dynamic system developing through provisional and dynamic systematizations' where there is no promise of an ultimate system.[29] Of 'the world [that is] called real, natural, including in this definition both the reality called physical and that called spiritual and human', Croce asserts 'All this world is intuition', 'is nothing but intuition or aesthetic fact.'[30] And since for Croce intuition is identical with expression and language, all the world is linguistic. Derrida's dictum '*Il n'y a pas de hors-texte*' purveys the same message that there cannot be 'a referent[,] ... a reality ... [or] a signified outside the text whose content could take place, could have taken place outside of language.' It is only the 'systematic production of [linguistic] differences, the production of a system of differences', and 'the systematic play of differences' which provisionally structure what we take the world to be, thus 'there is nothing outside of the text.'[31]

Moreover, for both Croce and Derrida, language not only constitutes the world, it is an unrestrainable creative power which is constantly transforming itself. 'Language', says Croce, 'is perpetual creation. What

[28] Derrida might point to the anxiety behind Croce's identification of intuition and expression, behind his assertion that 'they are not two, but one'; viz. 'He who separates intuition from expression never succeeds in reuniting them'. See B.Croce, *Aesthetic*, trans. D.Ainslie (London: Macmillan, 1922), 8, 9.

[29] For a brief account of this aspect of Croce and its criticism of Hegel, see J. Passmore, *A Hundred Years of Philosophy* (Harmondsworth, U.K.: Penguin, 1968), 300-301. (The translated citation from Croce's *Saggio Sullo Hegel* appears on page 300). Cf. J.Derrida, *Positions,* trans. A.Bass (London: Athlone, 1980), 27-29.

[30] *Aesthetic*, 30, 26.

[31] See J. Derrida, *Of Grammatology*, trans. G.Spivak (Baltimore: Johns Hopkins University Press, 1976), 158; and *Positions*, 28, 27.

has been linguistically expressed cannot be repeated ... The ever-new impressions give rise to continuous changes of sounds and meanings, that is, to ever-new expressions. To seek the model language, then, is to seek the immobility of motion.'[32] Croce's continually creative, category-defying intuition-expression adumbrates Derrida's irrepressibly disseminating *différance* which 'is incompatible with the static, synchronic, taxonomic, ahistoric motives in the concept of structure' and which 'marks an irreducible and generative multiplicity' that 'cannot be summarized into an exact conceptual tenor ... and ... explode[s] the semantic horizon.'[33] Further, as both Croce and Derrida regard meaning as determined by context, and context as unbounded and ever-changing, it is not surprising that both reject the possibility of translation, admitting only transformations or 'approximations'.[34]

Closely connected with their anti-realism and views on language, Croce and Derrida share a fundamental and pervasive position which might be called anti-taxonomism. This position maintains that there is no firm and unchallengeable rationale or justification for the distinctions which we standardly employ but which are readily shown to have problems of application and validation. It maintains that these distinctions are intrinsically imperfect and wobbly because they lack ontological grounding, that although they seem natural and reasonable they are really conventional and arbitrary. For Derrida there are no natural kinds or distinctions based on real ontological differences outside of language's free play of differences. Any distinctions or categories we seem to find 'do not have as their cause a subject or substance, a thing in general, that is somewhere present and itself escapes the play of differences'.[35] Building on Saussure, Derrida maintains that there are no positive terms or concepts, and he warns against the metaphysical response to supply them, 'to respond with a definition of essence, of quiddity, to reconstitute a system of essential predicates'.[36] Deconstruction, of course, is largely the product of undermining and displacing such traditional and allegedly essential distinctions, not merely by reversing the present hierarchy of the terms of distinction (e.g. philosophy versus literature), but by

[32] *Aesthetic*, 150. See also 68, 124-125 for Croce's assertion of the endless change of context which effects meaning and of the historically conditioned and conventional nature of all signification, themes central to Derrida.

[33] *Positions*, 27, 45.

[34] See *Aesthetic* 68, 73; and *Positions*, 20. Such considerations lead Croce and deconstructors to question the possibility of true interpretation or recovery of original meaning. But Croce ultimately affirms this possibility, either through an almost mystical appeal to the power and 'intuitive absoluteness of imagination' or through a pragmatist theory that history and 'original meaning' are simply what they are reconstructed to be (*Aesthetic*, 122-135). Both these interpretations are elaborated in my 'Croce on Interpretation: Deconstruction and Pragmatism', *New Literary History*, forthcoming 1989.

[35] See J.Derrida, *Speech and Phenomena and other Essays on Husserl's Theory of Signs*, trans. D. Alison (Evanston, Ill.: Northwestern University Press, 1973), 141.

[36] *Positions*, 58.

showing that there is ultimately no essential difference between them and that their apparent opposition conceals and is based on actual complicity and common ground. With the same aim of discrediting traditional essentialist distinctions, Derrida launches his discussions of 'undecidables' (e.g. the *pharmakon*, the *supplement*, the *hymen*), where the undecidable defies the classification of the binary distinction it inhabits, thus 'resisting and disorganizing it, without ever constituting a third term'.[37] Further, with similar intent, Derrida works to dissolve all the long-standing distinctions and oppositions of metaphysics by maintaining that all these rival doctrines assert the same essential 'metaphysics of presence', 'that all the names related to fundamentals, to principles, or to the center have always designated an invariable presence'.[38] And again in the same spirit, Derrida challenges, not by mere precept but by the example of his own writings, the traditional distinctions between philosophy, literature, and literary criticism.

Many years earlier, Croce had similarly attempted to undermine entrenched essentialist distinctions which dominated aesthetics and much of general philosophy. His deconstructive program was obviously far less radical and comprehensive than Derrida's, but the strategy was the same: pointing to a distinction's inadequacies of application and inconsistency, and asserting the absence of any real essence, property, or necessary principle which justifies the distinction in question. In his famous attack on the rhetorical categories of traditional criticism, Croce maintains that 'a philosophical classification of expressions is not possible', since there are no essential properties or firm 'formal differences' to justify such distinctions. He likewise denies any essential differences between the aesthetic activities of the artist, the critic, and the ordinary man; the apparent differences being only 'quantitative', conventional, and deriving from 'diversity of circumstances'. The same goes for the distinction between art and non-art. 'The limits of the expressions and intuitions that are called art, as opposed to those that are vulgarly called non-art, are empirical and impossible to define. If an epigram be art, why not a single word?'. Challenging standard distinctions between disciplines, Croce affirms that *'philosophy of language and philosophy of art are the same thing'*, an extraordinarily prescient motto for deconstruction's proposed union of philosophy and literary theory.[39]

My comparison of Croce and Derrida is not meant to deny their obvious difference. But it should make plausible my claim that Derridean-Yale deconstruction is to French structuralism and the New Criticism very much what Croceanism was to the aesthetic positivism of Taine (and

[37] *Ibid.*, 43.

[38] J. Derrida, 'Structure, Sign and Play in the Discourse of the Human Sciences' in *Writing and Difference*, trans. A.Bass (London: Routledge & Kegan Paul, 1978), 279-280.

[39] See *Aesthetic*, 13-14, 67-70, 87-92, 114-115, 120, 142.

others) and to the tradition of rhetorical analysis. Both are largely revolts against closure, attempts to discredit and break free from some entrenched constraining normal science that was felt to be unsatisfyingly restrictive yet devoid of any ontological grounding or incontrovertible principle of reason to justify its repressive authority. In order to defy restrictive science, a more potent and fundamental force is invoked, a supreme and subversively protean principle of creative generative freedom: intuition-expression, disseminating *différance*. Further, it is shown that the restrictive science's constitutive distinctions have no real validity; since not only do their terms lack independent, positive essences or content, but the distinctions themselves cannot be clearly and consistently drawn, and their hierarchical order can be reversed. Croce's dismantling reversal of positivism's privileging distinction of historical reality versus art (the latter epiphenomenal to the former) is a reversal performed by maintaining that historical reality is itself the product of aesthetic intuition and thus a form of art. This is surely a striking precedent for Derrida's deconstructing reversal of the philosophy/literature opposition, performed by treating philosophy as a form of writing.

But for all its attacks on fraudulent essentialist distinctions, Croce's aesthetic was later rightly attacked by Eliot and analytic philosophers for its essentialism.[40] To see why is to reveal a problematic common to Croceanism and deconstruction. One may sceptically and anti-essentialistically deny that accepted distinctions can be justified by appeal to any ontologically grounded essences inherent in the terms of distinction, which are instead explained as but the play of differences, context, and convention. But in denying such essences one is tempted (but not compelled) to go on to reject as necessarily improper the distinctions these essences were supposed to justify. Rejecting these distinctions, however, seems only to lead us to a much wider and pernicious essentialism, an engulfing and unstructured monism of expression or textuality. ('Expression is an indivisible whole'; and 'there is such a general text everywhere [that the limits of discourse] ... are overflowed, that is everywhere.')[41]

Of the many traditional critical distinctions that Croceanism and deconstruction threaten to undermine, perhaps the most central is that between literary art and its criticism. What today's deconstructors celebrate as innovative and powerful misreadings, the Croceans praised as creative criticism. In 1926 we find a book purveying that message. Written by an American critic, J.E. Spingarn, it was appropriately entitled *Creative Criticism* and bore a dedication to Croce as 'the most

[40] The later analytic critique of Croce, which was far more thorough and sustained than Eliot's very brief and incidental critical comments, is discussed in my 'Analytic Aesthetics, Literary Theory, and Deconstruction', *Monist*, 69 (1986), 22-38.

[41] *Aesthetic*, 146; *Positions*, 59.

original of all modern thinkers on art'. In reviewing the book for the *TLS*, Eliot expresses his opposition to the Crocean (and, by speculative extension, deconstructionist) manifesto of distinction-defying freedom.[42]

Eliot does not try to defend traditional critical distinctions as inviolable, sharp, or foundationally grounded. He had always maintained that criticism was an essential part of creation, and in his later hermeneutic stage came to recognize the role of the reader's creative imaginative response in interpretative criticism. Moreover, he repeatedly emphasized that critical distinctions like 'romantic' versus 'classic', poetry versus mere verse, imagination versus fancy get the limited validity and meaning they have only in certain contexts in terms of pragmatic purposes of marking differences. Eliot's point is simply this. Even if the distinctions we have made or want to make lack ontological and epistemological warranty, even if they are makeshift expedients, we need distinctions and criteria of some sort to structure our critical discourse, to give it point and focus; and the old ones we share can provide us with a fruitful, common structuring matrix until we can fashion better ones (which in any case would have to be fashioned largely from what we already have). For an unpartitioned, undifferentiated general text is an ungraspable abstraction. We can form no real idea of it, and thus it is utterly empty despite its suggestion of plenitude.

Therefore, the Crocean comminatory 'recitation of all the distinctions and classifications which art and criticism are now to repudiate' does not really help us in better structuring our critical discourse; and 'the phrase "self-expression" ' just like Derrida's term '*différance*' is not a magic name which obviates all need for shaping discourse in a relatively stable, coherent, and shared manner. Affirming in his review that 'the test ... of any critical programme or platform ... is the sort of criticism which it produces', Eliot feared that dismissing all structuring distinctions in the unfettered pursuit of self-expression was more likely to produce a tedium of ephemeral effusion than criticism of enduring worth. He was right. Croce's essential message of freedom soon came to be seen as an empty essentialism, generating a dreary, monotonous rhetoric of theory and practice.

This could be the ultimate fate of Derrida's emancipatory message, important and valuable as it has been, if deconstruction does not realize, with Eliot, that freedom is never fruitful if unconstrained and unstructured. Though distinctions between valid interpretations and misreadings of a text are not eternally fixed by a determinate object-meaning, though traditional distinctions between disciplines are neither ontologically given nor perfectly clear, these distinctions are none the less crucial in structuring productive discourse. Now that deconstruction has helped reveal their human origins and alterability,

---

[42] See T.S. Eliot, 'Creative Criticism', 535.

such distinctions need to be critically sustained and developed rather than simply and globally undermined, if they are to continue to be helpful. Even Jonathan Culler, perhaps the most cogent of deconstruction's apologists, is wary of the danger of distinctionless monistic essentialism and asserts that 'a distinction between literature and philosophy is essential to deconstruction's power'.[43] Unfortunately, however, Derrida's effective philosophical repudiation of any ontologically grounded distinctions or essences and his convincing rejection of any presence of fixed meaning for valid literary interpretations to mirror have too often led his literary cohorts and disciples to a monotonous essentialism in which all texts, regardless of genre or style, are aporetic and self-reflexive, and all readings are essentially misreadings.[44] The essential aporetic nature of all texts has been transformed into an interpretational theme which generates programmatic readings whose uniformity and predictability are already tedious and provoking to some deconstructors.[45]

On the other hand, the necessity of misreading (in the mirroring sense) and the rejection of any foundational division between literary art and criticism have incited major deconstructors like Hartman and Barthes (and sometimes Derrida himself) to ludic extremes, at once to pursue maximal structureless freedom and to escape the empty boredom that such freedom characteristically incurs. It is not for nothing that in celebrating the unfettered pursuit of textual pleasure, Barthes closely links its supreme manifestation of *'jouissance'* with the boredom of indeterminacy and unstructured unreadability: 'Boredom is not far from bliss'.[46]

Deconstruction is a very complex, sophisticated, and multiform body of

---

[43] See J. Culler, *On Deconstruction: Theory and Criticism After Structuralism* (Ithaca, Cornell University Press, 1982), 149-150, 184.

[44] If Derrida sometimes seems to hold that all the world is one general text, so de Man and Miller assert that all particular texts (to the questionable extent we can call them particular) share a common essence of deconstructive self-division: 'a wound of fracture ... lies hidden in all texts', where 'every literary text ... performs its own self-dismantling', and 'like all texts is "unreadable"', since it can support mutually inconsistent interpretations rather than issuing in a particular, definitively valid one. See Derrida's *Of Grammatology*, 158-129; *Positions*, 59; and 'Living On: Border Lines' in H. Bloom *et al.* (eds.), *Deconstruction and Criticism* (London: Routledge & Kegan Paul, 1979), 82-83; P.de Man, 'Shelley Disfigured', in *Deconstruction and Criticism*, 67; J. Hillis Miller, 'Stevens' Rock and Criticism as Cure, II', *Georgia Review* 30 (1976), 330; and 'The Critic as Host', in *Deconstruction and Criticism*; and, on the necessity of misreading, H. Bloom, *A Map of Misreading* (London: Oxford University Press, 1975); and Culler's *On Deconstruction*, 175-180. A more extensive list of deconstruction's essentialist pronouncements can be found in G. Graff, 'Deconstruction as Dogma, or Come Back to the Raft Ag'in, Strether Honey!', *Georgia Review*, 34 (1980), 410-411.

[45] See, for example, R. Gasché, 'Unscrambling Positions: On Gerald Graff's Critique of Deconstruction', *Modern Language Notes*, 96 (1981), 1015-1034.

[46] R. Barthes, *The Pleasure of the Text*, trans. R. Miller (New York: Hill and Wang, 1975), 25. See also Culler's account of this aspect of Barthes in J. Culler, *Roland Barthes* (New York: Oxford University Press, 1983), 98-100.

thought which powerfully resists any thumbnail sketch or facile refutation. To portray all deconstruction as simply a battle-cry of freedom, pleasure, and playful sceptical irreverence that relies on a monistic textualization of reality into the play of linguistic differences would be unfair and distortive. It would also fail to account for deconstruction's enormous appeal to some of criticism's most tough-minded, rigorous, and disciplined close readers. Many second-generation deconstructionists, like Culler and Norris, are indeed severely critical of the ludic and hedonistic excesses of some deconstructors and instead lean towards Paul de Man's intense seriousness, suggesting an ideal not of freedom and pleasure but of rigorous discipline and demanding argument in relentlessly pursuing the self-divisive truth about all texts.

But though they are right to repudiate the ultimately dreary and empty pursuit of pure freedom and frolic, it seems an equally baneful extreme to elevate deconstruction's 'demonstrable rigour' and the 'knowledge and feelings of mastery' its dismantling analyses afford as the privileged, overriding aim or highest goal of criticism.[47] Apparently disturbed by his admired Barthes' excessive claims for the privileging of pleasure and the body, Culler too quickly embraces the other extreme of ascetic rigor, rejecting the traditional critical goal of 'enriching elucidations' aimed at constituting the work as a satisfying, rich organic unity, as if such a goal was necessarily a sin of logical lassitude. With rigorous and relentless close questioning of texts his only ideal of reading, Culler puritanically 'refuse[s] to make aesthetic richness an end'.[48]

Thus for all its sceptical challenging of distinctions, deconstruction seems itself bedevilled and bifurcated by the very dubious knowledge/ pleasure or understanding/enjoyment dichotomy. Because we can meaningfully distinguish the two terms through contexts where they diverge (e.g. when we understand a poem but do not enjoy it or when we enjoy it but do not understand it as much as we wish to or should), this does not mean that they are necessarily sharply separable and fundamentally conflicting principles which admit of no balanced unity. As Eliot was seen to argue in Chapters Five and Six, the enjoyment and understanding of literature are instead very intimately, indeed conceptually, linked, so that, holistically speaking, we cannot dissociate the idea of enjoying poetry from understanding it and vice versa; even if understanding and enjoyment diverge in particular instances. In this chapter we saw how Eliot became aware of the pendulum swings of critical imbalance between hedonistic impressionism and joyless scholarship, and realized that any attempts to redress the balance by shifting allegiance to the undervalued term would only tend to generate an imbalance in the other direction.

[47] See C. Norris, *Deconstruction: Theory and Practice* (London: Methuen, 1982), 92-108; and *The Deconstructive Turn* (London: Methuen, 1983), 6-7 (quotation from p. 7); and see J. Culler, *Roland Barthes*, 91-100; and *On Deconstruction*, 132n., 225.
[48] *On Deconstruction*, 220-221, 240.

Eliot apparently concluded that the only way to stop such damaging pendulum swings of hedonism and cognitivism is to insist emphatically that enjoyment and understanding are not essentially opposed but ultimately are inseparable features of the activity of reading. This is precisely what he urged in 'The Frontiers of Criticism', where his more specific goal was to rescue criticism from the professional scientism of the university scholar by legitimating the personal and the pleasurable in our critical response. In this, of course, he anticipates Barthes and other contemporary hedonists, though with characteristic prudence he avoids their extremism. Eliot realized that the issues in criticism (and elsewhere) do not admit of such facile one-sided resolution; that (as Wilde said) the truth is rarely plain and never simple; that the right way, the way of right reason or *phronesis* is a difficult interpretative mediation of complexities, including those of changing circumstances.

All this, one might argue, could be applied to the proper understanding of Eliot's own critical thought, which is far from plain and never simple. Its complexities, tensions, and developments are sometimes frustratingly hard to follow and grasp coherently. But they are surely destined to inspire continued study by Eliot scholars and literary historians. My hope is that more of today's forward-looking critics and theorists will come to recognize and better appreciate the enduring value of Eliot's complex, pragmatic philosophy of criticism, even if the arguments of this book have not fully succeeded in making this value eminently evident.

Bibliography

Since the writings of Eliot and on Eliot are legion, I shall list here only those works which are cited in my text or are otherwise particularly related to the issues I discuss. More complete bibliographical information can be found in:

Gallup, Donald. *T.S. Eliot: a bibliography*. Second edition, London: Faber, 1969.
Martin, Mildred. *A Half Century of Eliot Criticism: an annotated bibliography of books and articles on Eliot in English, 1916-1965*. Lewisburg, Pa.: Bucknell University Press, 1972.
Ricks, Beatrice. *T.S. Eliot: a bibliography of secondary works*. Metuchen, New Jersey: Scarecrow Press, 1980.

Major works by Eliot

After Strange Gods. New York: Harcourt, Brace, & Company, 1934.
The Complete Poems and Plays of T.S. Eliot. London: Faber,1969.
Essays Ancient and Modern. London: Faber, 1936.
For Lancelot Andrewes. London: Faber, 1970; first published in 1928.
The Idea of a Christian Society. London: Faber, 1982; first published in 1939.
Knowledge and Experience in the Philosophy of F.H. Bradley. London: Faber, 1964.
Notes Toward the Definition of Culture. London: Faber, 1962; first published in 1948.
On Poetry and Poets. London: Faber, 1957.
On the Metaphysical Poetry of the Seventeenth Century with special reference to Donne, Crashaw, and Cowley. Unpublished Clark Lectures, delivered at Trinity College, Cambridge, 1926. Typescript in Kings College Library, Cambridge.
The Sacred Wood. London: Methuen, 1968; first published in 1920.
Selected Essays. London: Faber, 1976; first published in 1932.
Selected Prose of T.S. Eliot, ed. Frank Kermode. London: Faber, 1975.
The Use of Poetry and the Use of Criticism. London: Faber, 1964; first published in 1933.
To Criticize the Critic, and other writings. London: Faber, 1978; first published in 1965.

Uncollected works by Eliot cited in the text

'A Brief Treatise on the Criticism of Poetry', *Chapbook*, 2 (1920), 1-10.
'A Commentary', *Criterion*, 2 (1924), 231-235.
'[A review of] *A Defence of Idealism*', *New Statesman*, 22 September, 1917, 596.
'A Note on Poetry and Belief', *Enemy*, 1 (1927), 15-17.

'Commentary', *Criterion*, 6 (1927), 289-291.
'Commentary', *Criterion*, 6 (1927), 385-388.
'Contemporanea', *Egoist*, 5 (1918), 84-85.
'Creative Criticism', *Times Literary Supplement*, 1280 (1926), 535.
'The Criticism of Poetry', *Times Literary Supplement*, 953 (1920), 256.
'Experiment in Criticism', *Bookman*, 70 (1929), 225-233.
'[A review of] *Fashion in Literature: A Study of Changing Taste*', *English Review*, 53 (1931), 634-636.
'The Function of Criticism', *Criterion*, 2 (1923), 31-42.
'The Idea of a Literary Review', *Criterion*, 4 (1926), 1-6.
'Introduction'. In E. Pound, *The Literary Essays of Ezra Pound*. London: Faber, 1960, ix-xv.
'Introduction'. In G. W. Knight, *The Wheel of Fire*. London: Methuen, 1962, xiii-xx; first published in 1930.
'[A prefatory note on] James Joyce'. In B. Gheerbrant, *James Joyce: sa vie, son oeuvre, son rayonnement*. Paris: La Hune, 1949.
'Literature, Science, and Dogma', *Dial*, 82 (1927), 239-243.
'The Local Flavour', *Athenaeum*, 4676 (1919), 1332-1333.
'Marivaux', *Art and Letters*, 2 (1919), 80-85.
'Mr. Middleton Murry's Synthesis', *Criterion*, 6 (1927), 340-347.
'[A review of] *The Name and Nature of Poetry*', *Criterion*, 13 (1933), 151-154.
'Poetry and Propaganda', *Bookman*, 70 (1930), 595-602.
'Religion without Humanism'. In N. Foerster (ed.), *Humanism and America*. New York: Farrar and Rhinehard, 1930, 105-112.
'The Silurist', *Dial*, 83 (1927), 259-263.
'Studies in Contemporary Criticism', *Egoist*, 5 (1918), 113-114, 131-133.
'Style and Thought', *Nation*, 23 March 1918, 768-769.
'Thomas Hardy', *Manchester Guardian*, 803 (23 June, 1916), 3.
'Why Mr. Russell is not a Christian', *Criterion*, 6 (1927), 177-179.

Other works

Ackroyd, Peter. *T.S. Eliot*. London: Hamish Hamilton, 1984.
Addison, Joseph. 'Criticisms on *Paradise Lost*'. Reprinted in E.D. Jones (ed.), *English Critical Essays (Sixteenth, Seventeenth, and Eighteenth Centuries)*. London: Oxford University Press, 1943.
Adorno, Theodor. *Minima Moralia*. London: Verso, 1978.
Allan, Mowbray. *T.S. Eliot's Impersonal Theory of Poetry*. Lewisburg, Pa.: Bucknell University Press, 1974.
Aristotle, *Nichomachean Ethics* and *Poetics*. In W.D. Ross (ed.), *The Works of Aristotle*, vols. 9, 11. Oxford: Clarendon, 1924-25.
Arnold, Matthew. 'The Function of Criticism at the Present Time'. In L. Trilling (ed.), *The Portable Matthew Arnold*. New York: Viking, 1949.
Ayer, A.J. *Language, Truth, and Logic*. London: Gollancz, 1936.
———. *Russell and Moore: the analytic heritage*. London: Macmillan, 1971.
Baker, G.P. and P.M.S. Hacker. 'On Misunderstanding Wittgenstein: Kripke's Private Language Argument', *Synthese*, 58 (1984), 407-450.
———. *Wittgenstein: meaning and understanding*. Oxford: Blackwell, 1984.
Barthes, Roland. 'Criticism as Language'. Reprinted in David Lodge (ed.), *Twentieth Century Criticism: a reader*. London: Longman, 1977.
———. *The Pleasure of the Text*. New York: Hill and Wang, 1975.

Bateson, F. W. 'Criticism's Lost Leader'. In D. Newton-DeMolina (ed.), *The Literary Criticism of T.S. Eliot*. London: Athlone, 1977.

Beardsley, Monroe C. *Aesthetics*. New York: Harcourt Brace, 1958.

Bell, Ian F.A. *Critic as Scientist: the modernist poetics of Ezra Pound*. London: Methuen, 1981.

Bell, Robert. 'Bertrand Russell and the Eliots', *American Scholar*, 52 (1983), 309-325.

Benziger, J. 'Organic Unity: Leibniz to Coleridge', *PMLA*, 66 (1951), 24-48.

Bergonzi, Bernard. *T.S. Eliot*. New York: Macmillan, 1972.

Bernstein, Richard J. *Beyond Objectivism and Relativism*. Oxford: Blackwell, 1983.

Bleich, David. *Subjective Criticism*. Baltimore: Johns Hopkins University Press, 1978.

Bloom, Harold. *A Map of Misreading*. London: Oxford University Press, 1975.

Bolgan, Ann. 'The Philosophy of F.H. Bradley and the Mind and Art of T.S. Eliot: An Introduction'. In S.P. Rosenbaum (ed.), *English Literature and British Philosophy*. Chicago: University of Chicago Press, 1971.

Bourdieu, Pierre. *Distinction: a social critique of the judgement of taste*. Cambridge, Mass.: Harvard University Press, 1984.

———. *Outline of a Theory of Practice*. Cambridge: Cambridge University Press, 1977.

Bradley, F.H. *Appearance and Reality*. Oxford: Clarendon, 1930.

———. *Principles of Logic*. Oxford: Clarendon, 1922.

Casey, John. *The Language of Criticsm*. London: Methuen, 1966.

Collingwood, R.G. *The Principles of Art*. Oxford: Oxford University Press, 1958.

Croce, Benedetto. *Aesthetic*. London: Macmillan, 1921.

———. *Saggio Sullo Hegel*. Bari: Laterza, 1948.

Culler, Jonathan D. *On Deconstruction*. London: Routledge & Kegan Paul, 1982.

———. *Roland Barthes*. New York: Oxford University Press, 1983.

Danto, Arthur. 'The Artworld', *Journal of Philosophy*, 61 (1964), 571-584.

———. *The Transfiguration of the Commonplace*, Cambridge, Mass.: Harvard University Press, 1981.

Davidson, Donald. *Inquiries into Truth and Interpretation*. Oxford: Clarendon, 1984.

De Man, Paul. 'Shelley Disfigured'. In Harold Bloom *et al.* (eds.), *Deconstruction and Criticism*. London: Routledge & Kegan Paul, 1979.

Derrida, Jacques. 'An Interview with Jacques Derrida', *The Literary Review* (Edinburgh), 14 (18 April, 1 May, 1980).

———. *Of Grammatology*. Baltimore: Johns Hopkins University Press, 1976.

———. 'Living On: Border Lines:'. In Harold Bloom *et al.* (eds.), *Deconstruction and Criticism*. London: Routledge & Kegan Paul, 1979.

———. *Positions*. London: Athlone, 1980.

———. *Speech and Phenomena and other Essays on Husserl's Theory of Signs*. Evanston, Ill.: Northwestern University Press, 1973.

———. *Writing and Difference*. Chicago: University of Chicago Press, 1978.

Dewey, John. *Art as Experience*, New York, Putnam, 1980.

Dickie, George. *Art and the Aesthetic*. Ithaca: Cornell University Press, 1974.

———. *The Art Circle*. New York: Haven, 1984.

Diffey, T. J. 'Essentialism and the Definition of Art', *British Journal of Aesthetics*, 13 (1973), 103-120.

Eagleton, Terry. *Literary Theory: an introduction*. Oxford: Blackwell, 1983.

Fish, Stanley. 'Consequences'. In W.J.T. Mitchell (ed.), *Against Theory*. Chicago: University of Chicago Press, 1985.

————. *Is There a Text in This Class?* Cambridge, Mass.: Harvard University Press, 1980.

Foucault, Michel. 'The Order of Discourse'. Reprinted in Robert Young (ed.), *Untying the Text*. Baltimore: Johns Hopkins University Press, 1981, 48-77.

Freed, Lewis. *The Critic as Philosopher*. LaSalle, Ill.: Purdue University Press, 1979.

Gadamer, Hans-Georg. 'The Hermeneutics of Suspicion'. In Gary Shapiro and Alan Sica (eds.), *Hermeneutics*. Amherst: University of Massachusetts Press, 1984, 54-65.

————. *Kleine Schriften*. Tubingen: Mohr, 1967.

————. *Philosophical Hermeneutics*. Berkeley: University of California Press, 1976.

————. *Reason in the Age of Science*. Cambridge, Mass.: MIT Press, 1983.

————. 'Replik'. In K.-O. Apel *et al.* (eds.), *Hermeneutik und Ideologiekritik*. Frankfurt: Suhrkamp, 1976.

————. *Truth and Method*. New York: Crossroad, 1982.

Gallie, W.B. *Philosophy and the Historical Understanding*. New York: Schocken, 1968.

Gardner, Helen. *The Art of T.S. Eliot*. London: Faber, 1949.

————. *The Composition of 'Four Quartets'*. London: Faber, 1978.

Gasché, Rodolphe. 'Unscrambling Positions: On Gerald Graff's Critique of Deconstruction', *Modern Language Notes*, 96 (1981), 1015-1034.

Goodman, Nelson. *Problems and Projects*. Indianapolis: Bobbs-Merrill, 1972.

————. *Ways of Worldmaking*. Indianapolis: Hackett, 1978.

Gordon, Lyndall. *Eliot's Early Years*. Oxford: Oxford University Press, 1977.

Graff, Gerald. 'Deconstruction as Dogma, or Come Back to the Raft Ag'in, Strether Honey!', *Georgia Review*, 34 (1980), 404-421.

Gray, Piers. *T.S. Eliot's Intellectual and Poetic Development, 1909-1922*. Sussex: Harvester Press, 1982.

Grene, Marjorie. 'Perception, Interpretation, and the Sciences: Toward a New Philosophy of Science'. In D. Depew and B. Weber (eds.), *Evolution at a Crossroads: the new biology and the new philosophy of science*. Cambridge, Mass.: MIT Press, 1985.

Hampshire, Stuart. 'Logic and Appreciation'. Reprinted in W. Elton (ed.), *Aesthetics and Language*. Oxford: Blackwell, 1954, 161-169.

Hare, R. M. *Moral Thinking*. Oxford: Oxford University Press, 1981.

Heidegger, Martin, *Being and Time*. New York: Harper and Row, 1962.

Hirsch, E.D. *The Aims of Interpretation*. Chicago: University of Chicago Press, 1976.

————. *Validity in Interpretation*. New Haven: Yale University Press, 1967.

Horkheimer, Max and Theodor Adorno. *Dialectic of Enlightenment*. New York: Continuum, 1986.

Hough, Graham. *An Essay on Criticism*. New York: Norton, 1966.

Hulme, T.E. *Further Speculations*. Minneapolis: University of Minnesota Press, 1955.

————. *Speculations*. London: Routlege and Kegan Paul, 1960.

Isenberg, Arnold. 'Critical Communication'. Reprinted in W. Elton (ed.), *Aesthetics and Language*. Oxford: Blackwell, 1954, 131-146.

James, William. *Pragmatism and Other Essays*. New York: Simon and Schuster, 1963.

Jay, Gregory S. *T.S. Eliot and the Poetics of Literary History*. Baton Rouge, Louisiana: Louisiana State University Press, 1983.

Johnston, W.M. 'Viennese Impressionism: A Reappraisal of a Once Fashionable Category'. In E. Nielsen (ed.), *Focus on Vienna 1900*. München: Fink, 1983.

Jones, A. R. *The Life and Opinions of T.E. Hulme*. London: Gollancz, 1960.

Kenner, Hugh. *The Invisible Poet: T.S. Eliot*. London: Methuen, 1965.

Kenny, Anthony J.P. *The Aristotelian Ethics*. Oxford: Clarendon, 1978.

Kermode, Frank. *Romantic Image*. London: Routledge & Kegan Paul, 1961.

Knapp, Steven and W.B. Michaels. 'Against Theory'. Reprinted in W.J.T. Mitchell (ed.), *Against Theory*. Chicago: University of Chicago Press, 1985.

Knight, G. Wilson. *The Wheel of Fire*. London: Methuen, 1962.

Kojecky, Roger. *T.S. Eliot's Social Criticism*. London: Faber, 1971.

Krieger, Murray. *The New Apologists for Poetry*. Minneapolis: University of Minnesota Press, 1956.

Kripke, Saul. *Wittgenstein on Rules and Private Language*. Oxford: Oxford University Press, 1982.

Lee, Brian. *Theory and Personality: the significance of T. S. Eliot's criticism*. London: Athlone, 1979.

Levenson, M.H. *A Genealogy of Modernism*. Cambridge: Cambridge University Press, 1984.

Lewis, David. *Convention: a philosophical study*. Cambridge, Mass.: Harvard University Press, 1969.

Lobb, Edward. *T.S. Eliot and the Romantic Critical Tradition*. London: Routledge & Kegan Paul, 1981.

Lu, F.-P. *T.S. Eliot: the dialectical structure of his theory of poetry*. Chicago: University of Chicago Press, 1966.

Lucy, Sean. *T.S. Eliot and the Idea of Tradition*. London: Cohen and West, 1960.

Lyons, John. *Semantics*. Cambridge: Cambridge University Press, 1977.

Macdonald, Margaret. 'Some Distinctive Features of Arguments Used in Criticism of the Arts'. Reprinted in W. Elton (ed.), *Aesthetics and Language*. Oxford: Blackwell, 1954, 114-130.

MacIntyre, Alisdair. *After Virtue*. London: Duckworth, 1981.

———. 'Epistemological Crises, Dramatic Narrative and the Philosophy of Science', *Monist*, 60 (1977), 453-472.

Margolis, J.D. *T.S. Eliot's Intellectual Development, 1922-1939*. Chicago: University of Chicago Press, 1972.

Margolis, Joseph. *Pragmatism Without Foundations*. Oxford: Blackwell, 1986.

———. 'Relativism, History, and Objectivity in the Human Studies', *Journal for the Theory of Social Behavior*, 14 (1984), 1-23.

Matthiessen, F.O. *The Achievement of T.S. Eliot*. New York: Oxford University Press, 1959.

Michaels, Walter Benn. 'Philosophy in Kinkanja: Eliot's Pragmatism'. In *Glyph* 8. Baltimore: Johns Hopkins University Press, 1981, 170-202.

Miller, J. Hillis. 'The Critic as Host'. In Harold Bloom *et al.* (eds.), *Deconstruction and Criticism*. London: Routledge & Kegan Paul, 1979.

———. 'Stevens' Rock and Criticism as Cure, II', *Georgia Review*, 30 (1976), 330-348.

Moody, A.D. *Thomas Stearns Eliot: Poet*. Cambridge: Cambridge University Press, 1979.

Moore, G.E. 'The Nature of Judgement', *Mind*, 8 (1899), 196-193.

———. *Philosophical Studies*. London: Kegan Paul, Trench, Trubner, 1922.

———. *Principia Ethica*. Cambridge: Cambridge University Press, 1903.

———. 'Wittgenstein's Lectures in 1930-33'. Reprinted in Moore's *Philosophical*

Papers. London: Allen and Unwin, 1959.

Mothersill, Mary. *Beauty Restored*. Oxford: Oxford University Press, 1984.

Nagel, Thomas. *Mortal Questions*. Cambridge: Cambridge University Press, 1979.

Newton, K.M. 'Validity in Interpretation', *British Journal of Aesthetics*, 25 (1985), 207-219.

Norris, Christopher. *The Contest of Faculties: philosophy and theory after deconstruction*. London: Methuen, 1985.

———. *Deconstruction: theory and practice*. London: Methuen, 1982.

———. *The Deconstructive Turn*. London: Methuen, 1982.

———. *William Empson and the Philosophy of Literary Criticism*. London: Methuen, 1978.

Passmore, John. *A Hundred Years of Philosophy*. Harmondsworth, U.K.: Penguin, 1980.

Pears, David. *Bertrand Russell and the British Tradition*. London: Collins, 1968.

Peirce, Charles S. *Collected Papers of Charles Sanders Peirce*. Cambridge, Mass.: Harvard University Press, 1931-35.

Polanyi, Michael. *Personal Knowledge*. London: Routledge & Kegan Paul, 1958.

Popper, Karl. *Objective Knowledge*. Oxford: Oxford University Press, 1979.

Putnam, Hilary. *Meaning and the Moral Sciences*. London: Routledge & Kegan Paul, 1979.

———. *Reason, Truth and History*. Cambridge: Cambridge University Press, 1981.

Quine, W.V. *From a Logical Point of View*. New York: Harper and Row, 1961.

———. *Ontological Relativity and Other Essays*. New York: Columbia University Press, 1969.

———. *Philosophy of Logic*. Englewood Cliffs, N.J.: Prentice-Hall, 1970.

Ramsey, F.P. *The Foundations of Mathematics*. London: Kegan Paul, 1931.

Richards, I.A. *Practical Criticism*. New York: Harcourt, Brace, 1956.

———. *Principles of Literary Criticism*. London: Routledge & Kegan Paul, 1970.

———. *Science and Poetry*. London: Kegan Paul, 1926.

Rieff, Philip. *The Triumph of the Therapeutic*. New York: Harper and Row, 1966.

Rorty, Richard. *Consequences of Pragamtism*. Minneapolis: University of Minnesota Press, 1982.

———. 'Freud and Moral Reflection'. In J. Smith and W. Kerrigan (eds.), *Pragmatism's Freud: the moral disposition of psychoanalysis*. Baltimore: Johns Hopkins University Press, 1986, 1-27.

———. *Philosophy and the Mirror of Nature*. Princeton: Princeton University Press, 1979.

———. 'Solidarity or Objectivity?'. In J. Rajchman and Cornell West (eds.), *Post-Analytic Philosophy*. New York: Columbia University Press, 1985, 3-19.

———. 'Texts and Lumps', *New Literary History*, 17 (1985), 1-16.

Royce, Josiah. *The Problem of Christianity*. Chicago: University of Chicago Press, 1968.

Ruskin, John. 'Of the Pathetic Fallacy'. Reprinted in E.D. Jones (ed.), *English Critical Essays (Nineteenth Century)*. London: Oxford University Press, 1946.

Russell, Bertrand. *The Autobiography of Bertrand Russell*. Boston: Little, Brown, 1969.

———. 'Logical Atomism' and 'The Philosophy of Logical Atomism'. In David Pears (ed.), *Russell's Logical Atomism*. London: Fontana, 1972.

———. *My Philosophical Development*. New York: Simon and Schuster, 1959.

———. *Mysticism and Logic*. London: Allen and Unwin, 1917.

———. *Our Knowledge of the External World*. London: Allen and Unwin, 1914.

————. *Philosophical Essays*. London: Allen and Unwin, 1910.

————. *The Problems of Philosophy*. London: Oxford University Press, 1971

Savile, Anthony. *The Test of Time: an essay in philosophical aesthetics*. Oxford: Oxford University Press, 1982.

Schmidt, A.V.C. 'Eliot and the Dialect of the Tribe', *Essays in Criticism*, 33 (1983), 36-48.

Schuchard, Ronald. 'Eliot and Hulme in 1916: Toward a Revaluation of Eliot's Critical and Spiritual Development', *PMLA*, 88 (1973), 1083-1094.

Scruton, Roger. *Art and Imagination*. London: Methuen, 1974.

Searle, John. *Speech Acts*. Cambridge: Cambridge University Press, 1969.

Sencourt, Robert. *T.S. Eliot: a memoir*. London: Garnstone Press, 1971.

Sharrock, Roger. 'Eliot's "Tone"'. In D. Newton-DeMolina (ed.), *The Literary Criticism of T.S. Eliot*. London: Athlone, 1977, 160-183.

Shusterman, Richard. 'Analytic Aesthetics, Literary Theory, and Deconstruction', *Monist*, 69 (1986), 22-38.

————. 'Convention: Variations on a Theme', *Philosophical Investigations*, 9 (1986), 36-55.

————. 'Croce on Interpretation: Deconstruction and Pragmatism', *New Literary History*, 20 (1989).

————. 'Deconstruction and Analysis: Confrontation and Convergence', *British Journal of Aesthetics*, 26 (1986), 311-327.

————. 'Eliot and Logical Atomism', *ELH*, 49 (1982), 164-178.

————. 'Eliot and Ruskin', *Journal of Comparative Literature and Aesthetics*, 7 (1984), 35-49.

————. 'Evaluative Reasoning in Criticism', *Ratio*, 23 (1981), 141-157.

————. 'The Logic of Evaluation', *Philosophical Quarterly*, 30 (1980), 327-341.

————. 'The Logic of Interpretation', *Philosophical Quarterly*, 28 (1978), 310-324.

————. *The Object of Literary Criticism*. Amsterdam: Rodopi, 1984.

————. 'On Knowing the Value of a Work of Art'. In Peter McCormick (ed.), *The Reasons of Art*. Ottawa: University of Ottawa Press, 1985, 368-374.

————. 'Osborne and Moore on Organic Unity', *British Journal of Aesthetics*, 23 (1983), 352-359.

————. 'Poetics and Recent Analytic Aesthetics', *Poetics Today*, 7 (1986), 323-329.

————. 'Remembering Hulme: A Neglected Philsopher-Critic-Poet', *Journal of the History of Ideas*, 46 (1985), 559-576.

————. 'Wilde and Eliot', *T.S. Eliot Annual*, 1. London: Macmillan, 1988

Sibley, Frank. 'Aesthetic Concepts'. Reprinted in J. Margolis (ed.), *Philosophy Looks at the Arts*. Philadelphia: Temple University Press, 1978, 64-87.

Slater, H. 'Wittgenstein's Aesthetics', *British Journal of Aesthetics*, 23 (1983), 34-37.

Smith, J.E. 'Josiah Royce'. In P. Edwards (ed.), *Encyclopedia of Philosophy*. New York: Macmillan, 1967, vol. 7, 225-229.

Spender, Stephen. *Eliot*. London: Fontana, 1972.

Steiner, George. *Heidegger*. Glasgow: Fontana, 1978.

Urmson, J.O. 'Aristotle on Pleasure'. In J.M.E. Moravcsik (ed.), *Aristotle*. New York: Doubleday, 1967, 323-333.

————. *Philosophical Analysis: its development between the two World Wars*. Oxford: Oxford University Press, 1967.

Walton, Kendall. 'Fearing Fictions', *Journal of Philosophy*, 75 (1978), 5-27.

————. 'How Remote are Fictional Worlds from the Real World?', *Journal of Aesthetics and Art Criticism*, 37 (1978), 11-23.

Weitz, Morris. *'Hamlet' and the Philosophy of Literary Criticism*. London: Faber, 1972.

Wellek, René, and Austin Warren. *Theory of Literature*. Harmondsworth, U.K.: Penguin, 1970.

Williams, Bernard. *Ethics and the Limits of Philosophy*. London: Fontana, 1985.

Williams, Michael. *Groundless Belief*. Oxford: Blackwell, 1977.

Wimsatt, William K. and Cleanth Brooks, *Literary Criticism: a short history*. Chicago: University of Chicago Press, 1978.

Wisdom, John. 'Logical Constructions', *Mind*, 40-42, 1931-1933 in five parts.

———. *Philosophy and Psycho-Analysis*. Oxford: Blackwell, 1957.

Wittgenstein, Ludwig. *The Blue and Brown Books*. New York: Harper, 1958.

———. *Lectures and Conversations on Aesthetics, Psychology, and Religious Belief*. Oxford: Blackwell, 1970.

———. *Notebooks: 1914-1916*. Oxford: Blackwell, 1961.

———. *Philosophical Investigations*. Oxford: Blackwell, 1968.

———. *Tractatus Logico-Philosophicus*. London: Kegan Paul, 1931.

———. *Zettel*. Oxford: Blackwell, 1967.

Wollheim, Richard. *Art and its Objects*. New York: Harper and Row, 1968.

———. 'Eliot and F.H. Bradley: An Account'. In C.G. Martin (ed.), *Eliot in Perspective: a symposium*. London: Macmillan, 1970, 169-193.

———. *F.H. Bradley*. Harmondsworth, U.K.: Penguin, 1969.

Index